DIE TRYING

DIE TRYING

One Man's Quest to Conquer the Seven Summits

BO PARFET

WITH RICHARD BUSKIN

AMACOM AMERICAN MANAGEMENT ASSOCIATION

NEW YORK ▲ ATLANTA ▲ BRUSSELS ▲ CHICAGO ▲ MEXICO CITY ▲ SAN FRANCISCO
SHANGHAI ▲ TOKYO ▲ TORONTO ▲ WASHINGTON, D.C.

Special discounts on bulk quantities of AMACOM books are available to corporations, professional associations, and other organizations. For details, contact Special Sales Department, AMACOM, a division of American Management Association, 1601 Broadway, New York, NY 10019. Tel: 212-903-8316. Fax: 212-903-8083.
E-mail: specialsls@amanet.org
Website: www.amacombooks.org/go/specialsales
To view all AMACOM titles go to: www.amacombooks.org

This publication is designed to provide accurate and authoritative information in regard to the subject matter covered. It is sold with the understanding that the publisher is not engaged in rendering legal, accounting, or other professional service. If legal advice or other expert assistance is required, the services of a competent professional person should be sought.

Library of Congress Cataloging-in-Publication Data

Parfet, Bo.
Die trying : one man's quest to conquer the Seven Summits / Bo Parfet with Richard Buskin.
    p. cm.
Includes index.
ISBN-13: 978-0-8144-1084-4
ISBN-10: 0-8144-1084-7
1. Mountaineering.   2. Parfet, Bo.   3. Mountaineers—United States—Biography.
4. Mountains. 5. Continents. I. Buskin, Richard. II. Title.

GV200.P37 2009
796.522092—dc22   2008035288

Printing number
10 9 8 7 6 5 4 3 2 1

To all who've been told they can't achieve their dreams.
It's never too late.

CONTENTS

It was March 5, 2004, and there I was, submerged beneath a tree in a churning, roaring river in Belize, thinking, "This is a really stupid way to die." Thanks to training that had taught me to surround myself with a "bubble of calm" whenever emergencies or tough situations arise, I wasn't panicked. Nevertheless, I knew I had about a minute and a half of available oxygen before I'd black out and drown. Luckily, that didn't happen. I was able to shift the boat that was on top of me, free myself from the tree limbs that were holding me captive, and swim toward the light, where the first image that greeted me was that of Bo Parfet hanging onto a branch.

Bo had surfaced about a minute earlier. It was day two of the La Ruta Maya race, and we were now last among a field of just under a hundred vessels, yet it was only the first of many adventures that he and I would share together. Often, the kind of life-threatening incident that we'd just experienced shakes people up, and I wondered how it was going to affect Bo. You see, in my mind, he was still untested. Little did I know that during the next few years he would witness a death on Mount Everest and have several brushes with death himself in some of the world's most exotic locations.

It is often said that the mark of real character in a climber is not how he stands on the summit while holding a flag, but how he pulls himself out of an icy crevasse. Expeditions have a way of revealing a person's true personality, not least because teammates spend so much time together at close quarters—and in often trying conditions—that any pretense is quickly washed away. Indeed, the value of being a good teammate is not to be underestimated. A group that works cohesively together will triumph over individual effort every time.

Bo is a great teammate. His sense of humor defuses tension at just the right moments, and time and again his amazing acts of unselfishness ensure that his colleagues keep pulling for one another. In short, Bo makes those around him better. And while he learned all about leadership at Northwestern University's Kellogg School of Management, it's hard to imagine that anything he was taught there could match the experiences he has been through on his many expeditions.

Not that everything Bo touches immediately turns to gold. He would be the first to tell you that anything that's worth achieving is tough. If it were easy, everyone would do it. Ask winners and leaders if they have ever failed, and most will tell you that they have failed spectacularly. That's because failure is part of the process of winning. It's just sad how many people sabotage their own lives through inactivity.

The easy road is safe and predictable. Trying to extend yourself in any field of endeavor is difficult, especially when you run the risk of looking foolish if you fail. The important thing is to learn from the experience, and also to understand that on those occasions when you put every ounce of energy and passion into achieving something, the exhilaration of realizing your ambition will be well worth the fight. As the Scottish resistance fighter Sir William Wallace once said, "Every man dies, but not every man truly lives."

Bo Parfet has led a life that we all can learn from, and *Die Trying* provides us with an intimate look at what it means to put your neck on the line and pursue your dream while your biggest nightmare stares you down.

Richard C. Wiese,
Explorers Club President, 2002–2006

In the year it took me to write this book I really wrestled with whether to include a discussion of my background. My family, being very private small-town people, strongly urged me to skip over our history and get straight to the mountains in case people might find the story less accessible or compelling. My feelings about this are complex.

Certainly, I am blessed to have come from an illustrious background and to have enjoyed the experiences, education, and opportunities it affords. Elements of this background have contributed to my being able to travel and climb without worry, while my legacy as the child, grandchild, and great-grandchild of successful entrepreneurs is also something I carry on my shoulders; at times as a stifling burden and at others as a tremendous motivator.

That having been said, although the adventure of the Seven Summits is such that the narrative stands on its own, I really want readers of this book to understand the transformative powers of mountaineering. When you are roped in, alone, freezing, scared, and vulnerable on the side of an icy slope, nothing protects you from the common denominator of your humanity. You are equal to all other people, the only differentiation being your will and God-given strength. Mountaineering is an equalizer, and I hope that my story will encourage others to pursue it no matter their economic status, location, or background.

In the end, I've decided that I have nothing to hide or to be ashamed of about my legacy. Faced with a number of different paths, I've chosen one that pushes my body and psyche to their limits, and in that regard I have been extremely lucky. However, as you're about to see in the coming pages, I can also be a real piece of work, plagued by very human problems—some physiological, like my dyslexia; others personal, like my stubborn ego and pride—and for this reason it's important to explain just how I became this way . . .

Bo Parfet, Chicago, 2008

THE SEVEN SUMMITS (All right, eight, if you're really counting.)

There are two different versions of the Seven Summits: the list first postulated by Richard Bass and another then compiled by Reinhold Messner, which replaces Australia's highest mountain with the tallest mountain in Oceania/Australasia. This includes Australia, New Zealand, and the Pacific island of New Guinea. Here are the peaks in the order in which I climbed them:

Mountain	Country	Continent	Elevation (ft)
Mount Kilimanjaro	Tanzania	Africa	19,341
Cerro Aconcagua	Argentina	South America	22,841
Denali (Mount McKinley)	United States	North America	20,320
Vinson Massif	—	Antarctica	16,050
Mount Elbrus	Russia	Europe	18,510
Carstensz Pyramid (Puncak Jaya) [1]	Indonesia	Australia/ New Guinea	16,024
Mount Kosciuszko [2]	Australia	Australia	7,310
Mount Everest	Nepal, China	Asia	29,029

1. Messner list.
2. Bass list.

DIE TRYING

DANGLING IN MIDAIR at the end of a 40-foot rope, looking at a 2,000-foot drop down a craggy mass of mostly vertical rock, I sucked in some air and tried to catch my breath. I'd witnessed death close to the 29,029-foot summit of Mount Everest, been stuck in 70-mile-an-hour winds on the side of Aconcagua, struggled with a crippling bout of food poisoning on Kilimanjaro, and slipped into a crevasse on Vinson Massif. But after somehow ascending more than 16,000 feet to reach a steep, awkwardly inverted wall near the top of Papua New Guinea's Carstensz Pyramid, the highest mountain in Australasia, I was faced with an altogether different kind of challenge.

Having already dealt with the elements, Indonesian terrorists, local militia, lurking cannibals, and near starvation to the point of physical and emotional exhaustion, I stared at that intimidating length of granite and, in its rugged gray complexion and skyward trajectory, saw yet another manifestation of the proverbial barrier that I'd faced all my life. As a dyslexic kid with a speech impediment, I had grappled with overwhelming odds to disprove the claims of my teachers and fellow pupils that I'd never graduate from high school. As an adult, I had worked hard to succeed in a mostly literate world and achieve what I'd been assured was impossible.

Now, swinging beneath a ridge on Carstensz Pyramid, technically my most difficult climb to date, I thought, "You won't defeat me, you sonofabitch."

■   ■   ■

I'VE HEARD PEOPLE describe near-death circumstances with the phrase "I saw my life flash before my eyes," but I question this. Anyone who has experienced extreme fear, physical or emotional, would say that each second becomes an eternity, that time slows to a crawl and there's an absorption of the minutest details. Instead, it's our everyday lives that flash before us. Our heartbeats, distant noises, and incidents just beyond our field of vision all go unnoticed as the days pass, one rolling into another. But that isn't the case on the side of a mountain, where there's a hyperfocus on the tiniest subtleties of wind and temperature and sweat. When you climb, you feel each and every second of being alive, and that is something I have come to crave.

Thanks to expeditions such as that to Carstensz Pyramid, I've learned that fear isn't about wondering how you'll ever reach the top of the mountain. It's about the times when you're gasping for air, attempting to defy gravity, and being thankful for every beat of your heart. That's what I love about climbing—what it teaches me about myself physically, emotionally, and spiritually, as well as the ever-present possibility of death. Not that I value life less than anyone else. On the contrary, I'd say I value it more, and I'll put it on the line only for what I consider to be the most worthwhile challenges, testing myself in far-flung environments before returning to daily life with a fresh perspective. For me, the entire climbing experience is about feeling *reborn*.

The vast majority of people have goals: They want to work out; they'd like to eat healthier food; they have their eye on a new job; they want to start their own company; they're trying to become better parents. They want to change, and they want to improve. Yet, while they talk about this, within themselves they usually remain the same, year after year. So, how do you change? One way is to make minor adjustments over the course of a lifetime. Another is the transition that occurs in response to the death or near death of a loved one. And then there are those individuals such as myself who want to change dramatically and relatively quickly. Born with limited ability, we achieve this by saying that we're sick and tired of living a regular existence, and we step outside the ordinary by knowingly putting ourselves in life-threatening situations, facing adversity like we've never done before.

No doubt about it, during a three-month climbing expedition that forces me to learn something new (and think about what I've learned) every day, I change for the better and move beyond the set of skills with which I began the challenge. For me, my freedom is worth more than a salary.

Still, while some people believe that divinity and immortality await those who reach the summit, I can't say I've ever aspired to those lofty attributes. The truth is, I just thought that hauling myself up the side of a mountain might be a good way of attracting girls. Little did I realize that, in the process of trying to climb that mountain, I'd sometimes spend months without showering, risk losing fingers to frostbite, see my body wither at high altitudes, and share a tent with five other guys.

My grand aspirations as an international man of mystery were shattered early, as were any notions of my returning from a mountain as some sort of shaman, imparting answers to humanity's greatest questions. Among the Dalai Lama's "Instructions for Life" is one that states, "Share your knowledge. It's a way to achieve immortality." I love that line, but unfortunately, I'm a far cry from the man who wrote it. Instead, I'm just an ordinary guy who was blessed with the opportunity to undertake an extraordinary journey of exploration and self-discovery—my quest to climb the Seven Summits, an exhilarating, sometimes excruciating, ultimately enlightening odyssey that, without endowing me with spiritual transcendence, has provided many unforgettable experiences.

"When man knows how to live dangerously, he is not afraid to die," William O. Douglas, the Supreme Court's longest-serving justice, wrote in his adventure memoir *Of Men and Mountains*. "When he is not afraid to die, he is, strangely, free to live. When he is free to live, he can become bold, courageous, self-reliant."

This is the story of how I became free to live.

CHAPTER 1

GETTING TO THE MOUNTAIN

I will persist until I succeed. I was not delivered into this world into defeat, nor does failure course through my veins. I am not a sheep waiting to be prodded by my shepherd. I am a lion and I refuse to talk, to walk, to sleep with the sheep. The slaughterhouse of failure is not my destiny. I will persist until I succeed.

—Og Mandino, *The Greatest Salesman in the World*

THE POWER OF the human spirit—that priceless intangible that can transform even the most shattered and seemingly defeated individual into an indomitable force. It's sometimes the only thing that will save you as a climber when you're challenged by the invincible spirit of the mountain, and in my case it has also helped me overcome adversity and inner demons that at one time led me to place little value on living. That is, until I perceived it specifically in contrast to dying.

It was thanks not only to my early life experiences but also to my lineage and some incredibly insightful and supportive people that I developed my own strength of spirit. It's a spirit that runs right through my family, from my mom, dad, and four siblings all the way back to my paternal great-great-grandfather, Dr. William Erastus Upjohn, the founder—and for nearly 40 years the president—of the Upjohn Company, which evolved from a small attic business into a worldwide provider of pharmaceutical products and health-care services.

William's father, Uriah, left Wales for America in 1828 and studied medicine in New York. He eventually became a well-known doctor in Kalamazoo, that Michigan city located halfway between Detroit and Chicago whose catchy, Native American name has been mentioned in the title and lyrics of numerous songs. (Uriah's English-born cousin, Richard Upjohn, designed the present-day Trinity Church in New York City, one of the oldest churches in the country, and cofounded the American Institute of Architects.)

Uriah and his wife, Maria, had twelve children. Among the four who followed him into the medical profession was William. Born in 1852, William graduated from the University of Michigan in 1875 and spent the next 10 years as a doctor in the practice of his father's brother, also called William, in the nearby city of Hastings. At that time, most medicines were in fluid form, and pills were like small rocks—hard and, because they did not dissolve, nearly impossible to digest, let alone swallow. W. E. began experimenting with alternatives in the attic of his home. By 1885, he had invented and patented the "friable" pill, which could be crushed to a powder. This, in turn, crushed the competition, and soon a thumb reducing a pill to powder became the trademark symbol of the Upjohn Pill and Granule Company, founded by W. E. and his brother Henry in 1886 and shortened to the Upjohn Company six years later.

W. E., who was elected Kalamazoo's first mayor and later eulogized as its "First Citizen," had three daughters and a son by his first wife, Rachel Babcock. After her death, he married Carrie Sherwood Gilmore, whose late husband, James, had cofounded the city's largest department store, Gilmore Brothers. Carrie had three sons, one of whom was Donald Gilmore. When W. E. Upjohn died in 1932, the responsibility for running the company passed to his nephew, Dr. Lawrence Upjohn. There was no way any of W. E.'s daughters could have been considered for such a lofty position back then. However, when one of them, Genevieve, married Donald Gilmore, he became a virtual shoo-in to take over as president upon Lawrence's retirement in 1944. Just think: Donald, with a short stint at Yale University, was not only the founder's stepson, but also his son-in-law! And regardless of any nepotism, he also proved to be absolutely the right man for the job, expanding the company and taking it international.

Like the marriage of W. E. Upjohn and Carrie Sherwood Gilmore, the union of Donald and Genevieve joined Kalamazoo's two most prominent families. It also produced three daughters. The youngest, Martha Gilmore, married her childhood friend Ray Theodore Parfet (better known as Ted) in 1945. Having joined Upjohn as a business manager after being awarded the Distinguished Flying Cross as a B-25 bomber pilot on no less than 60 missions in World War II, Ted steadily worked his way up the company ladder to become Chairman and CEO in 1969—the last family member to do so—and he and Martha had four children: William, Sally, Donald, and Jane.

William Upjohn Parfet, my father, was born in 1946 and grew up in Kalamazoo. He attended Lawrenceville High School in New Jersey, received a B.A. (with honors) in economics from Lake Forest College, just north of Chicago, in 1970, and received an M.B.A. in international finance from the University of Michigan two years later. Bill (as he is better known) and my mom, Maury Lyon, were neighbors from the time he was three and she was four, and after their friendship led to marriage on March 31, 1968, they had four children: Teddy in 1973, Jenny in 1974, me in 1977, and Emily in 1980.

The year Teddy was born, Dad joined the Upjohn Company as a staff auditor. By 1985 he was a member of the board of directors, and he became Executive Vice President a short time later. Theodore Cooper succeeded Ray T. Parfet as chairman and CEO in 1987, and when Cooper died in April 1993, my dad was considered a leading candidate to replace him. But his ideas on how to lead the company didn't match those of his fellow directors, and within a few months he had resigned, although he remained on the board. Three years later, having helped one of his best friends to turn around a struggling medical devices firm, Dad did the same for MPI Research, a Michigan-based pharmaceutical/biotech-related company. Purchasing it at age 50, he worked long hours for the next five years, and the result was a flourishing organization of which he is currently the Chairman and CEO.

Meanwhile, in 1995, Upjohn merged with a Swedish pharmaceutical giant and its name was changed to Pharmacia & Upjohn. A subsequent merger with the American bioindustry company Monsanto resulted in the Upjohn name disappearing altogether. In 2003, Pharmacia was bought by Pfizer, at which point all ties with the Upjohn family were severed, along with any chance I might have had of following in my ancestors' footsteps. It was the end of one era and the start of another, one in which I would eventually attempt to create my own legacy, while mountaineering would help me find some answers to who I wanted to be.

My Upjohn heritage is now a part of history, and as such it has only a slight connection to my own need to achieve. Regardless of family background, one's drive comes from within, from the same place as the human spirit, as evidenced by my father's post-Upjohn accomplishments. And although my mother has proved that she is equally strong, talented, and resourceful, there is no doubt that the two of them are polar opposites.

Dad believes in tough love. At the same time, he's also a jovial guy who can communicate with anybody, from a gardener to the CEO of a big company, and I've always tried to learn by observing his excellent people and leadership skills. From him I undoubtedly inherited a larger-than-life personality together with the spirit of adventure, as he loves cars and likes to ski, fish, and hunt ducks.

Mom is the kind of person who finds great pleasure in helping people. She does a lot of philanthropic and civic work, was chairman of the board of trustees at Western Michigan University, and has always been extremely patient, kind, and caring, almost to a fault. I'd like to think that I inherited from her the thoughtfulness that has manifested itself in the philanthropic endeavors with which I've been involved on my mountaineering expeditions. She loves me unconditionally, and in her eyes I can do no wrong. Tough love just isn't a part of her nature, even though her strength in many other regards—both as a mother who would do anything to protect her children and as a businesswoman who excelled first as an antique dealer and then as a Realtor®—has made her a true hero in my eyes.

I didn't get much physical affection from my parents. Both of them were busy working, although I do remember my mom rocking me in her arms when I was upset, hugging me when I wasn't on the move, and rubbing my legs when I got muscle cramps as a result of running and riding my bike for hours on end. I had so much energy as a kid, I was always on the go.

It was in first grade at the small, private Kalamazoo Academy that my problems began, and this wasn't just because of a speech impediment that made it difficult for me to pronounce the letters r and s. (Two years of speech therapy cured that problem.) Within days I was struggling, sitting in class and feeling really uncomfortable when the other kids recited the alphabet each morning. The strongest kids would always go first while the others practiced, but I couldn't get past d, and I'd be frightened that everyone would realize this. Before long, I hated going to school. I was the only kid who just couldn't learn how to read or write. Since a lot of the letters were back to front in my mind, this is how they appeared when I drew them, and I would get confused when I saw them the right way around.

My teacher soon noticed that something was wrong, and after she informed my parents that their kid was dyslexic, I did a whole day of tests at the Specialized Language Development (SLD) Center in Kalamazoo. Man, did I hate that. Confused, angry, and frustrated, I screamed and threw books at the tutors and broke the pencils they gave me. Nevertheless, they analyzed the areas I needed to focus on—attention span, word identification, sight word vocabulary, and pattern recognition—and assigned a specialized tutor to my case.

Gayle Ahleman was great. A short woman with light blonde hair and a peaceful presence that gave me the impression she just floated wherever she went, she immediately said she could help. When I now look back on what she did for me, I could cry like a baby—in fact, just writing her name or thinking about her has the same impact. She was really special, and I had tremendous respect for her. Learning was tough as hell, but in a twisted way I liked the struggle of learning. It made me feel like a regular human being, and for her part, Mom also set about trying to help by communicating with my tutor, attending seminars, watching SLD videos, and reading the relevant books. However, the very public manner in which I was taught by Miss Ahleman was, for me, excruciating.

My first-grade classroom housed about 15 students, and a huge glass window separated it from an adjacent back room where she and I sat in full view of the other kids when they were learning German. Actually, it was just a bunch of Teutonic songs, but this hardly mattered, because considering the difficulty I was having with my own language, why would I be asked to wrap my vocal cords around another? Miss Ahleman and I would sit in the back room, and everyone else would turn and stare. I'd be mortified; my skin felt like it was boiling hot, and my body wanted to implode.

My special lessons lasted an hour each day, Monday to Friday, even during the summer. Initially, Miss Ahleman taught me all the consonant sounds. Then, when the vowels proved to be a lot more difficult, she poured dry rice into a cookie tray and asked me to draw the letters with my forefinger. This really kicked things into gear. Being able to actually *feel* the letters did something to my brain, and by the time I finished second grade, I'd remedied the problem of seeing certain things back to front. At home, I would spread our couch pillows along the length of the living room floor, and each time Mom gave me a word to spell, I'd shout out the letters, run around the pillows like I was on an obstacle course, and hustle back to the start. I just loved the challenge.

Years later, Gayle Ahleman would recall how, when I was struggling to climb an outdoor jungle gym, I continually rebuffed her efforts to help me when I slipped. "I can do this myself," I kept saying until I made it to the top, and Miss Ahleman included this in a report of that session, since it showed my independence and inner drive to succeed. "Who knew it was your first mountain?" she now remarks. Not that any of this dissuaded my teacher, Mr. Principé, a 6'8" cross between a stork and a geek, from telling Mom and Dad that I'd never graduate from high school—right in front of me.

For me, having a learning disability was like getting kicked in the face every single day. And one of the first things I did learn was how to pick myself up after each failure and try again, knowing that when I got up, it was only a matter of time before I'd get kicked and fall down once more. Screaming with frustration, tears rolling down my face, I would beat the crap out of anyone who called me stupid while telling myself over and over that it wasn't true, and that I could learn to read and somehow make my way in the world. (I still do this, just in different ways.) It was one thing trying to deal with the put-downs of teachers who should have known better, but what made life unbearable was contending with the kids who followed their lead. Every time my personal tutor appeared, I'd be petrified and pretend I didn't see her. Why couldn't it have been arranged for me to meet her out of sight in a neutral area? Instead, she would enter the back room and wait for me, sometimes for five or ten minutes, until finally she would come out, touch me on the shoulder, and say, "Bo, are you ready?" I just wanted to disappear.

When the other kids teased me—saying things like "You're stupid. Why do you need a tutor? Are you a retard?"—my reaction was to whack them. I was relatively tall for my age, and I was also strong thanks to all of my physical activity, so no one got the better of me in a fight. And neither did the teachers when anger at my own learning disability and frustration with their attitude resulted in me smart-mouthing them, refusing to sit down, and making it clear that I couldn't care less if they threatened me with a visit by the principal. When the principal did haul me out of class and sit me alone in another room, I'd have a time-out for half an hour and then, once I'd calmed down, return to class and fall back in line until the next time someone or something riled me.

On one occasion, when we were having music class in third grade, the teacher was calling out the students' names, and he pronounced mine "Bo Barf-it," prompting the whole class to laugh. Since this guy had already taught Teddy and our sister Jenny, the mispronunciation was clearly done on purpose, so I shouted, "Fuck you!" Then, when I realized that this had been drowned out by all the laughter, I turned completely obnoxious, doing the opposite of whatever he asked us to do, loudly playing the wrong notes on my recorder, and generally pushing all his buttons until he kicked me out of class.

Mom has told me that when she was contacted and came to the school, my older brother, Teddy, would say, "He just needs time to calm down." He knew what I was like, and he was right. But my frustration at my inability to learn was never really handled personally by our parents. I can hardly remember them ever reading to me, even though I myself read to Mom after things began to click for me in Mrs. Crawshaw's third-grade class. Those were really my formative years, and I was on my own the entire time, which is why I learned to self-motivate and constantly look for the next challenge while also challenging authority.

I continued to get into trouble through the fourth and fifth grades, but by that time, whenever I was really upset, I was allowed to stand up and tell the teacher I was going to take a time-out. No questions were asked; I could leave the room and just walk around the school until I had calmed down. It was like I had the run of the place! Then again, my fifth-grade teacher, Mrs. Perrino, was fabulous—kind, patient, and well versed in every subject. For the first time I got a lot of As and Bs and really hit my stride.

Over the years, I'd be sent home from time to time, and when that happened, I'd get to see my dad. That was actually kind of cool, since I didn't see him as much as I would have liked after he and Mom divorced when I was in second grade. That whole thing just snuck up on me. I hadn't been aware of any problems between them, but then all of a sudden the shouting started, and the next thing I knew, Mom had filed for divorce and Dad was gone. He rented a house in Kalamazoo, about 20 minutes' drive from our home, and my siblings and I would see him every other weekend. However, things were never the same. Within a year he was remarried, and this changed the family dynamic forever.

Dad's new wife, Barbara, had two sons, Kiley and Ryan. Kiley was a year older than my brother Teddy, Ryan was a year older than I, and for some reason Kiley was always picking on Ryan and me. I couldn't wait until I was bigger and able to stand up for myself. My time eventually came; Kiley picked on me for what felt like the hundredth time, and I flattened him with one punch. I admired him for subsequently admitting that he deserved it, but the bottom line was that he never messed with me again. My spirit was my strength.

By then, our family had expanded. When I was in fourth grade, Mom married Dick Reed, a really wonderful, trustworthy guy whose integrity and strong sense of justice has served as bedrock not only for her and his sons, Kevin and Brad—both of whom are more than 10 years older than I—but also for me and my siblings. And at around the same time, Barbara gave birth to our half sister, Sarah. However, even though I took that in my stride, the confusion of moving back and forth between two homes and two different family setups played its part in my becoming more rebellious and compiling a laundry list of misdemeanors that, despite the progress in my schoolwork, finally caught up with me in seventh grade.

First I was suspended after several of us guys were caught checking out the girls' bathroom. Then, having shown three kids the cool art of ripping the hood ornament off a Plymouth station wagon, I was called upon for guidance when an attempt to emulate my feat on a Mercedes ended in failure. "Yes, yes, in some cases you need to use wire clippers," I expertly informed one of the kids. He heeded my advice. The very next day, during recess, he and his pals removed the hood ornaments from every single car in the teachers' parking lot. When they were subsequently apprehended and questioned as to how they'd been able to do this, one of them blurted out, "Bo showed us." I was booted out of school a month before taking my final exams, which I took at home along with a total dressing-down from my dad.

It was at this point that my parents finally concluded that I'd probably outgrown Kalamazoo Academy. Kalamazoo Academy had certainly outgrown me, so in eighth grade I went to a bigger school, St. Monica's, which offered not only more kids, but also more diversity in terms of their ethnicity. I liked that. And I also had one of my favorite teachers in Mrs. Hillis, a sixty-something veteran with graying red hair and the build of a linebacker. She got the measure of me right away. "Bo, you can fight me all year long," she said the first time I smart-mouthed her, "but in the end I'll win and you'll lose." There was something different about her, and I knew it. She meant business, the classroom was her domain, and from that moment on I never talked back to her or to virtually anyone else. She set the tone, and it changed me.

Although I spent my freshman year of high school at Hackett Catholic Central in Kalamazoo, for my sophomore year Dad ensured that, like him, I went to boarding school. I ended up attending Brewster Academy in Wolfeboro, New Hampshire, which was a solid place to advance my burgeoning skills and aspirations as a basketball player (inspired by the Gene Hackman movie *Hoosiers*). There I played basketball on both the varsity and junior varsity teams. The first seven players on the varsity team were all Division 1 athletes, postgraduates who were basically doing a fifth year of high school in order to improve their SAT scores so that they could enter such colleges as Syracuse, Indiana, or North Carolina. They were already men, whereas I was only 15, so I didn't play all that much on varsity, but I did get to practice with those guys, serve as the eleventh man, and at least participate in a few games.

Still, when I went home and saw all my buddies, I realized that I wanted to stay in Kalamazoo, play on the local basketball team, and see if we could win a state championship. I therefore returned to Hackett Catholic Central, although not for long. I was easily the best player on the team, but because I wasn't a senior, the coach wouldn't start me. Frustrated that I wasn't in the starting lineup and self-destructive as a result of self-pity, I began smoking pot before the start of some games. Dad didn't know this, but Mom noticed something was up. "You're reacting slower than you normally do," she said. "What are you doing? What's wrong?"

When the season ended, I told my mom, "I'm hanging around with the wrong crowd. I need to go back to New Hampshire. I really want to play college basketball." Before mountaineering came along, basketball was a major physical and emotional outlet for me. However, when we talked to Dad, he refused to pay for this. He was sick of my flitting back and forth between the two schools, and Mom ended up paying for me to go to yet another New Hampshire high school called New Hampton Prep, where the basketball program was superior to that at Brewster Academy. Mom dug into her limited savings to ensure that I went to the best.

In the spring term of my junior year, I was allowed double time to take exams—and also to speak the answers—because of my dyslexia. As a result, I became a straight-A student. (To this day, I can formulate answers in my head, but a lot happens when these answers travel from head to pencil. Some things get lost.)

Athletically, I also had a great junior year at New Hampton, being the leading scorer on the lacrosse team. I was into all kinds of sports—ice hockey, football, skiing—but basketball was still my first choice. From the sixth through the tenth grades, it meant nothing for me to spend four or five hours at a time doing push-ups, sprints, dribbling drills, and shooting drills all on my own, even shoveling the driveway so that I could shoot hoops during the winter months. Nevertheless, during my senior year, I was the sixth man on the varsity B team. Again feeling frustrated, and with extra practice and personal drills still not turning things around, I made a big decision: I quit basketball. Until then, basketball had been my life, and while I'd never quite get over giving it up, I now did a lot more skiing, just not in New Hampshire.

Having already received a warning after I was caught smoking pot toward the end of my junior year, I was kicked out of school when a friend and I were busted for smuggling beer into our Draper Hall dorm. That meant going back to Kalamazoo and Hackett Catholic Central for the last semester and graduating with all of my friends back home.

On the recommendation of my dad, and paid for by me by working long hours writing parking tickets, working as a busboy in a restaurant, and investing in the stock market so that I could attend college full-time, I went to Colorado State University in Fort Collins, at the base of the Rocky Mountains, to study economics. It was important to me that I was holding down a couple of jobs to help pay for my tuition as well as my room and board, instead of relying on the financial assistance that Mom and Dad would have been happy to offer.

"Go where you want to live for four years," Dad advised me when I asked him which school I should apply to. Since I loved the mountains and skiing was a passion, Colorado seemed a natural choice. Still, life there wasn't easy. Buoyed by my high school graduation and believing that my dyslexia was a thing of the past, I tried to swim with the rest of the student body and racked up a string of F grades during the first semester. Immediately I told my mom, my sister, my close friends, and myself that perhaps college wasn't for me; perhaps those elementary school teachers had been right all along. My back was against the wall, and for two or three weeks I was pretty depressed.

Everyone advised me to work less, so I quit the parking ticket job and took three classes instead of four while still working in the restaurant 40 hours a week. My grades did improve a little, but with a 0.5 GPA I was on big-time academic probation and clearly not going to make it; by the summer, I was out of Colorado State, which required a 2.0.

During my sophomore year, I enrolled in a continuing education program at Colorado State University and looked into resources for disabled students. I found a facility where exams could be taken in a quiet room with no distractions. It was just what I needed. Quickly the Cs and Ds turned into As and Bs. What's more, with the help of a counselor, I was able to explain to Colorado State that, assuming I was no longer dyslexic, I hadn't taken advantage of the necessary resources while I was there and had practically turned myself into a straight-F student. This, in turn, led to what is known as a retroactive withdrawal, whereby the F grades were nullified and my GPA soared to 2.7. I was back in college.

It was around this time that I began getting into climbing. During my first year at the college, I went hiking and mountain biking with friends, and the hiking fairly quickly turned into rock scrambling, where you don't use a rope to climb the hill, but you do need to be on all fours. I was good at this, always way ahead of my friends while carrying their food and water to help them speed up. Then, because Colorado State required me to get sporting as well as elective credits, I killed two birds with one stone by taking a military skills class that offered a couple of credits. I'd always secretly wanted to join the military and had considered the Reserve Officer Training Corps (ROTC), the Marine Corps, or becoming a Navy SEAL. This class was a handy way for me to test those waters.

It was run by an ROTC captain who, during the course of extensive physical training drills, taught us how to tie knots, rappel off mountains, and navigate using a compass and a map. It was a lot of fun, and I overheard someone say that after the class ended, some ROTC guys were going to climb Longs Peak, one of the most popular of Colorado's "fourteeners" (independent mountains that are at least 14,000 feet above sea level) and the only one in the Rocky Mountain National Park that's located within the state's north central region. Boasting a steep east face, surmounted by a massive sheer cliff that is known as "the diamond" because of its shape, Longs Peak is a fairly technical climb that can prove dangerous for those without experience. This was what the ROTC guys had been training for.

I asked the captain if I could go, and after some hesitation because I wasn't part of the ROTC program, he agreed. A group of around

12 of us left at midnight, riding for over an hour in a military truck, my fellow travelers with all their military gear, me with just my ski clothes and a small backpack. On my previous hikes, it had been a case of the lighter I packed, the better, but those had been up to only 10,000 feet, not 14,000. Now I heard everyone going on and on about the altitude, and it still didn't cross my mind that what I was doing could actually be dangerous. I mean, c'mon, a hike is a hike.

All of us were wearing head torches in the dark, and about three of the guys walked really fast and raced ahead. Initially, I was among them, despite having been advised to hold back, but then I saw a few people start to poop out, and I fell in with a group that was following just behind. When they, too, began to accelerate, I slipped back to a third group and discovered that the guys in that group had already climbed Longs Peak and knew how to pace themselves. "Just watch," one of them told me. "We'll catch the others in three or four hours." I stuck with him as he walked slowly and steadily, sometimes stopping for water, and sure enough, by the time we reached the boulder field, everyone else was there. At that point, five people decided that they'd had enough and started to descend, but even though I was really tired, I had (thanks to those guys at the back) conserved my energy and felt able to carry on.

Near the top, we traversed a ridge with a sheer drop before scrambling up a steep slope to the summit. For me, that ridge was really frightening—one slip and it would be over—whereas the slope amounted to using ropes and just digging in, three people per rope, for about 100 feet. On a normal summer day the ropes wouldn't have been necessary, but on this occasion there was moisture. The problem was, I couldn't "rope up," or put on a harness and attach myself to the other climbers. The wannabe captain told me, "Since you're not ROTC, I can't be responsible for you," and that meant that if I fell, I'd drop by myself. He couldn't risk my dragging down (or being dragged down by) any of the guys under his "command." That was fair enough. If I had fallen and killed two other people, their families apparently could have sued both Colorado State and the ROTC.

As a result, I climbed solo, and I was scared, not least because it was snowing. Still, I did it because, having gone this far, I didn't want to give up. Making it to the summit was an accomplishment that no one could take away from me. And this was also the first time that the risk of dying actually made me feel more alive, doing something out of the ordinary by pitting my limited skills against a colossus of nature. Never before had I been so aware of my will to live, whereas some crazy stunts that I'd pulled in the past had been more like the death wishes of a depressed and angry teenager.

When I was 16, I'd sometimes drive straight through two-way stop signs at junctions where any possible cross traffic with the right of way was concealed by trees and heavy foliage. Blasting through there at around a hundred miles per hour, I experienced one extremely close miss, and although I was not specifically on a suicide mission, I was basically playing Russian roulette just for the hell of it, with little regard for my own life or, I'm ashamed to say, the lives of others. I was just so fed up with my home, school, and disability that in a moment's madness I was quite prepared to spin the gun barrel and find out if there was a bullet in the chamber. No fear, just exhilaration. The climb up Longs Peak was totally different.

That experience immediately humbled me. The spirituality, the energy—being on the side of a mountain was just magical, and it still is. It increases your consciousness, and I remember thinking, "Man, this is so much fun, I don't want to fall and die. I want to do it again." Kilimanjaro, which I initially overheard the ROTC guys talking about climbing when we were back on campus, would take that feeling to a whole other level, but without a doubt Longs Peak was like seeing the light for the first time.

Some people never forget a road trip across America that they took with their parents when they were six years old, but I never had anything like that. I experienced it on a mountain when I was 19, and when I returned, I knew that there was something different about me. Having acquired some sense of my potential, I suddenly wanted to aim higher in all facets of my life. During my remaining two years at

Colorado State, I hiked up another "fourteener," Pikes Peak, near the eastern edge of the Rockies. But most of my time was taken up studying for exams and improving my GPA to over 3.0, and in 1999 I graduated and set about becoming an investment banker by attending the University of Michigan, where I embarked on a two-year master's degree course in applied economics.

Because U of M is a Wall Street feeder school, I had several job offers for summer internships, and between my first and second years I worked as an investment banker at Goldman Sachs in both Chicago and New York. Then, a few months before graduating, I applied to become a research fellow at the Financial Accounting Standards Board (FASB), a private, not-for-profit organization whose mission is "to establish and improve standards of financial accounting and reporting for the guidance and education of the public, including issuers, auditors, and users of financial information."

While working on a couple of projects at FASB, I decided to give Wall Street investment banking another try, and I secured a job offer from J. P. Morgan. For me, at that time, it was definitely the right move. With a master's degree, I could easily expect to earn over $100,000 during my first year in return for working 100 hours per week, and I signed a contract with J. P. Morgan a few months before completing my fellowship at FASB.

While I was still at FASB, Gog Boonswong, the brother of my roommate, Brig, told me about a star-studded cross-country car rally called the Gumball 3000. Having seen films like *The Cannonball Run*, I had actually fantasized about racing from coast to coast. As it happens, the Gumball 3000 echoed the Cannonball Baker Sea-to-Shining-Sea Memorial Trophy Dash (or "Cannonball Run"), which had taken place on public roads between New York and Los Angeles during the 1970s. Celebrating the U.S. Interstate Highway System while also serving as a protest against its traffic laws, the race had been canceled in 1979 because of concerns about—surprise, surprise—road safety. Nonetheless, it had also inspired the *Cannonball, Cannonball Run*, and *Gumball Rally* series of movies. Exactly two decades later, rally organizer Maximillion Cooper revived and relocated the concept in the form of the Gumball 3000, which through 2001 featured celebrity drivers and classic cars competing in London-Europe round trips.

In April 2002, the "rally" (so called to give it an air of greater legitimacy) was staged in the United States for the first time, starting at the Plaza Hotel in New York and ending at the Playboy Mansion in Los Angeles, where Hugh Hefner and assorted Playmates handed out trophies. This was after the contestants had passed through a checkpoint at Grand Central Station in Washington, D.C.; partied at Elvis Presley's Graceland Mansion in Memphis, Tennessee; received a Dallas Cowboys welcome in Texas; and made stops at the Cadillac Ranch in Amarillo; Santa Fe, New Mexico; the Grand Canyon; and Las Vegas, Nevada.

Actors, models, millionaires, and billionaires were among the participants, while the lineup of 175 classic and supercharged cars included an award-winning 1960s Corvette painted in the Stars and Stripes and a 1959 Ferrari California Spider (similar to the one in the movie *Ferris Bueller's Day Off*) that had been bought for more than $1 million to take part in the rally. My own 1971 black-on-black Ferrari 365 GTB/4, better known as the Ferrari Daytona, boasted a top speed of 179 mph, acceleration from 0 to 60 mph in just 5.4 seconds, and a V12 engine at the front that positively rumbled. Loud and angry, its sound was magnificent, as befitting a car that came with a $90,000 price tag.

I had managed to save a fair amount of money and make some profitable stock market investments. Added to my earnings at FASB, this gave me the funds to buy the car. Then one of Dad's friends who owned a classic car dealership in Canada offered me the Daytona for much less and promised to buy it back a week later, following the race. Indeed, my Daytona was almost identical to the midnight-blue Daytona that racing legend Dan Gurney had driven from New York to Los Angeles in 1971 to win the second Cannonball Run.

With the competition's co-organizer, Brock Yates, as his codriver, Gurney had set a record by traveling the 2,863 miles in 35 hours and

54 minutes, collecting only one fine along the way. I knew I'd be lucky just to match that number of speeding tickets. Never mind all the radar detectors and satellite navigation systems, or that Maxmillion Cooper had tried to smooth the way with local authorities by informing them that many of the participants would be contributing heavily to the recently established 9/11 fund—some drivers actually had planes flying ahead and radioing them to warn of lurking cop cars.

Not me. The night before the race, the Daytona's alternator went bye-bye halfway through the Holland Tunnel, which connects New York and New Jersey. The resulting traffic jam in the smog was an unforgettable experience, and the subsequent last-minute repair somehow disabled the car's gas and oil gauges, radio, RPM dial, and even its cigarette lighter, meaning that there was nowhere to plug in my newly purchased GPS and "fuzz buster." The speedometer dial was just about the only device that still worked, so I was basically driving by the seat of my pants alongside a "copilot" from Cleveland named Jonathan Leebow who, I discovered at the last minute, had never even learned how to use a stick shift. I was furious. I'd have to stay behind the wheel the entire way and try to follow those cars that had two drivers in addition to all the necessary gadgets.

On the first leg of the race, we traveled from New York to Memphis, arriving at eight in the morning, and heard about one guy who had managed to collect 15 speeding tickets by the time he'd reached Washington, D.C. A couple of others had spent the night in jail, and there were plenty of spinouts and high-speed chases. For me, though, it was a case of so far, so good. That was, until the next morning, en route to Dallas, when at around 8:30 I was in a group of cars being chased by a cop. All of a sudden, speeds of 110 mph on the open road soared to 150 and 160 mph, as the cop was determined to take the last guy, and I was determined that that guy wouldn't be me. The police reinforcements and helicopter surveillance would come later.

Racing a car as fast as I could was just like a video game, and the adrenalin rush was incredible. Sometimes, at 110 or 120 mph, there would be other Gumballers racing straight past me, with cop cars in hot pursuit. It was total craziness. All of this action disappeared from view, however, when my buddy Jonathan volunteered his services as a navigator and managed to add a couple of hundred miles to our journey. Without any radar-equipped fellow racers to follow, I could only drive about eight miles above the speed limit in pitch darkness, and by the time we made it to Dallas—not at the intended seven in the evening, but at one in the morning—I was exhausted, although not enough to miss the Dallas Cowboys party, which was still in full swing.

The trip to the Grand Canyon was relatively without incident, but for me the race ended when a blown muffler en route to Vegas caused my copilot to be hospitalized with carbon monoxide poisoning. I ended up flying to L.A. in order to make the Playboy Mansion party, and although the Daytona didn't accompany me there, I did at least receive a "Spirit Award," presumably for never having given up—doing all the driving myself, surviving with hardly any electronics, talking the cops out of giving me tickets when I eventually did get pulled over, and even jumping on a plane to reach the finish line. Today, I still have the car, and to my surprise its value has increased exorbitantly.

For me, the 2002 Gumball 3000 was an amazing experience, and one that whetted my appetite for further, much more daring adventures. In June of that year, I began working at J. P. Morgan, and having done some ice climbing in New York's Adirondack Mountains the previous winter—navigating frozen waterfalls with a pair of ice axes and traction-supplying crampons (spikes) attached to my boots—I wanted to have an expedition to look forward to in order to stay motivated. Something to live for. Then I read an article on the Internet about global warming and how the glaciers atop Mount Kilimanjaro, Africa's highest peak, could be gone within 20 years. Since I was familiar with the aerial photographs that my Great-Aunt Margaret Upjohn had taken of this natural wonder during the 1940s, I now knew where my life was immediately headed.

KILIMANJARO

Twenty years from now you will be more disappointed by the things that you didn't do than by the ones you did do. So throw off the bowlines. Sail away from the safe harbor. Catch the trade winds in your sails. Explore. Dream. Discover.

—Mark Twain

I REALLY NEEDED a vacation. And not just any vacation. During the six months that I'd been at J. P. Morgan, working 100 or more hours per week on corporate finance for public companies—mergers, acquisitions, public offerings, debt offerings—I'd spent only sleeping time at the small, rat-infested loft near the corner of West Broadway and Canal Street, where SoHo meets Chinatown. Although I was paid well for being stuck inside an office cubicle from 9 every morning until 2 A.M., I had ballooned from 180 to 230 pounds thanks to a desk-bound diet of hotdogs at noon and a steakhouse takeout at 9 or

10 at night, punctuated by a daily 5 P.M. jog during which I'd pick up a couple of cheeseburgers, an order of fries, and a Coke from McDonald's. Cholesterol City. And all the while I was preparing for my trip to Kilimanjaro.

A lot of people are unhappy with their lives, including some who stay in a job they don't like for 30 or 40 years. Others do something about it. Bored and stressed out with the Wall Street rat race even though it was enabling me to earn good money, I began thinking, "Is this what my life's about, just work and sleep, sleep and work?" Spending my few moments of free time on the Internet, I read about the world's largest freestanding mountain, a Tanzanian colossus featuring three dormant volcanoes (Kibo, Mawensi, and Shira) as well as Kibo's summit, Uhuru Peak, which rises to a height of 19,340 feet. Okay, so I was completely out of shape, and using the StairMaster for an hour a week couldn't compete with two tons of Big Macs. However, climbing Longs Peak had consisted of one long 12-hour day, and when I read that trekking up Kilimanjaro comprises many days of only half that length, I idiotically figured that I should be able to handle it easily.

In need of something to look forward to, an experience that would be out of the ordinary, I booked my place on an expedition being organized by Adventure Peaks, an English company with a broad-based European clientele. I didn't want to climb Africa's highest mountain—a stratovolcano comprising multiple layers of hardened lava, as well as volcanic ash and fragments—with only people from my own country. I wanted a different perspective. And, following the altruistic lead of my great-great-grandfather Dr. William Upjohn, I also wanted to contribute something to the troubled region I'd soon be visiting.

To that end, after I'd secured nine days to make the trip (five days' leave from work, plus the weekends on either side), I focused on setting up a scholarship that would send two poor African students from shantytowns to medical school, enabling them to become doctors and really help people in a part of the world that is racked with AIDS and malnutrition. I learned about the South African Institute of Race Relations (SAIRR) through a friend, Wayne Safro. Run by a guy named John Kane-Berman, SAIRR had once given Nelson Mandela his law school grant, and I learned that this wonderful research and policy organization tests kids in really poor tribal areas and helps those with above-average skills to become doctors, lawyers, accountants, you name it. Linking up with SAIRR, I learned that all it would cost for me to provide a couple of medical school scholarships would be about $12,000, so I immediately began asking all of the people at work if they'd help me achieve this through small sponsorship grants. It was about wanting to make a change, my colleagues responded, and our joint efforts would subsequently yield tangible results.

There's an old African proverb: "If you educate a boy, you educate an individual. If you educate a girl, you educate a community." That's because, according to certain research studies, many of the educated young men in Africa leave their villages to further their careers, whereas the young women remain behind, raise children, and often do jobs that help their communities. My charitable endeavors have never specifically targeted women as the beneficiaries, and my Kilimanjaro-related sponsorship of African college graduates initially enabled a pair of young men to attend medical school. However, after one of them struggled and dropped out, the SAIRR contacted me to say that a young woman named Lungile Dlodlo, who was from a very humble background, needed my consent to use the remaining funds for a two-year course to obtain a national diploma in chemical engineering. My reply: "Absolutely."

In 2006, both Lungile and the remaining medical student, Tendani Mutambi, graduated. Although I had previously corresponded with them only via e-mail, I met them after they had completed their studies. Lungile had become an engineer for a reputable company in South Africa, and Tendani was a doctor dealing with HIV and pediatric patients in the shanty neighborhoods of Johannesburg. Both were really appreciative, and I was thankful to learn that Lungile had been sending money home to her family while encouraging her siblings and cousins to also get an education. For his part, Tendani is saving lives every day.

Back in 2002, when work was slow during the Christmas/New Year's period and my mind was increasingly consumed with thoughts of Kilimanjaro, I worked out three days a week at a local gym in a belated attempt to fight the flab. Having read plenty about altitude sickness, and being on a tight schedule that was allowing me just five days to climb and descend this giant mountain (Adventure Peaks also organized nine- and twelve-day treks there), I obtained a prescription for Diamox, which, if taken as a preventive measure, can help with acclimatization. Then, after also getting malaria pills and shots for tetanus, typhoid, and yellow fever, in early January 2003 I flew from New York to Amsterdam, and then from Amsterdam to Kilimanjaro International Airport in Tanzania. A lot of my fellow passengers were also going to climb the mountain, and on the way I kept overhearing comments like, "I've been taking my malaria pills for three days," and "I've been taking Diamox for a week," as well as terms such as AMS (acute mountain sickness), cerebral edema (swelling of the brain), and pulmonary edema (fluid in the lungs). By the time we landed, I was freaked out. I'd swallowed my first pills in midflight. Oh, yeah, I was real prepared.

The United Republic of Tanzania, located in East Africa and bordered on the north, west, and south by Kenya, Uganda, Rwanda, Burundi, the Democratic Republic of Congo, Zambia, Malawi, and Mozambique, is named after its mainland territory of Tanganyika and the Zanzibar islands, which sit within the Indian Ocean off the east coast of Africa. Home to some of the oldest human fossils so far discovered, as well as footprints estimated to be around 3.6 million years old, Tanzania is just over twice the size of California and is loaded with resources such as gold and natural gas. Nevertheless, while agriculture accounts for the bulk of its exports and employment, the country has struggled economically in the face of droughts, as well as a topography that limits cultivated crops to only 4 percent of the overall land area. The rest of the country includes Kilimanjaro in the northeast, the wildlife-rich Serengeti Plain in the northwest, and numerous other national parks and preserves.

Accordingly, with a free day before the climb and no desire to spend more time than necessary bonding with the mosquitoes in my crappy little hotel room, I went on a short safari around the Tarangire National Park, close to the spectacular Ngorongoro Crater—the world's largest unbroken, unflooded volcanic caldera—and was just knocked out to see all of the free-roaming wildebeest, rhinos, buffalos, elephants, lions, leopards, impalas, gazelles, zebras, and giraffes. Then and there I was captivated by my first African experience. All of my senses were heightened.

On the way to Tarangire, I had looked through the cab window and asked the driver, "Is that Kilimanjaro?" "Yes," came the reply. "Wow," I exclaimed. "It's really huge."

Catching sight of me in his mirror, the man saw where I was looking and started to laugh. "What's so funny?" I asked. "That's Mount Meru," he said, referring to a sub-15,000-foot live volcano located to the west of my planned destination. "*That's* Kilimanjaro!" Looking where he was pointing, I didn't know what he was talking about. Sure, I could see a small mountain topped by clouds. Then I looked above the clouds and saw a snow-capped peak. Holy shit! Was that where I'd be heading in less than a day? To say I felt intimidated would be a huge understatement. "There's no way I can do it," I thought. Still, the majesty of Kilimanjaro was sharply contrasted with bleak African reality when a kid was hit by a bus while I was traveling through a town called Arusha, on the way back from Tarangire.

It was getting dark, and one moment I saw a flash of white as a little girl—she couldn't have been older than five or six—darted across the street, and the next, the bus in front of us screeched to a halt. Then it began to move again and kept going, at which point I saw the child on the side of the road, lying on her front in a crucifix position. It was rush hour, and the place was packed with traffic and pedestrians, yet nobody rushed to her aid, so I told my driver, "Stop, she just got hit by a bus!"

"No, no, no," he insisted. "If we stop here, we could get robbed or murdered. We're not stopping."

"Fucking stop!" I screamed. "We can't just leave her there!"

But that's exactly what happened. The driver didn't want to know. And neither did two young boys who simply walked around the seemingly lifeless body as we drove past. I couldn't believe it. This kid had just been ploughed by 30,000 pounds of metal and nobody could give a damn. Was this sort of thing an ordinary, everyday occurrence in this part of the world? The next morning, I saw a photo of the child on the front page of a local newspaper, so obviously someone thought the incident was newsworthy. But no doubt about it, I had planted myself in a strange place with values and challenges that were poles apart from what I'd been used to up until now. And if this was yet another part of the African experience, then I couldn't wait to get away from the city to the relatively safer climes of Kilimanjaro.

The people with whom I'd be doing the climb were way better qualified than I was. There was Richard Thorby, a born-again Christian from South Africa who'd become an accountant in Geneva, Switzerland, after giving up gang life on the streets of Johannesburg. (Some might view this as a logical transition). Tall, dapper, and in his early forties, with dark hair and a neatly trimmed beard, he'd read a lot about Kilimanjaro, was very well organized, and, in true accountant fashion, had labeled all the items in his backpack: medicines, vitamins, everything. By way of preparation for the thin air up ahead, he and Tony Cain, a shorter, fortyish, balding British prison warden and former marine, had even done an acclimatization climb of Mt. Kenya, at 17,058 feet the second-highest mountain in Africa, and suffered AMS, projectile vomiting, weight loss, and ataxia (loss of muscle coordination) in the process. In Tony's case, pulmonary edema had finally necessitated traveling through the night to get him to safety.

Try to imagine, therefore, what these two guys must have been thinking when they first set eyes on me, a brash American with a big belly and gas-station sunglasses (offering no capacity to block harmful UV light) who'd simply thrown some toiletries into a bag, purchased a pair of climbing boots, and brought along his ski clothes. As

Richard later told me, "You looked more fat than fit, even though you'd subsequently prove us wrong."

Another member of the team who probably doubted me was "Oliver" (renamed for reasons that will become clear), our 29-year-old Adventure Peaks guide, whose technical climbing experience and tall and wiry mountaineer's body were offset by the fact that he'd never previously been to Kilimanjaro. The rest of us were kind of nervous about that, and justifiably so, especially since the highest he'd ever climbed was 15,774 feet up Mont Blanc in the French/Italian Alps. After learning this, I remember saying, "Shit, this is over 19,000 feet. What if you don't make it?"

"I'll make it."

"How do you know?"

"Trust me; I'll make it."

Since the law stipulates that there has to be a local guide to help people climb Kilimanjaro, Oliver's African counterpart was August, and he had things all set. Short in stature—only about five-foot-one—and skinny as could be, this 48-year-old man looked 10 years younger, and after we'd obtained our climbing permits, he reassured us that everything was in hand. Setting off in our van on the four-hour drive from the Kilimanjaro Airport area to the base of the mountain, we were informed by August that we had to get some meat for the trip. "I must go to the butcher," he told us, and when the van stopped about half an hour later, it was in front of a guy sitting behind a plastic table. Next to this guy was what looked like a clothesline, and hanging from it were these pitch-black sheets, six inches thick, six feet high, and three feet wide. I didn't have a clue what they were (clothing, perhaps?), and I also didn't realize that we were at the butcher's.

When the man brandished a machete, I thought he was threatening August, but then he picked some newspaper off the ground, spread it across the table, and grabbed hold of one of the black sheets, at which point millions of flies took to the air, revealing a slab of bloody red meat. Goat, gnu, buffalo—who knew what it was? For sure, this wasn't Kroger, and forget about any health and safety standards. After our master butcher had hacked away at the meat, he wrapped it in the newspaper, and August put it in his backpack. The rest of us looked on as if to say, *"What the hell is this?"*

"Is that going to be safe?" someone asked.

"Oh, yes, yes, it's okay," August reassured us. "We cook the meat real well."

Where was a McDonald's now that we needed one? There was sufficient meat to "satisfy" our rapidly diminishing appetites for the next three days. After that, halfway up the mountain, porters would bring us fresh supplies.

Many such porters were milling around when we arrived at the base of Kilimanjaro, along with hundreds of other locals who were following our van and begging us to hire them. "Secure your wallets, keep them hidden, and don't let go of your possessions," August warned us before we got out of the vehicle. "When you open these doors, you will be attacked." Which we were. I made sure that the front and back pockets of my shorts were empty, yet I could still feel hands rummaging around inside them as we tried to push our way through the crowd. One guy was even down on the ground, checking my socks to see if I had any money hidden there. I tried to keep my composure amid the pandemonium, aware that a hostile reaction on my part could provoke a free-for-all.

As my fellow climbers and I stood alongside numerous other trekking groups, August told us, "I have my team." This meant seven porters. Unlike the Sherpas working on Mt. Everest in Nepal, the porters at Kilimanjaro aren't experts at climbing. Instead, they can hike and carry massive loads—tents, stocks of clothes and food, and, in the case of one of our porters, a stove on his head that must have weighed at least 80 pounds—to the high camp while the trekkers carry day packs containing items such as raingear, a packed lunch, and several liters of water. Thereafter, it falls to the guide and his assistants to transport the tents and lighter loads of supplies the rest of the way. The thing was, looking these porters in the eye, I wondered if they could be counted upon in times of trouble any more than those people who'd walked by the motionless body of that girl who had been hit by the bus. As time would tell, they could, but the bus incident had certainly shaken my confidence in the locals.

Mt. Kilimanjaro, whose name is of unknown origin and uncertain meaning—Mountain of Greatness, White Mountain, Hill of Caravans, take your choice—boasts a summit, the highest in Africa, that was first conquered by a trio of explorers in 1889. Getting there involves one of the most beautiful treks on Earth, a long and demanding 45-mile climb through five different climatic zones: a humid, muddy rain forest that starts at about 6,500 feet and encircles the mountain; a heath at around 9,000 feet where there's heather that grows over 30 feet high; a grassy moorland, above the clouds at 10,500 feet, featuring unusual-looking plants that are resilient to the hot days and frozen nights; an alpine desert at around 15,000 feet, where the thin air probably explains why there are bones of dead animals that somehow strayed too far; and the windswept and bitter cold arctic region at 18,000 feet, just below the summit, where glaciers are just tiny remnants of the massive icecap that crowned the mountain thousands of years ago. It's as if you've walked all the way from the equator to the North Pole in a matter of days.

We navigated this by taking the picturesque but often less-utilized Machame route, which starts at the Machame Gate (elevation 5,718 feet) and quickly ascends through the rain forest and heath zones. Then it's on to the Lava Tower (15,000 feet) before descending back to the Barranco Camp (12,700 feet) on the same day, adhering to the "climb high, sleep low" ideal that enhances altitude acclimatization. All of which would have been fine had I been properly equipped.

"Aren't you using trekking poles?" Richard asked me just before we set out from the Machame Gate. He had brought his own pair, and some were on sale nearby. "Why would I need them?" I asked. "We're hiking."

"Well, they'll help to disperse some of the weight," he said, as I noticed him glancing at my midriff. "They'll save your knees and your back, especially on the way down."

"Nah, I'm okay," I replied, not yet realizing that I was grossly underprepared in terms of gear, food, and clothing. The guides for this expedition didn't really check what we were taking—that would change when I undertook more dangerous climbs—and they also had no idea about my lack of physical training. I, of course, was more than aware of this (hell, I couldn't even see my own feet), and it made me nervous. Yet, like everybody else on that first day, I was also excited.

We spent six hours trekking through the dense vegetation and short, steep climbs of the montane rain forest, and we were moving fast, with Oliver, our guide, cruising ahead of us, evidently trying to demonstrate his manhood after we'd emphasized that the highest he'd ever climbed had been Mont Blanc. When it poured, we had to don our raingear, and there was some serious mud, but we just kept going while I struggled to stay with the pack. Every time my co-trekkers rested or stopped for a drink, I'd catch up, only to have them set off again. I really had to focus, and I remember thinking, "I've come all this way, and I may not make it."

August and the porters were bringing up the rear, having initially told us to go ahead while they sorted out all of our baggage. The fact was, the distance we traveled in six hours they could probably have managed in two, even when carrying full loads, and they were on hand to set up our tents when we reached the Machame Camp at the end of the first day. There I ran into a middle-aged Californian woman named Becky, whom I had met on the plane, and who had told me that she'd been training for Kilimanjaro for the past year. She had just climbed Longs Peak, and having ascended to 14,000 feet in five days, she was concerned about going to 19,000 in just a day or two more. Now, when I saw her at the camp, she was bent over and massaging her head.

"Hey, how are you doing?" I asked.

"I've got a really bad headache," she replied, "and it's at the front of my head, so it's probably due to the altitude."

She was worried, but there wasn't much I could say aside from echoing everyone else's advice to keep drinking plenty of water. Then I struck up a conversation with "Lorna" (again renamed for her own protection), a gorgeous young Australian woman in her mid-twenties who was climbing by herself, and invited her to meet the rest of my small group. She and Oliver hit it off within about 10 minutes, and there was plenty of suspicion that they had also *had it* off after they quickly disappeared into his tent. This was despite the fact that each of them had a partner back home. Gossip spreads like wildfire on the side of a mountain, and Oliver's line about having something to help the blister on Lorna's right hand only helped fuel this, especially when they didn't emerge for over an hour.

After Lorna left, a few of us naturally asked Oliver what had been going on in his tent. (Hey, there was no TV.) "Oh, nothing," he replied. "I just really like her." But then, following a dinner of the tough, chewy, now-overcooked meat that August had purchased, Oliver immediately popped over to Lorna's tent, and I began to wonder (behavioral analyst that I am, yet still unaware of how common mountaineering shag sessions are) whether two people could actually fall for each other so quickly. It was like magic. And so were my delirium-filled dreams when the malaria pills began to take effect.

That night, in between sleepless bouts of tending to my aching legs, I dreamed about a baby drowning in the lake in front of my dad's house in Kalamazoo, Michigan. When I saw it fall into the water, I dived in, pulled it out, and gave it CPR. The dream was vivid, and I had it at least three times before I concluded that the baby was my younger sister, Emily, whom I'd twice saved from drowning—once in a pool, another time in the Atlantic Ocean—when we were kids. Only later, at the top of the mountain, did I realize that it was really about me. I was the one who for many years had felt helpless and needed saving, and now I was pulling myself out of the water, opening my eyes, and seeing the world in a different light. Not that I was in any way aware of this while I was making my way up Kilimanjaro.

Day two, which commenced with us sleeping in, entailed just four hours of trekking between the trees and bushes of the colder, dryer heath and moorland, accompanied throughout by Oliver's paramour, Lorna, as well as by plenty of croaking white-necked ravens. The trees, many of them beautifully draped in hanging moss, grew smaller and sparser the higher we climbed, and we could therefore see below us by the time we reached the Shira Camp, while also enjoying an unobscured view of Mt. Meru to the east. What we still couldn't see was our ultimate goal, the top of Kilimanjaro.

Again I ran into Becky, who this time was lying down with a couple of people watching over her. She was really, really sick, and when I asked her if this was limited to headaches, she said, "No, I think I've got a cerebral edema. My brain is swelling. I have to go back." Shortly afterward, I saw her being placed on a stretcher that had one huge central wheel underneath, and a porter then transported her down the mountain. Because of the increasingly thin air, only about 40 percent of the roughly 15,000 people who attempt to climb Kilimanjaro each year actually make it to the summit, and that percentage drops on the shorter treks like the one I was undertaking. Day two's slower pace had certainly suited me better, and regular doses of Motrin had helped ease the soreness in my legs. But I also knew that at 15,000 feet, the highest I had ever been outside of an airplane, I'd be entering the twilight zone.

Marking that point was a 40-foot-high, fang-shaped column of volcanic rock known as the Lava Tower (the core of a volcano that once erupted from the side of the immensely larger Kibo), and on day three we'd acclimatize by having lunch there before going back down to the Barranco Camp, where we'd spend the night. For me, this proved to be a test in perseverance, especially once Richard's altitude wristwatch informed us that we had ascended above 14,000 feet. Everyone has his or her maximum altitude, and after matching my personal record, I was almost waiting for my body to shut down. That's not a good idea. (Keep worrying about a heart attack and you'll probably give yourself one.) But I knew nothing about mental training at that time. While I was happy with my progress, I was also freaked out by the thought of crossing a major threshold, and the psychosomatic result was that for the final thousand feet before we reached the Tower, I felt like The Mummy, lumbering forward with three-second pauses between each lead-footed step, and gasping—sometimes gagging—for breath every step of the way.

Gasp-gasp-gasp-step—it was a monotonous rhythm, but one that I religiously adhered to as we traversed the mountain instead of ice-climbing a steep face. That would have been out of the question for me back then. And besides, I was already in enough trouble. All I could do was look straight ahead and think in the moment. Previously, I had focused on getting through the day. Now, with my chest tightening, my lungs seemingly shrinking, and every joint in my body giving me pain, it was all about whether I could make the next step. Fortunately, August led the way, and at 14,000 feet he had wisely set a sluggish pace. So, when Tony asked him to go faster, I countered with, "Can you go slower?" I'd already reached my limit, and Tony understood. Only Oliver, our other guide, raced ahead. He was sick of going so slowly. The rest of us were in this together—with the right mix of people, mountaineering's adversities and triumphs can make for a very unifying experience. Over time, I would learn the value of picking the right climbing partners.

Day two had been an enjoyable stroll through the moorland, yet right now I was in a fight, with myself as well as with the mountain, and I didn't like it. This wasn't fun, just exhausting, agonizing work, yet I never actually considered turning around. Perhaps it was about pride. Perhaps I would have thought about quitting if my friends and work colleagues hadn't already known about the climb. But then, perhaps it was about me, about not giving up on myself. Despite other mountaineers' recollections of spiritual awakenings and feeling closer to God, climbing is not always full of exalted thoughts. It can also be incredibly monotonous, and although I've experienced moments of feeling heroic—an ordinary guy doing something extraordinary, standing in a place between Heaven and Earth—there have been many more when I've been focusing on the drudgery and torment of the overall process.

In this case, I struggled on, and, just as sitting in a painful position will prompt you to change your posture, the fact that I was tortured encouraged me to experiment with my breathing: short pants, long breaths, so many breaths in, so many breaths out, through the mouth, through the nose. Consequently, I learned that slowly breathing in through my mouth and out through my nose calmed my body and reduced the overall sense of panic. And accordingly, together with August, Richard, and Tony, I just about made it to the Lava Tower.

By then, simultaneously shivering and sweating from overworking myself in the cold climes, I was in a pretty rough state. Having drunk all of my water (which is a big no-no), I was dehydrated, and while the resultant thickening of the blood could lead to heart failure, I was also increasing my chances of succumbing to acute mountain sickness. For the first time, I had a headache, and I was worried. My lack of preparation had virtually overtaken me, and I was so grateful to Richard when he generously let me have some of his customized energy drink when we sat down (or in my case slumped down) to lunch.

"It's not Gatorade," he informed me. "It's a special formula that I've researched, and it's really good for you."

No kidding. I took a couple of shots, and—bang!—life returned to my body. No wonder he still felt great. Whereas I'd been drinking dirty river water, he had this fancy concoction with vitamins and minerals. It was amazing. And after I had a short rest to regain some strength, I was ready along with everyone else to trek 2,000 feet back down the mountain to the Barranco Camp, where, thanks to our porters bringing fresh supplies, we had a chicken dinner. Nobody asked where the chicken had been caught or bought, or whether it had been coated with flies. At least it made a change from the meat.

One of the good things about Kilimanjaro was that, unlike certain other mountains that I later climbed, there were designated toilet facilities all along the route, holes in the ground similar to the public squat toilets that still exist in many parts of France, Italy, Greece, India, the Balkans, the Middle East, and southeast Asia. Of course, Richard had brought along several rolls of toilet paper (and, I'd like to point out, so had I), but he also had a heart monitor that revealed an interesting poop-related fact. According to him, when he crouched over the hole and balanced there with no seat, his heart rate soared to between 150 and 160. That's really humming. So I borrowed the monitor when I next took a dump, and sure enough, my heart rate was right there, too. That guy was just full of invaluable information.

On day four, we climbed back up to 15,239 feet and slept at Barafu, the high camp before the summit. To get there, we scrambled up the Barranco Wall, crossed small streams while trekking up and down the mountain—with the emphasis on up—and traversed rocky ground within the alpine desert. And, surprisingly, it wasn't too bad. By now, having become acclimatized to the high altitude, I felt a lot better, and once we'd reached the camp at around two in the afternoon, I was ready for the summit. That journey, August informed us, would commence at midnight. Sure, we'd be traveling more than 4,000 feet within about seven hours. But again, in line with the adage "climb high, sleep low," it's better to trick your body by doing a quick alpine ascent rather than risk AMS by sleeping and having your heart slow down at, say, 16,000 feet, where there's half as much oxygen as there is at sea level. (On Everest, I'd sleep at 26,000 feet without an oxygen tank, but it took me months to get to that point. Acclimatizing quickly is a whole different ball game. Then again, some climbers who are far more skilled than I am will never see some of the peaks that I have, simply because, for some physiological reason, I can cope with far higher altitudes than they can.)

In the meantime, at around four o'clock that afternoon, I treated myself to a little more of the chicken that we'd eaten the night before. Because of the altitude, no one else had much of an appetite (Richard was just stuffing himself full of Snickers bars), but I chomped on that chicken even though it didn't look too good. I fell asleep at around five, and when I woke up at ten that night, my stomach was absolutely killing me. A Pepcid AC did nothing to relieve the pain, and neither did a half dozen more. Bent double in my sleeping bag, I was sweating like a pig, yet when August rang a bell to wake everyone up— "Okay, get ready! We'll be leaving in 45 minutes!"—I somehow managed to get dressed.

Donning head torches and cold-weather gear, my fellow trekkers and I were among at least 150 people setting off at the same time across ground that, although moist during the day, is frozen at night, making it difficult to keep a foothold. This was the trickiest part of the climb, so the last thing I needed was food poisoning so bad that I was alternating between hot and cold flashes every few seconds. It made me feel as if a knife was being plunged into my stomach. The pain was excruciating, and the time I spent fighting it was undoubtedly the hardest three hours of my life. But what was the alternative?

Here I was, following the guy in front of me as we made our way across the rooftop of Africa—going back down in the pitch dark would, quite frankly, have been scarier. And thankfully, an explosive bout of diarrhea eventually signaled an end to the ordeal. Aware that Lorna was just a few paces back, I dived behind a rock, dropped my pants, pulled out the handy wipes, and let nature take its ugly course. This was just the first of at least eight violent and angry outbursts, but over the next hour my stomach pain slowly subsided. And, believe it or not, all the pooping also served as a handy distraction for my fellow climbers, an amusing conversation piece to punctuate the boredom.

Given the bug-infested locales in which many climbs take place, poop talk is a common means of helping the participants to bond. And in this case, as my stools gradually increased in firmness, so did the morale of our team. However, just getting through that whole affair was agonizing. I don't even remember what the ground looked like or anything else that went on around me. It was pure torture.

On and on we hiked, until finally the sun began to rise. It was a wonderful thing. As a warm glow enveloped the mountain, I looked to my left and saw an absolutely huge, monolithic slab of ice that resembled a long white tongue slithering near the summit: the ancient Furtwängler Glacier that, because of global warming, as well as an ongoing chemical process of sublimation, is rapidly vaporizing into the atmosphere. This is what I had looked at in awe on my way to the Tarangire National Park just a few days earlier. Now I was up close and personal, in the shadow of a natural wonder that may well be gone by the year 2020. It was a humbling experience. And so was looking down into the crater after we'd walked along the rim at Stella Point. Its sheer size was yet another of so many awesome sights on this trip that emphasized our insignificance when juxtaposed with the forces of nature.

When we arrived at the rim, everyone was celebrating. August shook my hand and said, "Congratulations, you've made it."

"I haven't made it," I replied. "The summit's still forty-five minutes away."

By then, I had devised "Bo Breathing": in through my mouth, out through my nose, 10 times; in through my nose, out through my mouth, 10 times; and so on. It was basically a little counting routine that helped me kill time and keep going. Then again, my feet were so cold because of my inadequate hiking boots that I couldn't stop anyway. I needed to be on the move, and helping me in that regard was Richard's souped-up water. My own water had frozen within the arctic region, so he let me drink some of his, and just a sip of that magic formula would keep me going for another half hour. Without it, without a doubt, I would never have made it.

When I reached the top of Mt. Kilimanjaro, for the first time in my life I said, "I can do anything." After climbing Longs Peak, I had thought that there was more for me out there. But now, staring at the great wide open, I was jolted by a feeling that nothing was beyond me. I'd return home with a new attitude. I knew I wanted to improve myself: to be a better son, a better brother, a better friend, a better professional. Climbing Kilimanjaro inspired these goals, and although I still wasn't sure quite how to achieve them, I knew that the next mountain would hold some of the answers.

On day two, Richard and Tony had informed me about the challenge of conquering the Seven Summits, the highest mountains on each of the continents. This was conceived in 1985 by the American Richard Bass, the oldest person to have climbed Mt. Everest, and then amended by Italian climber Reinhold Messner, the first person to make a solo ascent of Everest without supplemental oxygen.

Whereas the Bass list includes mainland Australia's Mt. Kosciuszko, the Messner list replaces this with a taller and altogether more difficult mountain on the Australasian continent, New Guinea's Carstensz Pyramid. Either way, the whole idea fascinated me. And since Kilimanjaro was one of the Seven Summits, I had asked Richard on that second day which one I should attempt to climb next.

"Aconcagua."

"Why?"

"Because it's like Kilimanjaro, just much taller."

Argentina's Cerro Aconcagua is, at 22,841 feet, the highest mountain in the Americas and technically an easy climb despite the risk of severe altitude sickness.

"It's another trek," Richard had told me.

"That's great," I'd thought. "If I can make it to 23,000 feet, I'll then know, at least from an altitude perspective, that I can try climbing Everest."

Ever since I had read in high school about Edmund Hillary and Tenzing Norgay conquering Everest, I'd dreamed about doing the same. And when I visited Nepal in 2000 and saw the mountain for the first time, I told my then-girlfriend, "I'm going to climb Everest. People have done it in their mid-forties, their mid-fifties, their mid-sixties, so I've got time. But I am going to take a shot at that mountain."

Now, discussing my options with Richard and Tony while standing atop Kilimanjaro, I learned that another of the Seven Summits, Alaska's Mt. McKinley, would provide me with excellent technical training for Everest. Then and there, I was sold on the Seven Summits concept. McKinley would have to be tackled in the not-too-distant future. Before that, however, I was headed to Aconcagua.

CHAPTER 3

ACONCAGUA

The higher we soar, the smaller we look to those who cannot fly.

—Friedrich Nietzsche

THERE ARE A number of personality traits that distinguish mountaineers from most other people. We can go without water for a couple of days, and without food and sleep for several more, and if this causes us to hallucinate, we'll still keep climbing. This is what we do; this is how we find out what we are made of; this is how—to our way of thinking—we become better people. It's an extreme form of behavior that also carries over into my professional life as an entrepreneur, which continues to see me working 100-hour weeks while forgetting to eat and missing out on sleep. Hey, if *you* regularly do these things, perhaps climbing is *your* calling.

That said, for the first five or six months after the Kilimanjaro climb, I didn't even think about attempting Argentina's Aconcagua, even though it was the logical next step in my quest for the Seven Summits. The descent of any mountain is always harder than the ascent because by that time you're exhausted; around 80 percent of fatalities and accidents happen on the way down. And although I'd run northern California's Napa Valley Marathon in 2000 and competed in several long-distance bike races, Kilimanjaro blew those endurance tests clean out of the water. Every day was a marathon, not least the final one, when it took 18 hours to reach the top and then return to the bottom. Since I was overweight and mentally not as strong as I would subsequently become, I really suffered through what was undoubtedly the hardest day of my life. So much so that, even though I'd been sold on the Seven Summits while standing atop the mountain, I vowed that I'd never climb again after limping all the way down without the aid of trekking poles.

Then, around June 2003, it hit me. As usual, I was working yet another 100-hour week at J. P. Morgan (sitting at my desk, I'd missed the entire spring season), and when one particular assignment required me to stay awake for 65 straight hours, my ordeals on the side of a mountain suddenly seemed a hell of a lot more enticing than those inside the office. In short, a public company was considering a hostile takeover of another tech company within a matter of days, and I and an associate named Battle Moore were assigned the task of producing a full mergers and acquisitions analysis from scratch, a 50-page pitch book explaining how a hostile takeover happens and how much the buyer should pay.

We started on Tuesday at 3 P.M., and our deadline was 10 o'clock Friday morning, when the managing directors of both our technology group and Mergers & Acquisitions would be leaving for the airport to meet the prospective client. Because of numerous additions and amendments, I had to pull three all-nighters to get the job done. Battle was a post-business-school associate and I was a mere financial analyst, so I took orders from him. What's more, he was able to go home, so when Friday morning rolled around, I was among the walking dead. At 9:55, I hole-punched and bound the last pitch book to come off the printer, and at 10:05 we received a call from the MDs: "We're in our limo on Park Avenue. Where the f—k are you guys?"

They wouldn't wait, and if we didn't get the material to them immediately, we could lose our jobs. In the end, each of us carrying five pitch books, we had to hail a cab and catch up with them en route to the airport. No thanks, no nothing. Still, I felt proud of the mission accomplished. Fueled by fear and a sense of duty, I had somehow managed to keep going while reminding myself that if I could climb Kilimanjaro, I could surely push through one more day. On my way back to the office, I remembered the three rules of mountaineering:

It's always further than it looks.

It's always taller than it looks.

It's always harder than it looks.

There are parallels between climbing and meeting many of life's challenges. And since I feel most alive in high-pressure situations with fire-drill deadlines, stretching my physical, emotional, and mental limits to the max, it's hardly surprising that I'm drawn toward both the mountaineering and business environments. Unlike people who lead structured lives, I have a high tolerance for the unknown, for change, even for panic. Welcome to the strange psyche of the climber.

When you're going up a mountain, you make a plan, and then life happens. What I now realized was that not only had I gained strength from my climbing experience, but I wanted to get stronger. According to what I read, I could probably hike to the top of Australia's 7,310-foot-high Mt. Kosciuszko in tennis shoes—in the summer, I might even do it in flip-flops. And Russia's 18,510-foot Mt. Elbrus also wouldn't be overly difficult, although it does have dangerous crevasses and I'd need crampons for better traction on ice and snow. Yet Aconcagua, as my climbing colleague Richard had informed me, offers a nontechnical route up its north face that's basically like a longer version of Kilimanjaro, one that can be trekked, with a little bit of scrambling, all the way to the top.

The fact that I'd need to climb an extra 3,500 feet really didn't faze me. For one thing, I wanted to break my own record, to keep moving onward and upward. And for another, I needed to get used to higher altitudes if Mt. Everest was my ultimate goal. As summer turned New York City into a concrete sweatbox, the nonstop grind of investment banking and the increasing pallor of my skin made me long for the Great Outdoors. Forget the agony endured on Kilimanjaro. (Okay, I couldn't, but the memory's rarely as bad as the real thing.) The idea of scaling the highest mountain on every continent fascinated me once again, and accordingly, I came to the same decision that I'd made some six months earlier: I was going to Aconcagua.

The question was, how could a financial analyst get three weeks off from work to participate in an 18-day expedition? No one in the history of investment banking had ever taken three weeks off to climb a mountain. But that's what I'd need for Aconcagua, which involves a three-day, 24-mile trek just to reach the Base Camp. Helping me slightly in that regard was the fact that, in addition to perceiving the Seven Summits as a personal challenge, I also wanted to benefit other people by setting up educational scholarships with the sponsorship money raised for each of the climbs.

When I relayed this plan to my managing directors at J. P. Morgan and asked them to help fund the cause, they were both fascinated and willing to contribute, not least because, in the case of Aconcagua, they knew where the money would be going. After linking up with the South African Institute of Race Relations for my Kilimanjaro scholarship fund, I'd learned from the head of J. P. Morgan's Latin American group that the company has a huge philanthropic arm that, among its many charitable activities, had donated money to Apoyo Escolar Nuestra Señora de la Paz (the Vocational Training Centre and School Support at Our Lady of Peace), a nonprofit organization linked to a church, in order to fund teachers in some of Buenos Aires's poorest neighborhoods.

My aim was to fund a teacher's salary for one year ($3,900), and 90 percent of the donations I'd receive would go toward that. The other 10 percent would help with administrative fees, as well as with my return to Argentina following the Aconcagua expedition in order to lecture students at the relevant school. As I've said, all of this helped *slightly* in terms of my securing time off from work. What it didn't do, however, was secure me close to three weeks. There was no way my bosses would agree to that. Instead, I obtained holiday leave from December 17 through 24, knowing that no business would be interested in having J. P. Morgan pitch it about mergers and acquisitions between Christmas and New Year's. That would make it a lot easier for me to delay my return.

In the meantime, I provided everyone at work with monthly e-mail updates about my training for the climb: two hours on the StairMaster each week while wearing a 25-pound backpack to prep for the fact that there'd be no porters. Aware that I couldn't climb Aconcagua by sheer force of will, as I'd done on Kilimanjaro, I thought my training was far better this time around. In fact, it was worse. Okay, so I was a much better trekker because of Kili, but Aconcagua is more of a climb, and for that, I soon discovered, I was extremely ill prepared.

My monthly e-mails also informed my work colleagues about the teacher we would be funding, while thanking all who were contributing. These included members of my own technology-related group and also people from the company's Latin American and health-care-related groups. Consequently, by the time I was ready to leave for Argentina, I'd magically been removed from all my projects—"Bo's doing his philanthropic climb." Even the J. P. Morgan newspaper ran a small article about what I was doing.

In 2004, I would actually meet the teacher whose salary was funded by our joint efforts. Her name is Isabelle, and at the school where she was teaching in Buenos Aires, I talked with her young students, all of whom had heard of America and one place in particular: Hollywood. Drawing an outline of the United States on the blackboard, I'd point to California in the west, New York in the east, and then circle the center of the country. "That's where *I'm* from," I'd state by way of a translator. Drawing a map of the world, I would also tell the kids that they could visit anywhere on Earth if they wanted to.

Never having been encouraged in this way when I was growing up (indeed, still pained and motivated by the memory of my second-grade teacher asserting that I would never graduate from high school), I not only gained self-belief and a sense of potential with each successive climb, but also learned about the need to determine my own destiny and direction, to *push myself,* rather than have them shaped by the people and events around me. That's why I told those kids to write their own stories in order to fulfill their dreams, dreams that had acquired a little color thanks to the monetary pledges of my bosses and colleagues at J. P. Morgan, as well as those of my relatives and friends.

On December 17, 2003, I flew to Buenos Aires before traveling north to Mendoza, the capital of Mendoza Province (one of 23 such provinces in Argentina), where the rocky heights of Aconcagua contrast sharply with the semiflat Cuyean plains to the east, which are crossed by tributaries of the Desaguadero River. Located in the middle-western part of the country, Cuyo (which also includes the provinces of San Juan, San Luis, and La Rioja) is one of its most popular tourist regions, thanks not only to the aforementioned mountain, but also to its largely dry and sunny climate, the Andean ski resort of Las Leñas, and plentiful wine tasting. Along with oil and uranium, viticulture accounts for much of Cuyo's industry, and the region produces over 70 percent of the nation's total wine production. To celebrate that fact, each year Mendoza Province hosts the world-renowned Fiesta Nacional de la Vendimia (Grape Harvest Festival) during the first week of March, featuring dancers, performers, and a beauty contest to select the Reina Nacional de la Vendimia (National Vendimia Queen).

The prestigious Universidad Nacional de Cuyo has its campus in Mendoza city, where wide streets and earthquake-conscious low-lying buildings conform to the innovative urban planning that took place following a devastating temblor in 1861 that claimed the lives of at least 5,000 people. Full of museums, hotels, restaurants, and, of course, wine bars, Mendoza is the preferred stopover for those wishing to climb Cerro Aconcagua, located about 70 miles to the northwest and 9 miles from Argentina's border with Chile. Aconcagua—part of the world's longest mountain range, the Andes, which stretches for 5,500 miles along the western edge of South America—is, at 22,841 feet, not only the highest peak outside Asia, but also the highest in both the Western and the Southern Hemispheres. Created by volcanic activity, yet not actually a volcano, it consists of rock and ice, with loose, crumbling scree, and while it is thought to have been named after Chile's Aconcagua River, the word itself may be derived from Ackon Cahuak, which in Quechua (a Native American language of South America) means "sentinel of stone."

The mountain has several glacial fields, the most significant of these being the northeastern Polish Glacier, named after a Polish expedition that, in 1934, accessed it en route to the summit. Today, while the nontechnical climb up the north face is by far the favorite among visitors to the mountain, the Polish Glacier Traverse is the second most utilized route. Only about 5 percent of climbers attempt the more difficult and dangerous south face approach, but on the next day's drive from Mendoza to Aconcagua, I suddenly discovered that I was one of those reckless adventurers.

Unlike Kili, the really dangerous mountains are in such remote locations or so deeply buried within a mountain range that you can't see them, and they take a long, long time to reach. Since Aconcagua matches these criteria, this was a red flag for me. What's more, I was scared when I heard the guides and others who clearly knew the mountain mention how treacherous it was. However, I couldn't back out now. I'd paid for my ticket on this roller-coaster ride, and I was locked in. So much for the "trek that's like a longer version of Kilimanjaro."

Whereas three-quarters of Aconcagua's climbers take the Horcones Valley approach to the 13,780-foot Plaza Argentina Base

Camp, my teammates and I were headed for the Vacas Valley. In addition to providing us with the longest and most picturesque of the approaches, this would also afford us a far less crowded experience—hardly surprising, since only a few lunatics choose to place themselves in such a precarious position.

Having again booked my trip through Adventure Peaks, I was this time accompanied only by Brits. These included Serena Brocklebank, a feisty middle-aged woman who worked for the British consulate in Nepal; Rhys Jones, a teenager who at one point was the youngest person ever to climb the Seven Summits; Bill Smith, a tall and wiry Welshman who coached high school basketball; Andrew Wilkinson, a professional triathlete and teacher at an all-girls school; Richard Fullerton, a powerful former military man whose wife was accompanying him on the climb; Steven Roberts, a college professor; Ed Parkin, a home builder; and Tim Hirst, a plump, jovial, 63-year-old dairy farmer who was making his third attempt to conquer Aconcagua, and who lightened our load with a constant stream of one-liners and racy jokes. In all, there were 14 climbers, yet our only guides were the husband-and-wife team of Andy and Helen Teasdale. Two guides for fourteen climbers—not a great ratio, especially since all of us were pretty green.

Ideally, the guide-to-climber ratio should be one-to-one or one-to-two, depending on the mountain. After all, if someone gets altitude sickness, gets hurt by a falling rock or avalanche, or falls into a crevasse, the guide is responsible for that person's care and, if necessary, taking him or her back down the mountain. With a group of 14 inexperienced climbers, there was a fair chance that at least 2 would end up needing such help, in which case the adventure would also be over for the other 12, many of whom had saved and trained hard to make this trip of a lifetime. That just isn't right, which is why I eventually came to dislike guided expeditions.

As it happens, everyone in my Aconcagua group had already been to Kilimanjaro except for Bill, the basketball coach, for whom this was his first climb. He was starting big. On day one—navigating a narrow, rocky trail, uneven scree terrain, several streams, and the Rio de las Vacas (River of the Cows) while llamas, mules, and cows grazed on nearby hillsides—we completed a five-hour, seven-mile hike to the 8,850-foot Las Leñas camp. Since this was the entry to Aconcagua Provincial Park, we were required to register here and have our climbing permits validated.

The next morning, after muleteers had roped and captured mules to transport our long-term supplies (no easy task), we set off on another seven-mile hike, carrying backpacks that contained the next two days' food, toilet paper, and change of clothes. And boy, were those mules fast. They and the muleteers raced ahead to Base Camp, while we started out by trekking barefoot across a fast-moving river in order to preserve our boots, then making our way through the brown and totally barren Vacas Valley, where a huge wind tunnel ensured that every inch of our exposed skin was totally coated in dust. With my face masked in a handkerchief and dark glasses, I probably looked like a bedraggled bank robber. And when I removed those items, the surrounding dirt spots resembled a badly planned suntan. In the intense daytime heat, this was tough country, especially for a guy who was still tipping the scales at 220 pounds.

To make matters worse, at one point Serena grew impatient and, apparently trying to emulate the mules, ran ahead on the trail, setting loose an avalanche of boulders. About 20 or 30 of them tumbled straight toward us, and although we heard a rumbling noise and managed to jump out of the way, Tim told Serena exactly what he thought, succinctly calling her a "stupid bloody cow!"

"How could I *sodding well know* that was going to happen?" she fired back, employing yet more Brit vernacular while commencing a back-and-forth that continued for the next half hour. For me, it was a lot of fun, like listening to a scene from an *Austin Powers* movie. However, I also knew that the fight stemmed from all of us trying to move as fast as we could. There was a lot of ego and very little teamwork—absolutely the wrong formula when climbing in a group. Adverse conditions would soon change all that.

When we reached the 10,500-foot Casa de Piedra camp and looked up past the valley wall, we had our first view of the rugged, snow-covered, ice-capped Cerro Aconcagua. What a spectacular, intimidating, and awe-inspiring sight it was—a heightened respect for the forces of nature coincided with a reining in of egos during the third day's 3,000-foot ascent to the Plaza Argentina Base Camp. Everyone was moving at a snail's pace during the final push up a steep and narrow canyon, the most precipitous part of the climb so far, when altitude-induced headaches began to affect several of the climbers. We had all earned our rest day, during which we could acclimatize, check our mule-delivered equipment, reorganize the loads for carrying, and generally kick back.

Rhys spent the entire day hanging out in the sun while wearing flip-flops, and his feet got so badly burned that they looked as if they'd been fried in oil. That night he was, as he put it, "bloody well pissed off," aware that there was no way he could make the following day's nearly-3,000-foot "cache" to Camp 1, which meant carrying equipment and food there and then returning to Base Camp. The rest of us sat around a table in the big mess tent, drinking whiskey and Coke, and the next morning we set off on a difficult climb that quickly turned dangerous.

Unlike on Kilimanjaro, where local cooks prepared everyone's food, for Aconcagua we had to bring our own groceries and make our own meals. As a result, I'd bought plenty of canned tuna—a personal favorite and a pretty dumb move, since it was really heavy and I needed to carry it in my undersized backpack along with elements of our tent gear. Even though everyone else's backpacks were much larger, they didn't look nearly as weighty, and they weren't, given that they were filled with much lighter foodstuffs such as freeze-dried noodles, thin pita breads, cheese slices, and boil-in-the-bag dinners. But hey, I was a macho guy, so no problem. No problem, that is, until we had to walk close to a frozen river where, through holes in the ice, we could see raging waters rushing downstream. Anyone who fell in there would be sucked under, with virtually no chance of survival.

The trail, immediately above, consisted of slippery scree. A few people nearly lost their footing, and what with my backpack making me wobble, I felt as if I was walking a tightrope.

Next came an area known as the Penatentes, featuring remnants of melted glacier on snow-covered, rocky terrain—millions of jagged, pointy ice stalagmites, many of them over six feet tall, that we had to navigate between while walking into high winds. Again, it was slippery, tough work, and after having lunch at Camp 1 and dropping off our food and equipment, we then trekked all the way back down to Base Camp. By now, I, too, had a headache, and my back was sore thanks to the heavy pack I'd been carrying. Not that this dissuaded me from loading it up with yet more cans of tuna and other snacks (tasty food for a growing boy) during the Christmas Eve rest day before we returned to where we'd just come from.

Because my backpack was so small, I even asked Andy, our guide, to carry some stuff for me. Dyslexic disorganization, lack of preparation—either way it was embarrassing, and so was my dumb-ass attitude toward climbing. "Bloody hell, this thing must weigh 90 pounds!" Andy exclaimed when he picked up my pack, and he immediately began removing many of the items, pointing out that I didn't need to be carrying 10 cans of tuna, the cardboard containers of my other food, and five pairs of socks. In no time at all, he eliminated about 20 pounds, but after repacking everything else, he said, "It's still too heavy. You'll just have to sort yourself out."

He was right. In fact, that backpack was so heavy, I couldn't even pick it up and put it on. Two people had to pick it up for me and set it on my back. I'd already pulled some muscles on the previous trip to Camp 1, and now I felt like I was carrying another person. "My trip's going to end right here," I thought. "I don't know if I can take five steps." The hump on my back was bigger than the gut on my front, but forget about asking anyone else what they were carrying in terms of food and clothes. This still wasn't a team effort, and my ego had shut me down. We were all into doing our own thing, and I was now reaping the consequences. The Christmas Day return to Camp

1 was really, really hard, but I just kept going: "I've managed 10 steps. Let's see if I can make 10 more."

Trailing behind with Tim, the dairy farmer who was more than twice my age, I only just managed to make the 16,400-foot destination. My back was absolutely killing me, I didn't think I could go on, and I didn't even have any "Christmas dinner." Tuna, schmoona. I didn't want to move from my tent. But then I needed to take a dump, and whereas Kilimanjaro has designated toilet holes all along the route, the only such facility on Aconcagua is at Base Camp (and filled to overflowing when I had the pleasure of using it). The rest of the way, people just wander off the main path (especially on barren land where there's nowhere to hide) and do their thing at a safe distance while hoping that everyone else is looking the other way. What's left behind is either toasted by the sun or cryogenically preserved in snow and ice, yet the unsavory sights and smells still don't match the situation at Camp 1, where, Andy informed me, "people just go around the other side of that little knoll."

Desperate to go, I ventured there and ran into an open-air cesspool, with hundreds of turds covered by toilet paper and small rocks. It was disgusting, and even the insects kept away. (On Aconcagua, where most vegetation ends far below, there's little to attract them at 17,000 feet.) Still, that was where I found myself, and so, with nose pinched and eyes closed, I added to the collection, unaware that I'd encounter even worse facilities on other mountains. Such thoughts rarely occur to novice climbers—just as few movie characters ever need to heed the call of nature, most mountaineering documentaries boast equally admirable bladder and bowel control. Unfortunately, at Camp 1 there was no such restraint in terms of personal behavior.

Since the outset, I had been sharing a tent with Bill, the basketball coach, and at high altitude the bitching really moved into high gear, not just between us, but among everyone in our group. Habits that had previously been tolerated now served as rich material for all-out bickering, and lying in my sleeping bag, I could hear raised voices coming from the other tents:

"You always remove your shoes, and that fucking pisses me off! Put them back on!"

"Do you have to brush your teeth while I'm trying to sleep?"

"You took our tent spot!"

The Yuletide spirit had disappeared on the other side of the poop knoll. Semistarved for oxygen, people were just plain edgy. Kilimanjaro had involved a smaller group and fewer days on the mountain. Here, with more characters and impending higher altitudes thrown into the mix, the atmosphere was altogether less friendly. In my case, I was sleeping in such tight quarters with the basketball coach that our Therm-a-Rest inflatable mattresses were about an inch apart. All night long, unable to sleep and nervous that he wasn't going to make the summit, he kept pushing away my leg through the sleeping bag and saying, "Can you scoot over?" There was nowhere for me to go, so at around three in the morning I finally said, "Will you stop touching my leg?"

"You're on my space!" he shouted in the pitch dark. Everyone could hear it.

"*What?*"

"You keep coming over to my space! Cut it out!"

"What are you talking about? We're like sardines here. At times I'm moving toward you, at others you're moving toward me. Who cares?"

Evidently Bill did, and he wouldn't back down, so the bickering continued until it was time to get up. Not that this was the start and end of our problems trying to play house together. From the get-go, he hadn't done a whole lot of cooking, and after our leg-pushing showdown, he basically left all of the "kitchen" chores to me. I'd go outside and break some ice for water, set up the stove, light it, put my Boil-in-the-Bag nondehydrated meal in the boiling water, and then sit back and wait for the food to cook, only to see Bill then get up, undo his own Boil-in-the-Bag, throw it in the pot, and lie back down. Boy, did that bug me, and so did the fact that when we made a cache to Camp 2, he refused to carry the stove. This, added to the bitching throughout breakfast, made the situation untenable. We were like an old married couple, sick of the sight of each other and angered by the most insignificant things—even the way one of us sipped his drink seemed to get the other all bent out of shape.

No doubt about it, the altitude really shortens your fuse, and when we headed for Camp 2, I moved way ahead of Bill because I didn't want to be anywhere near him. As it happened, the scree, icy snow, and wild swings in temperature on the steep ascent to 19,356 feet required step-by-step concentration, so there was less conversation among the group members before we arrived at our destination for lunch. Then, having dropped off food, clothes, and equipment, we descended just over 5,500 feet all the way back to Base Camp. What with the lack of oxygen at Camp 1, our bodies were slowly dying, so we slept at Base Camp instead in order to recuperate. It was there that I used Andy's satellite phone to call my friend Cara in New York.

Before leaving there, I had been in the process of compiling business school applications. I'd been waiting for two letters of recommendation, and so I asked Cara if these had arrived and if she'd then mailed my applications. "Yes," she replied. "You're all set." I'd also had to write my business school essays while working at J. P. Morgan, and this had necessitated staying up until 3 or 4 A.M. on a daily basis for close to five months during the summer and fall. I was applying to four schools, the competition was tough, and everything had to be done correctly, so in each case the essays and transcripts had required about 150 hours of work. Hearing Cara now tell me that everything had been taken care of alleviated a lot of extra stress, and I was really grateful, but there was still one more favor that I needed to ask of her.

"Please call José in Buenos Aires," I said, referring to Adventure Peaks's Argentinean representative, who had acquired everyone's climbing permits. I now needed him to call my boss at J. P. Morgan and tell him in a thick Latino accent, "Bo's stuck in a snowstorm and can't get back down. We don't know how long that will take. There is a complete whiteout."

It was now December 26, people had returned to the office, and I needed to buy extra time to complete my Aconcagua expedition. Once Cara took care of business and José called my boss, news of my being stranded on the side of a mountain spread like wildfire throughout J. P. Morgan. Never mind the "Save Ferris" campaign for the title character's supposed kidney transplant in the 1986 Matthew Broderick hooky-playing movie *Ferris Bueller's Day Off.* Suddenly it was "Save Bo." The financial analyst who had asked for contributions for his charitable climb might die on a mountain. The whole thing got blown way out of proportion.

Meanwhile, about 5,000 miles away, December 27 saw me and my fellow Aconcagua climbers return to Camp 1, and that night in our tent Bill and I got into a huge fight. Again, he kept nudging me: "Move over; you're hogging space."

"Cut it out!"

"Look, you're getting on my fucking nerves!"

"Oh, *really?* I carry the stove, I carry the tent, I'm boiling our water . . ."

There were cries of, "Shut up!" from the other tents, but Bill and I were going at it like a pair of prospective divorcees. No one could have gotten much sleep, so there were several sighs of relief the next morning when Andy announced that, because of snow and wind up ahead, we'd be having a rest day.

Pointing to the Polish Glacier, he said, "When we leave Camp 2 for the summit, we have to cross a snowfield, and it's very steep. So, if you fall, you'll be going for one helluva ride. I told everyone to bring their crampons, and we'll need them."

I'd worn crampons when ice climbing in New York's Adirondacks a couple of years earlier, but that was very different from navigating a glacier at high altitude and trying to avoid crevasses. Andy therefore taught us how we could walk flat-footed straight up a hill on the lower-angle ice and then, as the angle increased, attain the necessary ankle flexibility by turning our toes outward and walking like ducks, while planting the sharp, pointed butts of our three-foot-long ice axes into the slope ahead for extra grip. On steeper slopes up to about 40 degrees, we could move diagonally or, when the going got tough, sidestep by employing the "French Technique": planting all the spikes of the uphill foot solidly in the ground, then crossing the lower foot over it and planting that one solidly, too. For example, left-foot sidestep, right foot over left, left-foot sidestep, and so on. Then you could turn around—right-foot sidestep, left foot over right—in order to work the other leg.

While you're doing all this, the "rest step" is of paramount importance. Starting with the weight on your downhill leg, you can lock that leg and relax in that position for about a second. Then you can lift the downhill leg, take a quick step up, transfer the weight to the other foot, pause, again rest your muscles for a second, and repeat the whole process. Over several hours, these moments of rest really add up in terms of conserving your energy, which is why the rest step often turns out to be the difference between success and failure when trying to make the summit. It's huge.

Andy warned us to be careful when we were using the French Technique: It might feel easier on the ankles to edge into a slope by planting only the inner row of spikes, but that would be a sure-fire recipe for a slip that could result in sliding all the way down. So would catching crampon spikes on the opposite boot, gaiter, or even our crampon straps. Again, digging the butt of an ice ax into the adjacent ground provides added grip, and in the event of a serious slip, the pick of that same ax is crucial to what is known as a self-arrest. An aggressive, last-resort means of recovery rather than a preventive measure, with the aim of stopping safely, face down in the snow, this involves holding the ax in a solid grip, with one hand near the end of the shaft and the other hand around the ax's arched blade, and forcefully pushing the pick into the ice or snow just above your shoulder, aided by simultaneously pressing your chest and shoulder down on the shaft. Your spine must be arched slightly away from the snow in order to place most of your weight on the ax head, and also on your knees, which can dig into the snow to force a stop; your legs should be stiff and spread apart; and your crampons must remain above the snow until you've nearly ground to a halt, or else a spike could catch on hard snow or ice and flip you over backward.

Self-arrest is especially difficult if your fall throws you into an awkward position, such as head downhill instead of uphill, in which case the pick must be thrust into the snow or ice and used as a pivot to help swing your body around. Either way, you must act quickly if you are to have any chance of survival; your odds are probably 50-50, and there's no way of truly testing your self-arrest skills until a critical slip actually takes place. "God, this is the real deal," I thought while Andy was running through his demonstration. And when he remarked that people who argue are wasting energy, I pulled him aside and said that I didn't want to share a tent with Bill at Camp 2: "He's sucking the energy from me, and I may not make it."

Like everyone else in our group, Andy was well aware of the situation. "Don't worry," he said. "Right now, you and Bill are in a two-person tent, but that's staying here. We're taking only the three-person tents up to the next level, and I'll put you in one of those with another twosome."

I didn't push my luck by asking if that twosome could be Serena and Helen. (It turned out to be Andrew, the triathlete, and Ed, the home builder.) Meanwhile, my last night with Bill amounted to more leg-nudging, but I just ignored him, and the next morning, while he was still getting ready, I set off for Camp 2. The bad weather had cleared, and there was probably an hour's difference between the two of us leaving, but halfway into the 5,500-foot ascent, Helen told me that she had a headache, nausea, and dizziness, and that she was returning to Base Camp. She'd reached the summit of Aconcagua several years earlier without any problem, but this time around she couldn't do it. The two of us were at the front of the pack, and when the others all caught up and heard the news, it really rattled the team. If one of our guides had acute mountain sickness, what were the prospects for the rest of us? And what about just one guide for 14 inexperienced climbers?

Andy, concerned about his wife, really didn't know what to do, especially after we arrived at Camp 2 that night and heard the next day's weather forecast: a storm, with 40- to 50-mph winds. We were supposed to sleep, get up at midnight, and leave for the summit by 1 A.M., not even stopping at the 20,300-foot Camp 3 like many other climbers. But if the weather prevented the climb from happening, we'd be stuck with only one day's supply of food. (At least, most people would—I, of course, had more than enough tuna.)

"We don't have enough fuel to spend an extra day up here," Andy told us via radio to each of our tents at around 10 that night while the wind gusted all around us. "Plus, Helen is sick, and I want to get back down to see her. So, we're still leaving after midnight."

The wind was already so powerful that the floor of our tent nearly lifted Ed, Andrew, and me into the air. Yet, what kind of extra clothing had I brought to protect me from the elements? A puny down jacket, purchased at Target, that might have been okay for low-altitude skiing. I soon regretted that idiotic decision. Within 45 minutes of our departure, Bill succumbed to the freezing cold and force eight gale and had to drop out. Then, when the rest of us reached the glacier, it took an hour just to put on our crampons. Doing it with bare hands in sunshine was one thing; doing it with gloves in crap conditions was quite another, and while I was able to fit one of my crampons, Ed had to help me with the other. Andy couldn't lead the way until everyone was ready, and when I looked at the terrain and said, "I don't think we need crampons; I have my ice ax," he turned to me, his head torch illuminating my face in the pitch dark, and screamed through the roaring wind, "Bo, if you don't put on your crampons right now, you can bloody well piss off home!"

I didn't think traversing the glacier looked all that difficult, but what the hell did I know? With Ed's help, I put on my crampons. Then, as soon as we got going, another person bailed out, and after the traverse under the north face to a northwest ridge (often referred to as the False Polish Glacier Route), our crampons came back off. We were now standing at over 20,000 feet, higher than I'd ever been before, and the air was noticeably thinner. Next came a dirt trail hike. Halfway up, I looked back, and a gust of wind almost knocked me to the floor. One of the women in our team did go over, but after falling on her back and rolling a few times she managed to catch herself. She quit then and there, as did her husband, who had formerly served in the British Army. Now there were 10 of us, and when my left foot started to freeze, I told Andy that I, too, might go back down.

"Take off your boot and socks," he said. "I'll put your foot in my armpit." Believe me, as strange as that may sound, it was an offer I couldn't refuse. It was starting to get light, and while we waited for everyone inside the 21,400-foot Independencia Hut (a small, ramshackle wooden construction that is reportedly the world's highest alpine "refuge"), he unzipped his jacket, lifted several layers of sweaters, and spent 20 minutes with my foot in his bare armpit. Incriminating photos might have ruined both of our reputations. Still, it was a really nice thing for Andy to do, even if my foot didn't warm up.

"Bo, you could get frostbite, and I don't want you to lose some toes," he told me. "You've got to go back down."

I said, "Andy, I *want* to go back down."

Just as he was telling everyone else, "Okay, get ready to leave," I saw a stranger hiking past, so I asked, "Sir, do you have a hand warmer?" referring to the small, sometimes disposable packets that produce heat on demand. "No," came the reply. At that point, I took about three steps to begin my descent when another guy appeared. Again, I asked if he had a hand warmer.

"No," he said, before hesitating, unzipping his jacket, and then correcting himself. "Actually, I do. I have one. Here, you can have it."

"Are you sure?"

"Yes."

"Thank you! Where are you from?"

"Colorado."

"Wow, I went to school in Fort Collins."

"I'm from Denver."

Again I thanked him. Then I took the hand warmer, shook it, threw it in my boot, and almost immediately began to regain some feeling in my toes. A stranger from Denver had rescued my expedition. Rejoining my colleagues, I climbed above the Independencia Hut to an area known as the Crusta del Viento (Windy Crust), an apt name in light of the ravaging 60- to 70-mph gusts that were now blasting us from the right side. Running as fast as we could, we all huddled behind a 50-foot-high rock and began pounding each other's backs to warm ourselves up. During our 10 minutes there, four more people decided to turn back, including Tim, who asserted, "It's just too bloody cold." In my down jacket, I was turning blue. Rhys and Ed were both feeling dizzy. And what awaited us was the biggest challenge of all, a climber's purgatory.

Taking a narrow path with a steep slope off to the side, we traversed to the Canaleta, a tight, concave, 35-degree-angle chute that stretches roughly 1,300 feet to the summit ridge. It was now around noon, and Andy looked at me, looked at his watch, and said, "If we hurry, we can make it." Then he took off. No one else heard him, including Andrew, the triathlete, who blindly followed close behind, so I relayed Andy's remark to the other four climbers, who were taking a break several feet away. I might as well have been talking to a brick wall. There was a 2 P.M. cutoff time when we'd have to turn around and start our descent, since the sun went down at five, and yet all I heard were comments like, "I'm just resting, getting some food."

"Guys, we've got to go," I persisted, but Ed and Rhys were unmoved. They had bad headaches, and they weren't yet sure about going any higher. Serena didn't even respond. So I headed off, scrambling behind Andy and Andrew up a chute that consisted of horribly loose scree, with unstable boulders the size of Buicks. This was what Aconcagua was all about. My water bottle was frozen solid, I hadn't had anything to eat or drink for over 11 hours, the wind was howling, there were small snow flurries, and the final push to the summit was, in a word, torturous. Yet, at this point, while scrambling on all fours, dodging tumbling rocks, and slipping a step back for every two forward, my only option was to gut it out and draw on all of my mental resources, along with whatever physical stamina I had left.

Having heard about Aconcagua a year ago, decided to climb it six months ago, thought about it, dreamed about it, planned for it (sort of), and made it this far, I now had summit fever. This was the last few miles of the marathon, the part that separates the men from the boys, the weak from the strong, and it served to test what I was really made of. How tough in mind and body was I? The summit fever was bad, because all I could think about was that ultimate goal. I hadn't yet learned to stay in the moment and just think about my next step. When you do that, all of a sudden you find yourself at the summit. I was wasting my mental energy thinking about it. And yet I still have to say, for all of the pain and torture that I had to endure, I was happy to be there. I didn't want to be anywhere else.

I'd make five or six moves, then find a rock and just lie against its side, gasping for air. At over 22,000 feet, I was far into unknown territory (at times too far), and, starving and dehydrated, eyes wide open, I began to hallucinate. I remember seeing my dad and my sisters, and hearing all of them talk to me: "Hey, Bo, how's it going?" I didn't respond. I just picked myself up, advanced another 10 or 20 feet, and collapsed all over again, feeling like I had nothing left to give. This continued, over and over. The hallucinations stopped when I was on the move, but as soon as I lay on my back, I would feel like a fly on the wall, watching my family members interact. Sometimes my siblings were still kids, sometimes they were all grown-up—it was just bizarre, and it happened at least half a dozen times.

Looking at my watch, I saw that it was 2:30. "Thank God, I get to turn around," I told myself, aware that the cutoff time was 2 o'clock. "I want to go back down. I'm exhausted." I was so exhausted that I was no longer thinking about the summit. My legs had turned to Jell-O, I'd given all I had, and the summit fever was over—this two-hour journey up the Canaleta chute had just crushed me. Then I saw Andy coming down. He'd made it to the top, and Andrew was almost there.

"Congratulations," I said with a weak smile, "but it's after 2 o'clock, so I'm turning back."

"No, no, no," Andy replied, "I've changed the turnaround time to 3 o'clock. If you hurry, you can make it, so keep going."

If he had told me to turn around, I wouldn't have objected; I'd have gone straight back down.

"Are you sure I can make it in half an hour?"

"Yeah. The others are too far behind, but you should go for it. Then again, if you don't feel capable, turn around now."

After everything that had led to this moment, I had to make an instant decision: Do I go for it, or don't I? He'd given me the choice.

"Well, I'll go for another 15 minutes and see how close I get."

Which is exactly what I did. When the Canaleta chute ends at the Cresta del Guanaco summit ridge, the mountain's south face drops about 9,000 vertical feet, and a cross atop the summit finally reveals itself. . . . I was pretty damned close. Then I saw the triathlete coming back down. "Bo, congratulations," he said, shaking my hand. "You're gonna make it. It's right there."

What a feeling: "Yeah, I *can make it!*" The fever had returned. Ten minutes later, I was at the top, and someone had an oxygen tank up there. Sitting cross-legged, his face completely covered with a scarf and goggles, he was sucking air while repeating some mantra: "Om, om, om . . ."

"I've got to get down right now," I thought while taking in the stunning 360-degree views of mountainous terrain below and off into the distance. So, tapping the guy on the shoulder, I said, "Hey, man, sorry to bother you. Can you take my picture?"

"Mmm-hmm. Mmm-hmm."

"Just hold the camera right here and push this button."

Click. "Could you take one more?" Click.

Putting the camera in my pocket, I began to head back down. I'd probably been on the summit for two minutes. Atop Kilimanjaro, I had thought, "I can do anything." Atop Aconcagua, I knew that I was on borrowed time. It was going to get dark soon, I'd had no food or water for more than 14 hours, and I was so tired that all I could think was, "I need to get down or I'm going to die." I had no energy left, and the summit was just halfway on the overall journey.

As I left there, my legs still like Jell-O—and in line with most accidents happening on the way down—I tripped, fell head over heels, tumbled three times, slid on scree, and slammed hip-first into a pile of rocks. Thank God I didn't get hurt. That was a wake-up call, and from then on I was really cautious, sliding down much of the Canaleta on my butt and taking every step very seriously. The descent seemed to take forever, and at one point I saw one of my teammates, a Ph.D. professor who had turned around earlier, just laid out on his back. Another guy was shaking him, "Wake up, wake up," which he did. But then, after getting to his feet and taking another four or five steps, he collapsed again. Once more, the colleague roused him, this time with a kick to the head, and once more the professor advanced about several feet before falling back down and receiving another kick to the head. I couldn't believe I was watching this. The guy was kicking him all the way down.

For my part, by the time I approached the bottom of the chute, whenever I blinked, I had to fight to reopen my eyes. I could have fallen asleep in a split second. And when I did reach the bottom of the Canaleta and hooked up with others on my team, I didn't even talk about having reached the summit. We all just took a rest, and within no time at all every single one of us was out for the count, including Andy. Then, about 10 minutes later, he was standing above us, yelling, "Everybody wake up!" There were grunts and groans. "Come on," he reiterated, "we've got to move! Let's go!"

All of us fought internally to somehow raise our heads and revive our weary bodies. Camp 2 was the destination, another 2,000-plus feet away, and for about half that distance we were pretty successful at just plodding on. Then we reached the steep little dirt trail where I'd nearly been blown over on the way up, followed by the northwest ridge where we'd ditched our crampons after traversing the glacier. Again we all had a short nap, and when we woke up, it was getting dark and Andy was screaming at us, "Let's go!" I don't know how he'd interrupted his own sleep.

Head torches on, we traversed the glacier, navigated a steep and rocky snowfield, and finally made it back to Camp 2. Andrew and I arrived there together, and Ed was already in our tent. As I sat down, my hamstrings tightened up on me: "Aaargh!" When I tried to straighten my legs, they were locked, quadriceps bulging with knots two inches thick. My body had no salt, no nothing, and within seconds my throat muscles began tightening up, too, cutting off my windpipe. I was in complete agony, croaking, "I need some water," and there was nothing I could do to immediately stop the pain. Ed, who's a good friend to this day, handed me a muscle-relaxing tablet, and I washed it down with two glasses of water that he'd already prepared by boiling some ice. Then I took a painkiller and ate some of his soup, and after about 40 minutes, my muscles finally began to ease up. Agony over. I slept like a log.

The next morning, having loaded up our backpacks (mine with all the excess food and clothes; heaven knows why I didn't throw that stuff out), we headed back to Base Camp. Still, if I thought the trip was over, I could think again. Cheeks, forehead, ears, and hands blackened by frostbite and windburn, struggling through the ice stalagmites of the Penatentes with that monster pack on my back, I fell over and couldn't get up. There I was, hands and legs in the air, flailing like a crab, and all because I was too cheap to give away some of my canned tuna.

Eventually I managed to get the pack off and have a couple of the guys lift it onto my back, and when we arrived at Base Camp, Helen was there, thankfully recovered from her bout of AMS, cooking French fries. Only then did I show everyone the summit photos on my digital camera, and after eating some fries, I went to my tent, lay down, and cried. At last it had hit me: "I did it!" Just three people out of sixteen had done so: a professional guide, a professional triathlete, and a flabby investment banker from New York, 50 pounds overweight but proud as hell. Who would have thought it possible? Don't count out the fat guy.

We completed the three-day, 24-mile trek from Base Camp to the trailhead at Punta Vacas in just two days, even though my feet were so sore that a donkey transported me on the final day. That night, back in Mendoza, we all went to an Argentinean steakhouse and got smashed at some dance club, yet all the while I was wondering whether I still had a job at J. P. Morgan. That is why I headed straight there in my travel clothes with the backpack after flying from Buenos Aires to New York the very next day, January 3. I had been away a total of 18 days. Beforehand, I'd e-mailed my boss to say that I had survived a severe storm and was heading back, and when I arrived at the office in the late afternoon, dead skin literally falling off my hands, people were touching my cheeks and asking, "Did you paint your face black?" There could be little doubt that I'd been through one hell of an ordeal. However, reading this chapter, they'll now know what really happened. The stuck-in-a-snowstorm story wasn't contrived to court sympathy, just to buy me time.

I'd learned a lot on Kilimanjaro. However, mountaineering is a big discipline, so learning a lot means that you still have a long way to go. On Aconcagua, still naïve, unprepared, and out of shape, I was taught several climbing techniques, not to mention how to pack lighter, and that whole experience should have humbled me. Yet, even though I'd learned that I could survive on a mountain, I hadn't yet learned how to manage a mountain. By the time I reached the summit, I had nothing left, and if I did the same on Everest, it would kill me. I still didn't know that. I also didn't know about not racing my fellow climbers and restraining my ego. I'd had little tastes of humility, but the really big lessons were still in front of me.

UP THE CREEK
A QUICK ADVENTURE

Only those who will risk going too far can possibly find out how far they can go.

—T. S. Eliot

IN MY LIMITED experience, I have noticed that people who consistently perform at a higher level have certain characteristics in common: They are committed to their endeavor, they have a passion for what they do, their goals are well defined, and they are more comfortable than most when taking risks. Indeed, their ability to take intelligent risks is an important ingredient in their success and a huge determinant of anybody's level of achievement.

Average performers settle into their comfort zone, fall into endlessly recurring patterns, and stop challenging themselves in significant ways. And that's fine if you're not striving for the extraordinary. If, on the other hand, you're reaching for the Moon, then I have some golden rules:

- ▲ *Make your intentions clear.* Putting people in the picture helps prevent confusion and conflict later on.

- ▲ *Be fully committed to whatever you do.* When you decide on something, go for it 100 percent.

- ▲ *Don't second-guess yourself.* Hesitation and overanalysis is a recipe for failure.

- ▲ *Show your ego the door.* Concerns about pride and self-image will only hold you back.

- ▲ *Learn from your failures.* Determine why things have gone wrong, try again, and never give up.

For me, these rules apply both personally and professionally. All of us take calculated risks in our everyday lives, whether we're crossing the street or changing jobs. But since we get to choose the risks we take, why not choose those that are most beneficial? That's why I love adventure sports that have a high level of inherent danger, take me beyond the ordinary, and make me feel alive. And that's also why, during my second year at J. P. Morgan, I set my sights on getting a master's degree in business administration, which would provide me with the tools to undertake calculated risks in terms of my career.

Having been placed in charge of some first-year analysts and summer analysts, I wanted to be a better manager and motivator of people. Sure, this would mean leaving the company and forgoing two years of income, but if I had an M.B.A., numerous new doors would be opened to me. I'd hone some of the more tangible skills, like entrepreneurism and business strategy; I'd develop insights into marketing and the elusive mind of the consumer; and, most importantly, I'd learn techniques for motivating and leading people. My hope was that these skills would place me on the path to one day becoming a

CEO. Accordingly, when I received an offer from the Columbia University Business School in New York at the end of January 2004, I was really excited. That's where I was going, even though there was a major issue I had to consider.

The bonus is a big part of Wall Street. The bonus was why I and many of my colleagues worked there 100 hours per week. However, if I told my bosses I'd be starting business school in September, they'd be less likely to give me the sweet projects, and consequently my bonus would be a lot smaller when I left the company at the beginning of July. I therefore had to make a decision: avoid telling them in order to walk away with a healthy lump sum, or tell them that I was leaving and spend the next five months doing less work for less money. After thinking long and hard, I decided to tell them. It was more honest.

Then, in early February, I received an offer from the Kellogg School of Management at Chicago's Northwestern University, and this forced me to make yet another decision. The top-ranked Columbia, one of six Ivy League business schools, is known for its close ties to Wall Street and has been affiliated with 12 winners of the Nobel Prize in economics. However, Kellogg, located on Northwestern's Evanston campus overlooking Lake Michigan, pioneered the concept of group projects as a mechanism for promoting teamwork and team leadership within the business world. Consistently ranked as one of the world's top business institutions by the likes of *Business Week* and the *Wall Street Journal*, Kellogg is known for training programs that provide management skills geared toward leadership roles in the corporate, public, and non-profit sectors.

Both Columbia and Kellogg were my target schools, so it was a really difficult choice. However, given my desire to develop leadership skills, as well as my goal of eventually returning to the Midwest to work for MPI Research (the Michigan-based pharmaceutical/ biotech-related company of which my dad is chairman and CEO), I ended up accepting Kellogg's offer.

In the meantime, the result of my handing in my notice was, as expected, a lighter workload. And so, with more time on my hands—not to mention a nose that was now fine-tuned to sniffing out any opportunity to indulge in unnecessary risks and activities involving physical torment—I flew to Central America on March 4 to take part in the annual La Ruta Maya Belize Endurance Canoe Race. Comprising a four-day, 170-mile paddle along the Macal and Belize Rivers that link San Ignacio in the foothills of the Maya Mountains with the port of Belize City, and including three-person teams from as far away as Canada, the United States, the United Kingdom, and Japan, this is the world's second-largest canoe race. For me, it was a totally different experience, and one for which—surprise!—I was largely unprepared.

I'd first heard about the race during a lecture at the Explorers Club, an international organization dedicated to the advancement of field research and preserving the instinct to explore. Founded in 1904 and headquartered in New York City, the club promotes the scientific exploration of land, sea, air, and space by supporting research and education in the physical, natural, and biological sciences. Among its members have been those responsible for some very famous firsts: first to the North Pole (Robert Peary, Matthew Henson, and Ootah in 1909), first to the South Pole (Roald Amundsen in 1911), first to the summit of Mount Everest (Sir Edmund Hillary and Tenzing Norgay in 1953), first to the deepest point in the ocean (Jacques Piccard and Don Walsh in 1960), and first to the surface of the Moon (Neil Armstrong, Buzz Aldrin, and Michael Collins in 1969). Membership enables networking in this kind of illustrious company, as well as attending members-only events, but acquiring it requires expeditionary or scientific accomplishments of your own.

I began attending public lectures at the Explorers Club headquarters on Manhattan's Upper East Side in 2003, shortly after returning from Kilimanjaro. One lecture was given by a woman who had explored the history of chocolate, another by a man who gave his front-line perspective from both sides in the Indian-Pakistani war over Kashmir. I joined the club after returning to Kili for a scientific research expedition in early 2005, but in February 2004 I heard other members discussing the La Ruta Maya race, and this immediately piqued my interest. Needing two more people to make up a crew, I first contacted my good friend Jonathan Leebow from Cleveland, Ohio, with whom I'd attended the Brewster Academy boarding school in Wolfeboro, New Hampshire, and partnered in the Gumball 3000 car rally, and who now worked in his father's steel company. He was up for the challenge.

Then I spoke with another friend, Richard Wiese, the youngest-ever President of the Explorers Club. An Emmy-winning documentary maker, he had tagged tigers in the Yucatan jungles, captured crocodiles and handled venomous snakes in Australia, participated in medical research on Everest, and cross-country skied to the North Pole. However, he'd never paddled in the Ruta Maya. So, inspired by his dynamic personality and inner drive, I asked him to come on board, and after initially declining my request, he eventually agreed to be counted in so long as this was purely for pleasure and not on behalf of the Explorers Club, which would have wanted him to be filmed by another member who was making a documentary of the event.

The race itself involved about 90 teams divided into seven categories: male, female, mixed, masters, intramural (members of a single institution), dory (small boats sometimes used for fishing), and pleasure craft. In our case, there should have been an extra classification for "slow," not so much because of our physical shortcomings as because of the deficiencies of the cheapo canoe that, due to our arrival at the last minute with no idea of how to enter the race, we rented from the organizers just half an hour before the event got underway. With me sitting at the front, Jonathan behind me, and Richard steering from the rear, we worked like dogs on that first day, paddling as fast as we could for about 10 hours along 49 miles of flat water, shoals, and small rapids on the way to the first camp at Banana Bank. Still, there were boats that just flew past us—it was as if we were traveling in the nautical version of a minivan while others were in Ferraris, cruising along with just a fraction of the sweat effort that we were putting in.

Having co-captained our basketball team in high school, Jonathan and I spurred each other on like a couple of drill sergeants, screaming, "One-two-three-four," all the way to 30 as we paddled on opposite sides of the boat, then screaming, "Switch!" and each paddling on the other side. The other competitors must have thought we were lunatics. And they were probably right. Our old-town canoe was heavy, like a big tank, and no amount of diligent toil would make it go faster. Not that we were alone—about half the boats were similar to ours, and so the field basically divided up into three packs, with the professional rowers way ahead of the intermediates, who were, in turn, way ahead of novices like us. That was fine; since we were timed each day, and these times were then compiled to determine the final standings, we were simply competing with others in our "class."

By the end of the first day, the three of us had massive blisters on our hands, but at least our boat hadn't flipped over like numerous others that we saw. We'd seen crocodiles in that river, so we knew that this was serious business, requiring all our powers of concentration. Following a quick meal, Richard and I just collapsed in our tent, desperate for sleep before embarking on the next day's grueling 16-hour ride on treacherous waters. Jonathan, meanwhile, was a ball of nervous energy, mingling with everyone else before showering with a hose attached to a spigot. "Hey, this shampoo's great," I could hear him tell some other rowers before emitting a series of short grunts that quickly rose to an ear-piercing "Aaaaaaaargh!"

Seconds later, our tent was ripped open and in he dived, his head full of shampoo, naked except for a pair of soaking wet shorts, yelling, "I'm getting bitten!" He sure was. Grabbing my head torch, I turned it on and saw about two hundred fire ants all over his body. Now they, too, were in our tent. After an exhausting day, this was the last straw. "You butthead!" I exclaimed as Richard and I began feeling the painful stings. Right on cue, Jonathan reached back and yanked a few more ants out of his butt. They were everywhere. It must have taken us an hour to kill most of those little red pests. The next morning all three of us were smothered in bites. In addition, Jonathan had a bandage around his head, courtesy of having smashed it against a tree branch while trying to escape from his makeshift shower. This would prove to be an eerie foreshadowing of what happened next.

Immediately after we set out on the second part of our canoe race, the river narrowed into a funnel. At one point, on the left bank, a semicircular clump of land jutted out into the water. Directly opposite, on the right bank, a tree that had fallen over was lying semi-immersed in violent rapids, about halfway across the river. This bottleneck provided the boats with about 15 feet in which to maneuver, and ahead of us we could see one after another flipping over. We therefore approached slowly from the right side, only to be swept up by the current and slammed side-on into the tree trunk. In less than a second, I felt the canoe just leave my body—it got sucked under, and my feet tried to follow while I grabbed some bark and held on for dear life.

There were other fallen trees in the water just beyond the one with which we'd collided, so as I struggled to hold onto the trunk, I knew that if I let go, I might get trapped beneath the surface. That's why, for about five seconds, the only thing I focused on was my grip. I didn't turn my head to see what had happened to Jonathan and Richard, and I didn't even have time to yell. It was so intense. I thought I was going to die, especially after my fingers began slipping. I didn't want to let go slowly and scratch my face on the underside of the trunk. If I was about to go, I might as well do so with some force, so I tried to push myself away from the tree. In a split second, I was sucked under, feet first. As the right side of my head hit a branch in the pitch dark, I opened my eyes and saw daylight up ahead. I had cleared the main tree, and within a second or two I somehow emerged head-first above the water and unsuccessfully tried to grab a branch of one of the other fallen trees.

Again I disappeared into the dark below the surface, before popping back up and this time managing to hold on to some foliage.

Looking around, I didn't see the canoe, I didn't see Richard, and I didn't see Jonathan. "Oh, my God," I thought. Sitting behind me in the boat when it hit the tree side-on, they had been closer to the riverbank, where the trunk and the foliage were even thicker and the water was more shallow. They could both have been trapped. Then, after about 30 seconds that felt like an eternity, Jonathan appeared above the surface, fighting his way through branches while shouting, "Help! Help me!"

"You're okay, you're okay," I reassured him. Richard, meanwhile, was still nowhere to be seen, and that was because when the canoe went under, it flipped over with him inside, before getting stuck underneath a branch and pinning him to the bottom of the river. Somehow he managed to squirm free, and when he emerged, he was close to the main tree. His face was purple and he was gasping for air, but he was alive. And as a result of what we'd just endured, he and I would bond for life. Believe me, after this kind of shared experience, you look at one another with a deeper feeling of friendship, as if you've almost just died together. The fake bullshit of a fluffy friendship is out the door forever. It's a real and raw camaraderie of the best kind, the kind I yearn for.

Meanwhile, back on the rushing river, none of the other competitors could stop to rescue us—they were having enough problems of their own trying to stay afloat. The three of us held onto some branches for nearly 45 minutes, wary of any crocodiles that might be ready for breakfast, until a rescue powerboat approached us from downriver. Thrown a rope, we pulled ourselves to safety, along with our canoe, which had been buried under a mess of trees and foliage.

Miraculously, aside from some scrapes, the boat was undamaged. Despite a delay of about two hours, we rejoined the race in last place, blistered but undaunted. Just catching up with another boat was exciting, which was lucky, because when we reached the finish line in Belize City at the end of the fourth day we were in sixty-ninth place.

All things considered, that was a minor victory. Literally and figuratively, we had been out of our depth, and it was fortunate that none
of us paid dearly for our lack of experience. Never, even during all
my climbing expeditions, would I come closer to death. This was yet
another episode that, as I'm now aware, provided me with a greater
appreciation for that precious, temporal thing we call life.

I like to ask people, "When in your life have you most felt alive?"
The answer I hear over and over again is when they have overcome
a fear. In the La Ruta Maya Belize Endurance Race, my immediate
survival was all I could think about during those few seconds when I
was desperately trying to hold on to the trunk of the tree, but the
heightened will to live that this engendered was permanently etched
on my psyche. And although I still enjoyed the canoe race and loved
the challenge, another lasting effect is that I no longer really like the
water. I prefer the mountains.

CHAPTER

5

DENALI

Good judgment comes from experience. Experience comes from bad judgment.

—Muslim-Persian cleric Mulla Nasrudin

LIFE OCCASIONALLY throws extreme situations our way that we're just not trained to cope with. Some of them we bring on ourselves; others hit us unexpectedly. Either way, when groups of people are faced with trying circumstances, they require leadership, and it's my belief that if you have the ability to lead, then you have the obligation to lead. A good leader knows when to lead, when to be a good teammate, and when to keep quiet and be a good follower. However, even though leadership was something that I definitely aspired to in light of my family background, my initial Seven Summits exploits emphasized that I still had a long way to go in terms of acquiring the aforementioned skills. I just hadn't realized this yet.

On Kilimanjaro, it was all about survival. When I wanted to slow down and another climber wanted to go faster, the three of us slowed down as a team, and when we hiked, we were never more than four feet apart. We really derived strength from being together. I felt that strength, and it felt good to me. Conversely, on Aconcagua, there were too many people and not enough guides, and when one of the guides succumbed to altitude sickness, there was real chaos. With insufficient leadership, no makeshift second-in-command, and the difficulties of a group fragmented by personal challenges, only 2 of 14 amateur climbers actually made it to the summit, including me basically doing it all by myself. If given the choice between being lucky and being skillful, I'm never quite sure which one to choose, but in this case, lucky suited me fine.

On a mountain, as in business, everyone can be on board, but someone has to lead, to motivate, to make the tough decisions, even when (or perhaps especially when) there's no way of knowing which choice is best. And when there's inadequate leadership, you have to forge ahead on your own. That's what I learned on Aconcagua. I didn't know where I was going or what was going to happen, but I earned the respect of the others who didn't make the peak despite being much better climbers than I was. Still, I would soon find out that a group with too many leaders is also not a good thing.

By the time I gave notice of my business school decision to J. P. Morgan in January 2004, I'd accrued enough vacation days for a June climb of the highest peak in North America, Alaska's Mount McKinley. This would be one last dance before business school, a final sponsored climb under the J. P. Morgan umbrella in a spectacular, nearly deserted setting where the inhabitant-to-land ratio is equivalent to about 100 people occupying all of Manhattan. Once again drawn to the Great Outdoors, I therefore booked my trip to the third mountain on my Seven Summits quest, a 20,320-foot ogre of rock, snow, and ice whose main attraction was its convenient geographical location.

Named after U.S. President William McKinley in 1897 (presumably in a fit of patriotic fervor, since the man himself hailed from Ohio), Mount McKinley is located within the Denali National Park and Preserve, which is home to many forms of wildlife, from grizzly bears, caribou, moose, wolves, and wolverines to assorted birds and fish. Denali, which means "the Great One" in the language of the local Athabasca Indians, is the mountain's official appellation in the state of Alaska, and this is certainly appropriate in light of its 18,000-foot vertical rise, which is far higher than that of Mount Everest.

Whereas Denali sits on a 2,000-foot plateau, Everest, despite boasting a summit that's about 9,000 feet higher above sea level, actually sits on a 17,000-foot plateau, meaning that its vertical rise is only just over 12,000 feet. Still, given the challenges that Denali presents in terms of severe altitude sickness because of its elevation and its high latitude, as well as the extreme cold that once caused a thermometer left at 15,000 feet to record a temperature of –100 degrees Fahrenheit (-73.3 degrees Celsius), several climbers had told me, "If you can't get up Mount McKinley, don't even look at Everest." It was yet another step that I had to take en route to my ultimate goal.

Unlike Kilimanjaro and Aconcagua, Denali offers no porters or mules to carry your gear. You are on your own, without the porter's climbing experience, physical support, knowledge of the mountain, and calm leadership during times of crisis. What's more, as on Everest, you're on a glacier the entire time. It's a treacherous place. However, although the Kilimanjaro experience had briefly discouraged me from attempting another climb, after conquering Aconcagua, my soul felt alive, and I immediately set my sights on Denali. For the first time in my life I thought, "I actually have some talent. I have some raw, natural ability that enables me to climb high," and I realized that I could be really good at this. Until then, I'd never even dreamed of being a professional mountaineer, and the awareness of this now being possible was empowering.

When I had informed my colleagues at J. P. Morgan that I'd be heading for business school, I had packaged the news with an announcement that I was setting up a scholarship for the Denali climb that would benefit the Alaska Native Tribal Health Consortium (ANTHC). This organization provides Alaskan Natives with specialty medical care, community health services, construction of clean water and sanitation facilities, information technology, training, and educational support, and I wanted to raise money for health-care-related college scholarships: $8,000 divided among four Native Alaskan students. In their case, a little money could go a long way.

After returning from the La Ruta Maya boat adventure in March 2004, I took advantage of my relatively light 80-hour workweeks at J. P. Morgan by using the other 20 hours to train for Denali. I did this at the Manhattan Athletic Club, which was located in our building, and since it was only a three-minute walk from my desk to the gym, there was no excuse for me to avoid exercise. (There never had been. It was just that at last I had recognized the need for adequate preparation.) On Saturday mornings, I would do a three-hour, all-cardio workout with a stationary bike, elliptical treadmill, and StairStepper while wearing a backpack that weighed between 50 and 60 pounds. It was really tough. Three days a week, I would also lift weights, and on several other days, from noon until one, I'd spend my lunch break playing basketball with a group of lawyers, accountants, and investment bankers.

Thanks to a diet that now consisted of salads for dinner and no more Big Macs, my weight dropped from 225 to 195 pounds, and by the time I flew to Anchorage, Alaska, on June 18, 2004, I was in pretty good shape. I'd need to be. Denali is a totally different animal from Kili and Aconcagua. It isn't a hike or a moderate scramble; it's full-on mountaineering, using ropes while traversing crevasse-covered glaciers made up of ice that cracks and slowly moves. At any time, without knowing it, you could be standing on a little snow bridge— a layer of icy snow—concealing a crevasse that's 500 or 1,000 feet deep. Then again, you might know that you're on a snow bridge because there are huge cracks at either end. Either way, if that snow bridge collapses, you're going for one hell of a ride, and it doesn't help your nerves when a bridge sags visibly. That's why, when you're walking on that glacier, you're not just hanging out; you're on high alert, and you've got to avoid the temptation to run or tiptoe, both of which will put more strain on the fragile surface. Instead, you must stick to your normal pace.

This is what the three guides from the Alaska-based expedition organizer, Mountain Trip, told me and my five fellow climbers when all of us assembled in a parking lot the day after my arrival in Anchorage. At least this time there was a far healthier guide-to-climber ratio than I'd experienced on Aconcagua, even if Ryan Campbell, our tough, tall, and wiry head guide, basically took no prisoners with his my-way-or-the-highway approach. He was assisted by Clark Fyans, a short, skinny ski and surfer dude (depending on the season), and by Bill Bilmeier, who was relatively new to this game but a total climbing geek with an in-depth knowledge of all the gear. No-nonsense honchos, the three of them presented a united front while setting us straight about the challenges up ahead.

Standing alongside me were Richard Thorby, my South African–born, Swiss-based friend from the Kilimanjaro trip, who had coordinated his Denali booking with mine; Mike Hsu, a smart, stocky, Chinese American navy pilot with a Southern drawl; Mike's friend J. P. Moorhead, a lean-built British triathlete and investment banker who lived in Australia; Alex, another Brit, who had recently married and was taking a year off from his job in insurance to tour the world with his new wife; and Phil Drowley, a British bobby from the Isle of Man. Aside from Richard, who was in his mid-forties, the other guys were all in their thirties.

"Okay," said Ryan, "let's see what gear you've brought for the climb. Who wants to go first?"

"I do," I said, proud of the fact that not only was I well prepared for the two-week excursion, but that I'd actually splurged on a full-body down suit instead of the down jacket that had been specified on Mountain Trip's gear list. Again, though, I'd got it wrong.

"You don't need that," said Ryan as he helped me unpack two large duffel bags and threw the down suit onto a pile of items that would stay behind. "If it's that cold, you're not moving. You'll be in the tent, or else you'll die. All you should have for your top layers is a quick-dry T-shirt, a light undershirt, a heavier undershirt, a waterproof jacket, a puffer jacket, and a major expedition down jacket."

In addition to the now-discarded one-piece down suit, I'd also invested in a high-quality down jacket, so that was okay. Nevertheless, I was informed that I'd need only three pairs of socks, not six. The others, some of which were either too thick or too thin, were therefore thrown into the stay-behind pile, and ditto my underwear. "You only need two of those," Ryan told me, stating that he'd survive with one pair of briefs, some long fleece underpants, and a windbreaker for his legs. After all, with no washing facilities, why bring more clothes? Handi Wipes would be our main means of hygiene.

Two of my four pairs of gloves were discarded, as was one of my two bottles of sunscreen. A couple of rolls of toilet paper were just fine, as were my snack foods—including Snickers and power bars—and my camera, but overall the weight of what I'd be carrying was reduced by at least 25 percent. That meant a revised load of about 50 pounds on my back, which didn't include the group supplies of tents, stoves, shovels, fuel, and food that we'd all be dragging with us on sleds attached to ropes that went around our waists.

On Kili and Aconcagua you can bring plenty of gear because it'll be carried to Base Camp by a porter or a mule. You can load up as much as you want and then be selective in terms of what you yourself carry from Base Camp. Since that's what Richard had experienced on his only other Seven Summits climb, he brought even more stuff to Denali than I did, a lot of it meticulously stored and labeled in plastic bags, only to have half of it be rejected by the guides. Nevertheless, having done his research, he stood his ground. "I need this," he insisted, citing the online and published advice of other climbers. Ryan, Clark, and Bill were clearly pissed. "Richard, I guide Mount McKinley," Ryan declared. "I don't care if you've read in books what other mountaineers do. For this mountain, you don't need all that gear."

"Well, I've printed this article that says I do," Richard persisted. "And so do the accounts of several extremely famous climbers." Talk about putting our guides' noses out of joint. Richard was challenging them, and the tension was palpable. "Fine," Ryan concluded. "Bring all you want, but don't blame us if you don't summit." Later on, while acknowledging that the guides had made some good points, Richard told me that he still intended to hang onto most of what he'd packed since he was sure he would need it.

After everyone's gear had been scrutinized, we were led over to a tree, a rope was attached to one of the high branches, and, wearing harnesses that were attached to that vertical rope, we each ascended it in order to learn what it would be like to climb out of a crevasse. This necessitated using a jumar (a handheld clamp that runs freely up a slack rope, but has teeth that tighten around that rope in response to weight applied from below) and a smaller, lighter hand-held ascender that, although without a handle, achieves pretty much the same thing. Both the jumar and the ascender have lengths of rope hanging from them, with loops at the bottom into which the climber can insert his feet. If, therefore, your right hand is holding the jumar and this is pushed up the vertical rope, you then put your right foot in the now-higher foot loop, pull yourself up, do the same with the left ascender and foot loop, and so on.

After falling into a crevasse, the first thing to do is to go to the bottom of the rope that's attached to your harness, tie a knot, remove your backpack, and clip it to the rope so that it's beneath you when you try to climb. Then, because hypothermia is a major risk inside a freezing cold crevasse, you should take the warm jacket that's at the top of your backpack, put it on, and then use your jumar and ascender to climb out. None of this is easy when you're dangling on a rope, especially if, as is common, you start spinning. Still, if you're conscious, this is how you get out of a crevasse. If you get knocked out, the guide is forced to take over.

Our group would be climbing in three-person teams, each with a guide at the front attached to the climber in the middle, who was attached to the climber at the rear. The distance between each would be about 30 feet, and the ropes should be fairly taut, with only about two or three inches in the middle actually touching the ground. That way, we had just enough slack to provide some freedom of movement, but if anyone did fall into a crevasse, he would fall in only up to his waist so long as the attached climber held his ground. This would hopefully avert the problem that arises when somebody drops a long way down a hole, and the rope that runs between him and the climber attached to the other end cuts into the edge of the crevasse at the surface, creating a further split in the ice. Dangling beneath the icy surface instead of the opening, the person in the crevasse is basically trapped, and using axes to break through that surface risks the whole thing caving in on his head.

If the person who falls into the crevasse is dangling beneath the opening but has been knocked unconscious or has broken a leg and can't move, the guide has to self-arrest, hitting the deck while digging his ax into the ice and snow. Then, once the situation has been stabilized, a carabiner (an oblong metal ring with an openable spring-hinged side) can be used to clip the other end of the rope that's attached to the fallen climber to a metal spike known as a piton. This, too, is driven into the ice and snow; two or three such anchors may be attached to the rope, freeing up the guide and the other climber so that they can wedge an ice ax under the part of the rope that is running over the edge of the crevasse. This should prevent it from splitting the ice further and trapping the victim underneath. Afterward, using a pulley system that disperses and lightens the load, the victim can hopefully be winched out of the hole.

Rope management and crevasse rescue techniques can save people's lives, and this is what we practiced before driving 120 miles to Talkeetna, the gateway to Denali National Park, on June 20. We then took a breathtaking 45-minute flight in a tiny, ski-equipped, single-engine bush plane over grassy land inhabited by moose, elk, and caribou to the snow-covered, 7,200-foot Base Camp. This is located on the southeast fork of the 36-mile-long Kahiltna Glacier, and there, having ski-landed in a snowy field that is affectionately known as "Kahiltna International Airport," we watched a safety video about the mountain that left us in no doubt as to the danger in which we were placing ourselves. On average, only about 20 percent of those who head for the summit actually make it, and there have been close to a hundred fatalities since the climb was first attempted in 1903. These statistics set off my internal alarm bells, and I felt even more panicky when, after the film ended, we saw climbers return with burnt and wind-battered faces that looked as if they'd been smashed with bats.

My only consolation was knowing that, since I had already climbed higher than Denali's 20,320 feet and done some good workouts at the gym, from an altitude and strength perspective I was better prepared than ever before. Without those two factors, I might well have had second thoughts. And even though I didn't, just seeing the video and those beat-up climbers within the space of an hour was all the incentive I and my colleagues needed to spend the next morning practicing our rope management techniques.

The first successful Denali expedition was organized in 1913 by an Episcopal missionary named Hudson Stuck, and it wasn't until 34 years later that a New Englander named Bradford Washburn devised an easier route than the one used by Stuck and his two colleagues. Washburn first utilized this route, known as the West Buttress Route, in 1951, and today this technically facile but physically demanding way of reaching the summit is by far the most popular. Certainly, it's the one that I and the eight others in my group would be taking, with three three-man rope teams consisting of Ryan, Mike the navy pilot, and J. P. the triathlete (easily the strongest trio) at the front; Clark, Alex, and Phil in the center; and Bill, Richard, and I bringing up the rear. That placed me at the very back, unable to move any faster than the pace that Richard was capable of maintaining. This arrangement ensured that Bill would slow down whenever he felt the rope around his waist being tugged, whereas if Richard had been behind me, I might have kept moving and attempted to drag him along.

On day two, after departing from Base Camp, we all descended three hundred vertical feet to join up with the main Kahiltna Glacier before heading up the Kahiltna for five miles until we reached the 8,000-foot Camp 1 at the base of Ski Hill. From the get-go, Richard had been struggling, hampered not only by the heavy load that he insisted on carrying, but also by being out of shape because of an ankle sprain that he'd sustained during a trail run several weeks before the trip. That had put the kibosh on his training program, and consequently our three-man rope team arrived at Camp 1 about an hour after the other two teams. This didn't bother me too much initially—going more slowly actually enabled me to take in the beautiful mountain views as we hiked up the lower part of the crevasse-riddled Kahiltna Glacier.

Every time we arrived at a camp, there would be a similar routine: while still roped together, we'd each use poles to probe for hidden crevasses on the site where we elected to set up camp. Then, when we determined that it was safe, we would carve a perimeter in the snow with our feet to delineate the area in which we could be unroped. At that point, some of us would collect snow to boil for water, while others would saw chunks out of the ice to make bricks so that an igloo-style wall could be erected around the tents, shielding us from high winds to help keep us warm. At the same time, a few people would dig a six-foot-deep hole in the ice and snow and carve out shelves there for the stoves, along with places where everyone could sit while eating dinner within a tent enclosure. What we created, in effect, was an insulated kitchen/dining area that was far more protected from the elements than if it were above ground. We would also build a toilet by digging a hole that was separated from the tents by another igloo-style wall. Since there are latrines at only two locations along the route—Base Camp and the 14,200-foot Camp 4—the park service states that in all other places climbers must poop into double plastic bags and throw these into deep crevasses.

Probing for crevasses, delineating a safe area, making ice bricks, erecting walls, creating a kitchen/dining tent, building a toilet, and setting up our sleeping quarters—most of these chores were repeated at every camp on our climb, and it was the fitter members who invariably did more of the work. When you dig out six feet of snow, you're really sweating, so it was never a case of arriving at camp and being able to relax. There'd still be several more hours of hard labor. That's why it was so important to take care of ourselves, eating regularly and drinking at least four quarts of fluid daily to help us avoid suffering not only from acute mountain sickness, but also from frostbite and hypothermia amid temperatures that, in the first week, averaged around 15 degrees Fahrenheit during the day and 5 or 6 degrees at night.

On day three, carrying 40- or 50-pound backpacks while pulling 50- or 60-pound sleds, we did what is known as a "single carry" up Ski Hill to the 9,800-foot Camp 2, transporting our gear and staying there instead of caching it and going back down. Again, my three-man rope team arrived long after the others, and that night I told Ryan that I didn't want to risk my chance of summiting by wasting energy accommodating Richard. "On another team I could go much, much faster," I remarked, not bothering to recall how Richard had slowed down for me on Kilimanjaro while donating some of his precious energy snacks.

"You're fine," Ryan assured me. "Everything's going to be okay."

Not true. I wasn't fine. And whereas Richard's a nice guy, I was being insensitive and thinking only of myself in a team situation (something that I regret to this day). Accordingly, after again moving at what felt like a snail's pace when ascending to the 11,200-foot Camp 3 on day four, I was even more frustrated, and Richard totally understood why. "This is really bothering me," I told the head guide. "We're now showing up to camp a couple of hours after you guys, and that means I'm on my feet a couple of hours longer. I can't move at the normal pace for which I trained, and it's exhausting me."

"Don't give me a hard time," Ryan replied. "Your summit chances won't be hindered by Richard."

Day five was difficult. Camp 3 marks the beginning of the West Buttress Route, and this is where the nature of the climb really changes, with snowshoes being replaced by crampons for the steeper slopes and wind-blown, hard-packed snow of the crevasse-congested ascent up Motorcycle Hill. This leads to a ridge that ends at about 12,000 feet, at the lower part of a broad plateau, but we actually went 1,200 feet higher and did a cache to the appropriately named Windy Corner, where a sharp left turn leads climbers along another ridge at the base of the West Buttress. Then we returned to Camp 3, and although I had tried to speed things up by carrying some of Richard's gear, our three-man rope team still arrived there more than two hours after everyone else.

When I'd asked Bill, our guide, to help me carry some of Richard's items, his response was, "Richard's gotta carry his own weight."

"Yeah, but he's slow. I'm taking some for him. Can't you help?"

After bitching and moaning, he'd agreed to take a couple of things, and when we had returned to Camp 3, I overheard Bill telling Ryan, "Bo got a little irritated at Windy Corner."

Nothing more was said that night. The next day the shit hit the fan.

During our 3,000-foot ascent to the 14,200-foot Camp 4, we returned to Windy Corner, and whereas the weather there the previous day had been absolutely fine, this time the place lived up to its name, with freezing winds of between 30 and 50 miles per hour roaring straight in our balaclava-covered faces. The sharp left turn to the ridge at the base of the West Buttress is a wind tunnel, and it was precisely there that Richard suddenly stopped and shouted, "I have a blister."

Since I was walking downwind, I could hear him, but up ahead Bill was unaware of the problem until he felt a tug on the rope connecting the two of them. "If you have a blister, you've got to fix it *right now*," I heard him shout. "Otherwise it's only going to get worse."

I couldn't believe it. Of all places to stop, this had to be the worst. The wind was absolutely howling, and we'd freeze if we didn't move, whereas if we just kept going another 20 minutes, the conditions would be a whole lot better. Sure, in that time Richard's blister would grow bigger, and if you have a hot spot, you should treat it immediately. But here we were on one of the most unfriendly parts of Mount McKinley, and I thought that even with a blister Richard should be tough enough to keep going another 20 minutes until we reached a safer place.

"Aw, geez, c'mon!" I exclaimed from 30 feet away, even though Richard and Bill probably couldn't hear me because of the wind. Then, already starting to feel cold, I put on another layer of clothing, sat on my backpack, and watched Richard slowly and methodically open up his own pack, put on a jacket, put on a warmer hat, take out a bag full of labeled items, and allow his water bottle to escape and fly toward me. I grabbed it. Next, he pulled out another bag with a glove stuck to it, and that glove just went bye-bye. It must have elevated a thousand feet as Richard watched it in disbelief.

"Hurry up!" I screamed. The methodical unpacking continued until Richard finally located his medical kit, laid it on the ground, and started breathing into his cupped hands to warm them up. "Freaking hell," I muttered while Bill waited patiently. On later climbs, I came to realize that Bill's attitude was intrinsic to teamwork and true leadership, yet at this moment my ego, impatience, and inexperience were running riot over all other considerations. And besides, it was *really* cold.

Unwrapping a Band-Aid and gripping it between his teeth, Richard slowly returned all of the items to his backpack, sat on it, removed a boot, took off two layers of socks, held up his foot, and then grasped the Band-Aid with both hands, only to have it be swept away by a gust of wind. "Aaaargh!" he cried in despair, arms outstretched as the plaster joined his flyaway glove somewhere in the stratosphere. Now he'd have to repeat the entire routine.

I was on the verge of having a fit. During a lull in the wind, Bill could hear me scream, "Hurry up! This is *nuts*! I'm freaking freezing!" By now, we'd been at Windy Corner for at least an hour, prompting Ryan and his teammates, who had been climbing the ridge at the base of the West Buttress and were well on their way to Camp 4, to come all the way back to see what was wrong. The next thing I knew, Ryan and Bill were talking, Bill was pointing at me, and within seconds Ryan was unclipping himself from the rope. Heading in my direction until he was about two inches from my face, he looked as if he was going to explode.

"What the f—k are you doing?" he shouted while grabbing my jacket. "Are you a f—king leader? Do you think you're a f—king leader? Answer me, dammit!"

"What do you mean?" I asked cautiously, unsure whether we might come to blows, while subliminally tempering my innate desire to lead with misgivings about my ability to do so. "It's freezing here. I'm just voicing how I feel."

"Well, a leader wouldn't voice how he feels! A leader would just shut up! You've got to quit harassing Bill! He knows what he's doing! Richard can't go any faster, and you're actually making the situation worse!"

The frozen air was turning blue with his curse words, and if I had returned the compliment, we probably would have fought. That was the last thing anyone needed. So I just stood my ground, expressing how I felt, and after about 10 minutes of back-and-forth and neither of us giving an inch, Ryan rejoined his team, everyone resumed the climb, and we eventually arrived at the 14,200-foot camp. By then, having had time to contemplate rather than react, I couldn't escape the embarrassing fact that, regardless of my convictions, I'd behaved like a jerk. On previous climbs, my difficulties had been related to a lack of preparation and overcoming physical limitations. Now I was being forced to incorporate the team dynamic into my way of thinking.

The next day we'd be able to rest and acclimatize, but this would be followed by a cache just beyond the 16,200-foot Camp 5, involving a 45-degree climb with fixed ropes to a section known as the head-wall. "Holy crap," I thought, looking up at it from Camp 4. It was time to state my case.

The three guides were in the kitchen tent when I entered, and after sitting down, I said, "Hey, listen. First and foremost, I want to apologize to you, Bill, for trying to push things. You're the guide, you have more experience, and you're going to do what's safest for the team. I was freezing cold and frustrated, but I want you to know I'll keep my mouth shut in future."

Next I turned to Ryan and told him, "I appreciate your voicing your opinions so politely and eloquently." He, Bill, and Clark all laughed. "I'm still new to this game and I'm still learning a lot," I continued, "and your yelling at me really woke me up."

My apology was accepted and cooler heads prevailed, enabling me to then say, "Richard and I don't have a problem, but moving so slowly is affecting me physically and mentally. Now that we have the hardest part to climb, is there something we can do?"

"Yeah," Ryan answered, "there *is* something we can do. From here on out, you're going to be on Clark's rope team, and Bill is going to guide Richard one-on-one."

"Oh, my gosh, that's *great*," I remarked while Ryan explained, "We couldn't do this before, because if someone falls into a crevasse, it's good to have a couple of people who are outside it and can pull the weight."

Now that the climb was growing steeper, crevasses would be less of a threat. Silently I wondered why I couldn't have been told this earlier or why we couldn't all have taken turns being with Richard, but it was good news nonetheless. Day 8's difficult cache, just past a rock known as Washburn's Thumb at 16,500 feet, went smoothly enough despite the extreme cold. But following a rest day at Camp 4, there was also a weather day that saw us held back by snow and wind. As Bradford Washburn himself has said, Denali can be relatively straightforward in good weather and a disaster if you're caught in a big storm. You must have respect for the mountain, go back down if necessary, and if you're delayed, then you shouldn't lie around. That's a prime way of succumbing to a cerebral or pulmonary edema. Instead, you should exercise in whatever way possible to keep your blood flowing.

During our rest day at Camp 4, we encountered a team that, because of raging winds, had been forced to turn around at the 17,200-foot High Camp, just over 3,000 feet from the summit. The climbers looked shattered, and after hanging out for a couple of hours and grabbing some much-needed food while telling everyone what the conditions were like above the headwall, they set off for Camp 3. A couple of hours later, we heard a pop and a rumble, and after Ryan received an SOS call on his walkie-talkie, we learned that some ice had thawed down below, freeing rocks the size of cars to slide down the mountain and hit the team we'd just spoken to. One of those guys was dead. Two others were badly injured.

Trained in CPR, Ryan and Clark rushed to the scene and took the climbers down on sleds to a place where they could be safely reached by a rescue helicopter. When our guides returned, there was blood all over their jackets and gloves. That really shook me up. Unlike the momentary feeling of being scared on a roller coaster or after narrowly avoiding a road accident, this has stayed with me to the present day. Mountaineering is often equated with being in the military—death does and will occur. While I struggled to come to terms with the fact that someone I'd just talked to was dead, I also wondered how the inevitable news of this incident would affect anyone who knew that I was doing the same climb. Maybe they'd think I was the one who had died. As well as being a little concerned for my own safety, I also found myself worrying about those who might worry about me, so it was good that we were provided with the resources to phone home and say that we were okay.

There was a somber atmosphere as we sat in our kitchen tent and discussed the accident. Although Ryan and Clark did a great job of talking philosophically about mountaineering's harsh realities while assuring us that they were doing everything they could to minimize our own risk, the eerie feeling of recent death was exacerbated by the bad weather that hit our camp the following day, as well as by a weird sight as we headed toward the 17,200-foot High Camp on day 11. A team that was already up there had been retrieving its deep-buried cache when it stumbled upon the frozen, preserved body of a climber who, judging by his clothes and ID, had died there in the 1960s. News of this discovery spread like wildfire, and while we were repeating our 45-degree climb up the headwall, we could actually see the dead body being lowered down a gully on a 3,000-foot rope that ran all the way to Camp 4. Death on the mountain—it suddenly seemed hard to avoid. And while this forced me to contemplate my own mortality, it again served to intensify my growing lust for life.

Having previously climbed the headwall in freezing conditions, I was wearing multiple layers of clothes that didn't take into account the now much warmer climate, and I was soon absolutely drenched in sweat. Still, now that I was on Clark's rope, I didn't want to say, "Hey guys, stop. I'm sweating." I wanted to show how strong I was, and thanks to this idiotic display of ego, I barely made it to the point where fixed ropes appear at about 15,200 feet. Overheating during a climb can kill you—you get dehydrated, your salt and carbohydrate levels plummet, your energy is zapped, and at high altitudes you're in deep trouble. However, while pride often comes before a fall, feelings of inadequacy tie in with the need to prove yourself. When you're comfortable with who you are, you don't have that need—at least, not on an emotional level. That's been a part of my journey.

In the meantime, unable to take the next step, I finally sat down, removed a couple of layers, drank a whole liter of water, and ate most of my food. I desperately needed some fuel, and by the time we reached Washburn's Thumb, I was out of water. Not good, especially since we were now breathing in fumes from a nearby forest fire. But after retrieving our cache and scrambling over rocks and snow along a ridge that narrows to about 15 feet—with a 4,500-foot drop on one side and a 2,500-foot drop on the other—we made it to the High Camp, which sits atop a saucer-shaped plateau. I was exhausted.

More bad weather delayed our push for the summit, and, while we were waiting around on day 12, the guides told us to unload the excess baggage that we'd been carrying despite being advised to leave it back at the Anchorage parking lot. In my case, this amounted to about three or four pounds of stuff I didn't need. Richard had at least twenty pounds. "Richard," Bill exclaimed, "no wonder you're slow!"

Day 13 was beautiful and sunny as we traversed the icy, 30-degree slope of the Denali Pass. Well rested, I felt good, and we really motored along the poorly defined ridge that led us to the 19,500-foot broad plateau that's known as the Football Field. Still, Alex, on the rope behind Clark and me, was starting to hurt, and while we were ascending the small headwall that leads to the 20,000-foot summit ridge, I told Clark that I was pulling Alex a little bit.

"Alex, are you okay?" Clark shouted.

"No, I'm not okay. I can't go on."

When you're tied to a rope and one guy can't make it, no one can make it. We were just a few hundred feet from the summit. This was really lousy.

"Bo, do you have any GU?" Clark asked, referring to a power bar that's ground up into an easily digestible milkshake consistency.

"Sure."

"Leave a packet of GU in the snow."

I did as he asked. "C'mon, Alex," Clark shouted. "Get to the GU."

We all climbed about 30 feet so that he could get to the GU. Then, after eating it and resting for about five minutes, he said, "Okay, I feel a little better."

"Bo, put another one in the snow, and also leave him some water," Clark instructed.

I did, and this routine was repeated three more times on the way to the ridge. From there, we walked the 300 feet to the summit. It was incredible—like one of those dreams where you're soaring above the clouds, which would have been handy since there was one hell of a drop on either side. Clark, Alex, Phil, and I were all teary-eyed as we reached our goal a short time after Ryan, Mike, and J. P.

Unfortunately, Richard had been forced to give up just past the Football Field. He was worn out.

Having taken our summit photos, we began our descent, and at the Football Field we saw a guy on all fours, puking his brains out. He was a doctor from Britain, and his colleagues were calling him Trumpy. A reading from a portable pulse oximeter (a medical device that, when placed under a finger, measures the oxygen saturation level of a patient's blood) showed that he had a heart rate of 160 beats and an oxygen saturation level of about 60 percent. A level of 96 to 100 percent is the normal range at sea level, and even with the lower amount of oxygen at around 20,000 feet, my own reading was 85. Trumpy, who was probably one of those people whose biology just isn't suited to high altitudes, was in serious trouble.

After Mike and J. P. joined our rope, making us a six-man team, Ryan short-roped Trumpy all the way down to High Camp, standing about four feet behind him so that if Trumpy fell, he could pull him back. The rest of us followed them there, bypassing Richard, who was genuinely happy that we'd made the summit. The next day, having loaded up the tents and stoves in huge packs, I rejoined his and Bill's rope for the remaining descent. There wasn't far to go, I told myself as Ryan and Clark each set off with his team. But then, as soon as we started to move, the clouds and wind came in from nowhere, and I couldn't even see Richard 30 feet ahead. In fact, I could barely see the rope.

Descending the headwall, Richard went first, followed by me, and as is normal for guides when going downhill, Bill at the back, enabling him to self-arrest if anyone else should take a tumble. That came into play when Richard suddenly fell and ripped me off my feet. I flew forward, head first, and when my jumar stopped my fall, I was left dangling with my feet facing up the mountain. Quickly I managed to maneuver myself the right way up, and all the while Richard was screaming, "Aaargh! Aaargh! I broke my leg! I broke my leg! Aaargh! Aaargh! I can't move!"

Unable to hear him, Bill shouted, "Bo, hurry up!"

"Richard's hurt," I shouted back. "He says he's broken his leg."

"Fuck!" Bill screamed. "That goddamn Richard!"

Richard, meanwhile, had reassessed his condition: "It's not my leg, it's my calf muscle. It's torn off the bone!"

When I relayed this to Bill, our guide's response was, "Tell him to keep going!"

"Richard, Bill says you should keep going." It felt so good to say that. After all, coming from Bill, it was okay. "Hurry your ass up!"

We were in whiteout conditions, and when I relayed Richard's request for Bill to go down and help him, the response was a definitive, "No! This is an area where we can't stop."

"C'mon, man," I yelled down to Richard. "Dig in! Just use your other leg."

Finally, he figured out a way of moving just one inch at a time, which was excruciating for all of us who were trying to keep our footing at a 45-degree angle. Consequently, when we reached the 15,200-foot level where the fixed ropes ended, I was more than a little miffed. That descent had taken us three or four hours. At the same time, I was concerned for Richard, who was clearly hurt, but when another team that had summited caught up with us, I asked Bill if I could hitch a ride on their rope and he said, "Sure, go ahead."

Aware that the hard part of the descent was over, and that only Bill was required to short-rope Richard down a mild slope for about 45 minutes, I hopped on the other team's rope and headed to Camp 4. Once we were there, the guides told Richard that although he couldn't walk, he certainly could hobble, and he was going to Base Camp right away. "I'll take him," Ryan announced, "and someone must come with us. We need three people on a rope."

"I've done my time," I thought. "Please don't pick me."

At that moment J. P., the triathlete, stepped up and said, "I'll go." I later learned that it took them over 20 hours to get all the way down.

The rest of us left about 10 hours after Ryan, J. P., and Richard, when it was dark and the snow was harder. A couple of weeks earlier, we had seen quite a few crevasses on the Kahiltna Glacier. Now there were hundreds of them. It seemed as if there was one every 10 feet. I almost fell in on numerous occasions, but somehow I managed to fling myself past the opening. The journey was brutal. However, after we made it back to Base Camp at around 8 A.M., flew to Talkeetna about three hours later, and were reinvigorated by the normal level of oxygen at sea level, we wasted no time in doing what many of us had been dreaming and even obsessing about for the past couple of weeks—stuffing ourselves with our favorite junk food. So it was that a late-afternoon lunch of burgers and fries was immediately followed by a visit to the pizzeria. Not the most exciting way to celebrate July Fourth, but as part of my mountain-based odyssey of sometimes gut-wrenching self-discovery, I wouldn't have had it any other way.

While it takes a lot of self-confidence to complete some of the climbs, too much self-confidence is no good. This usually relates back to ego, and on Denali my ego was ultimately reined in a little when I began to grasp the concept of being a good team player, along with some of the qualities that are required to lead. Thinking before I speak, occasionally speaking my mind, at other times knowing when to shut up and follow—it's a fragile balancing act, and although you can never be perfect, you can still try to perfect what you're doing. That's what I learned. But there was a lot more to learn. There always is.

ELBRUS, FIRST ATTEMPT

Success is not final, failure is not fatal. It is the courage to continue that counts.

—Winston Churchill

UPON RETURNING to New York from Alaska, I went straight to J. P. Morgan, and within an hour my computer had been removed, I'd cleaned out my desk, and there was a party for me in the conference room. Afterward, as I was about to walk out the door, I looked back at all the analysts with their heads down, hard at work, and I felt like a soldier who was leaving to go fight another battle. There they were, still stuck in the trenches, while I was headed to business school and the Great Unknown.

I was still trying to acquire what amounted to a master's in climbing, and I'd really started to hit my stride on Denali. Never before had I spent the entire time on a mountain moving up a glacier, using ropes, an ice ax, snowshoes, and crampons, and I'd loved it. By my standards, I'd prepared well, and afterward I felt strong. However, that expedition was also the last time I'd use a multiguide service. From now on, whenever possible, I wanted to challenge myself by going it alone, or with experienced climbing friends.

I was always independent. I can still remember playing ice hockey as a five-year-old, at a time when, inexperienced and dyslexic, I didn't yet understand the complexities or strategies of the game. Nevertheless, while the other kids tended to gather in a bunch and move all over the ice en masse, if I got the puck, I'd stick-work it toward the opponent's goal by whatever means possible, and on one occasion I scored a hat trick. When it comes to expeditions, I'm basically more of an individualist than I am someone who strives for acceptance within a wider group, and that's why I love the fact that you can climb however you want—you can do group guided climbing, which is fine; do individual guided climbing, so that you can go at your own pace; climb with friends; or go it alone with no guides whatsoever. When you sign up to be part of a group, you have no idea whom you'll end up with, and my experiences on Denali had forced me to think about the attributes that make a good teammate as well as those that make a good team leader. What's more, those experiences had also made me contemplate my own qualities in that regard and whether or not they were compatible with certain types of people.

Gaining perspective on myself and my personality traits was vital to my maturation as a person and as a mountaineer (not that the two are mutually exclusive), especially since I'd already planned my next expedition. Back in May, about six weeks before the Denali trip, I'd had a conversation with Rich Birrer, one of my colleagues at J. P. Morgan, who, together with his mom, his dad, his sister, Danielle, and his twin brother, Chris, had spent the summers of 1988 through 2000 climbing the "50 Highpoints," the highest-elevation point in each of the 50 states. Rich, Chris, and Danielle had even coauthored a book about this—*Climbing Across America: A Family Guide to*

Highpointing the 50 States—and in addition to each having a first-degree black belt in Kyokushinkai karate, they had also received the bronze, silver, and gold Congressional Medals for community volunteer activity. Now, having already tackled Kilimanjaro, Rich told me that he, Chris, and their father were focused on climbing the Seven Summits. Next up: Russia's Mount Elbrus.

Located in the Caucasus range between the Black and Caspian Seas, near the border of Georgia, Elbrus is, like Kilimanjaro, a stratovolcano. Its name means "woman's breasts" in one of the Caucasian languages, and this makes sense when you see its two summits: the eastern, first ascended by a local guide in 1829, stands at 18,442 feet; the western, first ascended by a British expedition in 1874, is just 68 feet taller, yet it's widely recognized as the highest point both in Russia and in all of Europe. According to ancient mythology, it was here that Zeus, the Greek king of the gods, chained Prometheus after the Titan stole fire from him and placed it in man's possession. The volcano has been dormant for the past 2,000 years and boasts a permanent icecap that feeds 22 glaciers; it has been a popular climbing destination since the early years of the Soviet Union. However, it has also been a death trap.

In the winter of 1936, a large group of inexperienced Konsomols (members of the youth wing of the Soviet Communist Party) attempted the climb and many of them suffered fatal slips on the ice. Still, the government continued to encourage ascents of the mountain, and in 1959 construction work commenced on a cable car system that, since its completion in 1976, has been able to transport visitors up to 12,500 feet, leaving a straightforward, almost crevasse-free ascent of about 6,000 feet to the west summit. Because of atrocious winter conditions that deter all but the most experienced climbers, this ascent is usually attempted during the summer, and although it is not technically difficult, it is still often hampered by strong winds and afternoon electrical storms.

This did not deter an adventurer named Alexander Abramov, who, in the late summer of 1997, earned a place in the *Guinness Book of*

World Records for traveling to the east summit with a 10-person team packed inside a four-wheel-drive Land Rover Defender. The team also made it back down, but not so the SUV, which skidded out of control when one of the team tried to drive it without chains, plummeted down the slope after the driver escaped, and impaled itself on some rocks, where it remains to this day. Over the years, other crazies have attempted to conquer Elbrus on motorcycles (so far without success), but even on foot this climb isn't always easy, as evidenced by the 15 to 30 people who lose their lives there each year. You have to know what you're doing.

When Rich Birrer told me that he, Chris, and their dad intended to climb Elbrus without guides and that they would be doing this in August, between my return from Denali and my entry to Kellogg, I was immediately interested in joining them. Three years younger than I, as well as shorter and more wiry, with brown, wavy hair and outgoing personalities, the twins had been proficient members of the Yale University diving team. Their father, Rich, Sr., also known as the Doc, was a stern, highly disciplined Air Force physician, a Fulbright scholar, and an award-winning medical researcher who ran marathons barefoot and didn't indulge in small talk. Since he and Chris intended to follow Elbrus by climbing Turkey's highest peak, Mount Ararat (which many people believe was the landing spot for Noah's Ark), they'd take care of their own flights. I therefore wrote Rich an $800 check and asked him to book me on the same flights as he, which is what he did. Then he e-mailed me the itinerary, and I saw us listed as "Bo" and "Rich" instead of "Robert" and "Richard."

"The names on our tickets have to match the names on our passports," I told him.

"Nah, that won't be a problem," he tried to assure me in a voice that suggested that he knew what he was talking about. I wasn't buying it.

"Let's call Swiss Air," I replied. When we did, we learned that not only were the tickets invalid, but there would be no refund. Now Rich was freaking out. Our only option was to keep calling Swiss Air.

The fourth time we did so, a manager finally agreed to waive company policy and, as a one-time favor, change our tickets after we went through the hassle of supplying our passports, backup IDs, and even our employment records. A small oversight had resulted in mucho bureaucracy, but I didn't realize that this was just an ominous sign of what lay ahead.

Acquiring a Russian visa also proved to be a little complicated, not least because of the stained photo on my passport, which I'd managed to soak during the La Ruta Maya canoe race. The visa was eventually issued, but after I'd heeded the Russian Embassy's advice to get a new passport, the old one was handed back to me at the New York passport office with holes punched through it and "void" stamped on the main ID page.

"My new passport has a different number, and it doesn't have the Russian visa," I complained to an official.

"That's okay," she replied. "Just show both passports. Each of them has your name and photo."

Unsure about this, I returned to the Russian Embassy and was told the same thing. Fair enough. I was all set.

My Denali trip followed shortly thereafter, and when I returned, I was fired up and ready for Elbrus. Since this one-day climb wouldn't be as high or as technical, I didn't need to train. I was fit and confident. And although crampons and an ice ax would be required for the glacier, I'd also read that crevasses really aren't a problem so long as a climber adheres to the clearly delineated main route that runs from the end of the ski lift up to the top of the mountain. Compared to Denali, Aconcagua, or even Kilimanjaro, it sounded dead easy.

On August 7, Rich and I took off from Newark International Airport and, after a stop-off in Geneva, arrived at Moscow's Domodedovo International Airport the following day, where Chris and the Doc were already waiting for us. Rich lined up at passport control just in front of me, and I could see him argue with the official, but eventually he was allowed to pass through and retrieve his luggage. Now it was my turn. I handed over my two passports and was quickly informed that the different numbers on the old one with the visa and the new one without meant that I couldn't enter the country.

"You must return to America," the female official calmly asserted, and this was confirmed by a supervisor when I tried to object. "There is the line for deportation," he helpfully explained. I couldn't believe it. Rich was out of sight, so there was no way I could tell him, and when I joined the deportation line behind about 30 other people, their hands-on-hips postures indicated that this might be a lengthy process.

"How long have you been waiting?" I asked a guy five places farther up the line.

"Two hours," he replied. Oh, my gosh, I could be standing here all day. Not that anyone was forcing us to—we could walk around as much as we wanted as long as we didn't enter the baggage area. I went to the bathroom and briefly tried to figure out if there was a way I might sneak through. Bad idea. Walking around the "new arrivals" zone, I then saw about 15 people standing in front of a small doorway, yelling and waving their fists, and when I asked one of them what was going on, he said that they all had problems with their tickets or their passports and weren't being allowed to enter the country. Aha!

Wondering what was on the other side of the doorway, I tried to weasel my way through, but without success. All of the protesters were absolutely furious—no one wanted to fly back to where they'd just come from. This underscored how life is what you make of it. Some people were standing timidly in the deportation line; others were kicking up a real stink. Then, all of a sudden, the seas parted where the near-riot was taking place, and everyone quieted down as a tall, dark, beautiful young Russian woman emerged from the other side of that crowded entrance to who-knows-where. She looked at me, I looked at her . . . the attraction was instantaneous. Cue the soft focus and slow motion of a love scene out of some made-for-TV movie. This had never happened to me before.

As she walked by, she kept looking back in my direction. "That," I told myself, "is an angel." It's pathetic how quickly I forgot about getting through passport control. Within a few moments she returned from wherever she'd gone. "How are you?" I asked, trying to break the ice. "I'm fine," she replied. "How are you?"

Not the most sparkling conversation, but hey, it was a start. "Well, I could be better," I commented as she continued walking.

Once again, the seas parted and she disappeared through the doorway. Immediately, the yelling and fist waving resumed. When a couple of people peeled away, I managed to sneak a peek into what I now discovered was an office with at least three computers, but the staff there continued to hold the line; nobody could get in. An hour went by, while I wondered what my buddy Rich must be thinking. Then the seas parted once more, the magnificent Muscovite reappeared, and this time I was ready: "My name's Bo, what's yours?"

"Katya."

"What's going on?" I asked.

"There are some real jerks," came the thickly accented reply.

"What's their problem?"

"Mostly their visas."

"So, where are you going?"

"I need to get out of here and have a cigarette. Would you like one?"

"Absolutely."

I had tried some cigarettes about 10 years earlier, but that had been it. Then again, had this stunning woman offered me a Snickers bar, I probably would have smoked that too if I thought it might impress her. I followed her upstairs to a deserted lounge where we smoked and chatted about where each of us lived. Then I got to the point and told her that I was in Russia to climb Mount Elbrus and I had a problem with my visa. When I showed her my two passports, she looked at her watch and asked, "Do you have cash on you?"

I did. "Well, I may be able to help you," she said. "We have a guy here who creates visas, but he left early today. However, at Sheremetievo the guy stays until six."

Sheremetievo is Moscow's other main international airport. It was 4:30. "How long does it take to get there?" I asked.

"Oh, the traffic will be bad now. Perhaps an hour, an hour and a half."

"That means I've got to get it now."

"Well, I'm not sure I should help you . . ."

As this last statement was said in an unmistakably seductive and flirty manner, I threw caution to the wind and kissed her on the lips. "Will you help me now?"

Although slightly taken aback, she didn't look horrified. So I kissed her again. "If you help me, I will be *really* grateful," I assured her. "Let's go out tonight. You can take me to dinner."

"Okay, okay," she said, wrapping her arms around my neck. "It's a hundred dollars for the visa." Then we kissed some more. Believe me, I wasn't trying to lower the price. This lady was like a guardian angel sent by Victoria's Secret.

After a guard accompanied me to the baggage area so that I could locate Rich, Chris, and the Doc—all of whom were wondering what the hell had been going on—I handed them my passports, the requisite signed immigration document, and some highly regarded American money, and I explained the situation and what I needed them to do. They took a cab to Sheremetievo Airport and returned about three hours later with my visa. In the meantime, Katya and I had exchanged phone numbers and other pleasantries, and since family commitments meant that she couldn't go out that night, I promised to call her when I returned from Elbrus. As things turned out, I should have persuaded her to accompany me on the next leg of the journey.

When the security official at Domodedovo Airport stamped my passport but not my departure card, I really didn't give it much thought. I was just glad to join the Birrers and head for our Moscow hotel. The next morning, we took off from Sheremetievo (while I sat, startled, on the john) for a two-hour flight on a decrepit old plane where rotting food was served on metal trays and the cabin door kept swinging open. Our destination: Mineralnye Vody Airport in Stavropol Krai. Just three hours' drive from the mountain, and located close to the Chechen border in a war-torn region of the Caucasus, this antiquated Soviet-era rattrap has been described as "a lower circle of hell" by the *Economist* and voted one of the world's five worst airports by *Foreign Policy* magazine. It isn't hard to see why.

As BBC News foreign correspondent Steve Rosenberg described it in 2005, "There are no trolleys, no porters—the check-in desks have been completely gutted. . . . Rather worryingly, there's a man selling Caucasian swords and daggers in the departure lounge, and opposite him, over on the wall, is a list of local criminals wanted for murder. . . . The 'VIP Restaurant' didn't have any tea or food. In fact, it didn't even have any tables or chairs, just a picture of a bottle of water on the wall. And a rusty sink full of cigarette butts."

At least the Moscow airports I'd seen were nothing like this. As soon as we disembarked from the plane and stood on the runway at Mineralnye Vody, Rich whipped out his camera and began taking photos of the shack that posed as a terminal. On the roof, there was a Cold War–friendly hammer and sickle. On the ground, mangy-looking feral dogs were running wild. Immediately some security guards appeared out of nowhere and grabbed both Rich and me, and while Chris and the Doc pretended that they didn't even know us, these armed gorillas hauled us toward the terminal, dumped us in a tiny, sweaty back room, and locked the door. Having demanded to see our passports, they then pointed out that although these *had* been stamped by the Domodedovo Airport authorities, our departure cards hadn't been. No doubt about it, even if those cards had been stamped, they would have found something else to justify them grilling us like hamburgers. This was a moneymaking scam, and we knew it right away.

"Big problem, big problem," the burliest guard kept repeating. And when he told us that we'd have to be deported, I quickly ran out of patience and shouted, "No freaking way!"

Rich and I were sitting at a table that, in line with the airport's other amenities, was nothing more than a cardboard box. Placing a pen and a piece of paper on it, the guard pounded it with a bloody-knuckled fist and barked, "You must pay!" The bartering had begun. The starting price: a very familiar-sounding $100.

"I'm not paying a thing," I insisted while Rich muttered, "Man, I don't know about this." Then I got up to leave, prompting the muscle-bound guard to grab me by the shoulder, push me, and shout, "Sit down!"

"This is bullcrap!" I fired back. "You guys are thieves! I want to see the police!"

"We *are* the police."

I stood up again, and this time I got into a tussle with the big guy, the two of us shouting at one another in our native tongues. He shoved me, I pushed him back forcefully, and for about three seconds we were engaged like a couple of bulls. Then, realizing that this could get really ugly, more for me than for my fellow wrestler, I said, "Okay, okay," raised my arms as a sign of submission, and sat back down. It was obvious that Rich and I weren't getting out of that room with our spending money intact.

"Goshdamit!" I exclaimed while picking up the pen. Then I crossed out "$100" and wrote "$50."

"Okay," both guards muttered approvingly.

How it worked, I have no clue, but that's all it took. Rich handed over the 50 bucks and we were out of there. As Churchill once said, "If you are going through hell, keep going." Not that we succeeded in having our departure cards stamped. There still had to be *some* fun in store for the return journey. I just couldn't believe all the crap I'd had to endure before even reaching the base of the mountain. Of course, patience was one of the many virtues that I still needed to acquire, but there's no way I'd ever try to develop a heightened tolerance for injustice, to me or anyone else.

Our next destination was Terskol, the little town at the foot of Elbrus, which has become a major tourist location thanks to not only the constant influx of climbers, but also the booming Russian ski industry. Indeed, while crime and corruption are widespread within Russia, and there are constant reminders of the old Soviet regime in the form of monolithic, characterless government buildings that appear to have been designed to intimidate the citizens and reduce them to mere statistics, the places that I saw were not without charm. Moscow is a fascinating, vibrant city that melds modern attractions with some incredible historic architecture, not least around Red Square, and even Terskol has plenty of bars and restaurants to keep people entertained.

Nevertheless, after Rich, Chris, Doc, and I laid out $200 (a price that seemed cheap compared to the $1,000 originally demanded) for a vodka-drenched cabbie to take us on a three-hour fun ride to the mountain's nearest town, we were treated to several more scams in the form of compulsory-purchase tickets and "special permits" at each stop on the cable car/chairlift ride to Garabashi, the 12,500-foot starting point of the climb. I just wanted to get this expedition over and done with.

Finding ourselves almost immediately on the glacier, we trekked for about an hour up the snowy slopes to the 13,800-foot High Camp and the burned-out ruins of the old three-story metal-sheathed hut that was once known as the highest "hotel" in the world—Priut 11, the "Refuge of the Eleven," named after a tent on that site that had previously housed a team of scientists. Perched off the end of a cliff and covered in ice, it now boasts only a hole-in-the-floor latrine that, having survived the 1998 fire, pours a nonstop supply of poop down the side of the mountain; this facility was justifiably proclaimed to be the "world's nastiest outhouse" by *Outside* magazine in 1993.

In 2001, basic bunk-bed accommodation for about 50 people was created close to the site of a ruined fuel store located some 60 feet below Priut 11. Known as the Diesel Hut, this serves as an alternative to the even smaller Shuvalova and Blue Huts situated nearby, as well as the relatively upmarket Garabashi "Barrels" (a line of cylindrical cabins), which are near the upper station of the Elbrus ski-lift system. Since we'd be melting snow for water, and the ground below and all around Priut 11 was smothered in excrement, we opted to pitch a tent near the Diesel Hut, where the snow was hopefully cleaner.

It was now about four in the afternoon on August 10 and the weather was perfect—sunny with no wind. When we asked people staying in the Diesel Hut where they got their water, they pointed to a pipe funneling melted glacier into a small stream. It sounded idyllic.

"Do we have to treat the water?" one of us asked.

"No, no, no, it's fine!"

While the Doc had three water bottles that he'd filled back in Terskol, Rich, Chris, and I had decided to carry lighter loads, so we just held our mugs below the hallowed stream and drank to our hearts' content. It tasted great.

The next day was a rest day. Waking up with a bad dose of the Hershey squirts, I sprinted somewhat gingerly over to Priut 11 and saw for myself what it was all about. It was absolutely disgusting. Turds squelched underfoot as I trudged toward the toilet hole, which looks down on an icy abyss. What's more, as I crouched over that hole, I was blasted from underneath by a gust of wind that very nearly knocked me off my feet. Just picturing myself doing an impromptu break dance on that crap-covered floor still gives me the creeps.

Outside, the weather was again terrific, so after I'd rejoined the others, we walked a short distance uphill to get a feel for the route and grow accustomed to the altitude. After all, going from sea level to nearly 14,000 feet had been a huge jump. Many people spend seven to ten days just acclimatizing on Elbrus, and they do so by initially basing themselves in Terskol and then hiking to and from the second cable car station, as well as to and from the third cable car station, before ascending to Garabashi. Being capable of acclimatizing more quickly, we'd done all this in just over an hour via the cable car/chairlift system, yet even though none of us had felt out of breath while we were being transported, we could really feel the altitude when we were hiking up to High Camp.

At some point in the afternoon, a mountain official approached us along with an armed soldier and announced, "You must pay the environmental fee." This was one of the additional charges that we'd managed to ignore while negotiating our way up the cable car system. The official was so pissed, he'd located a soldier and hiked up to High Camp to ensure that we each laid out another $10. Those guys were relentless.

In the meantime, we had estimated that the climb to the summit and the return to Terskol would take us anywhere from 12 to 15 hours. When we heard that rough weather was heading our way, the Doc decided that we should go to bed at 9:00 P.M., get up at 2:45 A.M., and set off at 3:00. He ran everything like a military operation. When he said, "Okay, guys, dinner is served in five minutes," that meant it would be served in five minutes and that his boys would be there. When he said, "It's time for bed," they were all in the tent at the same time. I was still sitting outside when they turned in at 10:00, and after their alarms rang in unison at 2:45 in the morning, they were up in an instant and ready to leave at 3:00.

The Doc, in fact, left at *precisely* 3:00 without saying a word to anyone else. "Guys, where's your dad?" I asked.

"He's gone. We're running a little bit late."

That meant that the twins left two minutes after the Doc. I, tardy as usual, left 15 minutes after them—my lifelong problems with punctuality and adhering to a disciplined schedule could be symptomatic of dyslexia or perhaps just a blasé attitude. Either way, the two-hour route to the Pastukhov Rocks at 15,840 feet was easy enough to discern: a broad, steadily ascending slope. From there, we would head east for a couple of hours to reach the 17,800-foot saddle between the two peaks, and then a direct, four-hour trek along steeper ground—on a gradient ranging from 40 to 45 degrees—would take us to the west summit. The only trouble was that at departure time the conditions were cold, cloudy, and really, really windy.

After trekking on my own for a while, I spotted Rich up ahead. He had stopped, and as I got closer I wondered why he was emptying the contents of his water bottle. Then I realized that he was basically pissing out of his rear end. He was as sick as a dog. Having heard him go in and out of the tent all night, I'd suspected he might have diarrhea, but this was really acute, and it soon turned out that Chris was suffering from the same ailment. As obvious as it may now seem, we didn't discover the cause until several hours later, when we were on our way back down the mountain. Taking another route that followed the stream of water that led to the pipe out of which Rich, Chris, and I had filled our bottles near the Diesel Hut, we saw poop everywhere. So much for assuming that it was confined to the area immediately surrounding good old Priut 11 and believing three different people who asserted that the water was "fine."

This would be another invaluable lesson: Whenever possible, doing your own research instead of just taking the word of others can not only make the difference between success or failure in all walks of life, but on the side of a mountain it can also be the difference between life and death. In retrospect, what we had done was really, really dumb. We could—and therefore should—have looked all around to see if anything might be contaminating the water. Had we done so, Rich and Chris wouldn't have been poisoned. In my case, after that first drink, I'd been treating the water with iodine pills, so even though I, too, had diarrhea, it wasn't as bad as theirs. And the disease-free Doc was still drinking his water from Terskol.

As the darkness began to lift it was clear that we were really fogged in, and as we approached the Pastukhov Rocks amid snow flurries and strong crosswinds, we saw more and more people turning back. The path was no longer easy to distinguish, and we knew that crevasses lurked to the left of the trail. During a powwow at the rocks, the Doc said, "I'm going down right now."

With that, he did an about-face and was gone. The twins and I decided that we would press on—if we kept going for another hour, the weather might clear. However, within five minutes both of the boys said that they were turning around. That left just me. Despite some lingering diarrhea, I was feeling good, and I knew I could make it. I'd made Kili, Aconcagua, and McKinley—this wasn't hard. Then again, unable to see all that far beyond my nose, I couldn't tell where I was going. Did I really fancy dying like a wannabe hero? Hell, no. Forget the summit. I turned around.

Back at High Camp, it snowed all day. We were scheduled to fly back to Moscow late the next afternoon, so we got up in the very early hours of the morning, and when we saw that the weather was still against us, we decided to head for home. This, of course, entailed paying our way at every stop of the cable car system, and we knew that, with unstamped departure cards, Rich and I would be hammered yet again at good old Mineralnye Vody Airport. Since he and Chris are twins, I suggested that Rich use Chris's passport to get past the officials with their dad, and then the Doc could return it to Chris so that the two of them would go through together.

That's precisely what they did. Rich went through okay and the Doc followed him, but then when I tried to do the same, I was stopped by an official, holding up a hand and going into his routine. Was this an organized scam or what? "It's okay," I said. "I know. I don't have the stamp. I have to pay. I must go back to the office."

As I started walking, he came after me. "Where are you going?"

"I have to pay. Don't worry. I'm going to pay."

After finding the famous back room, I sat down with another security guy, and reluctant to pay $50 yet again, put $20 on the cardboard-box table and said, "This is more than enough."

"Okay, okay," he said, pocketing the money before signing—but not stamping—my departure card. The whole thing took a few minutes. It was much easier just playing the game, especially now that I knew the unofficial rules. And at the same time, the three Birrers had passed through security using only two passports.

Fed up after the entire Russian ordeal, I flew back to Moscow. Once there, I paid a marginal amount to have a three-day stopover in Geneva so that I could climb the Matterhorn in the Swiss/Italian Alps, and I also spent a great night in the Russian capital with Katya, my guardian angel. Nevertheless, when she told me that she had to work the next morning, I remarked that I'd be flying out in the evening. In truth, my flight was scheduled for 8:00 A.M.

I knew that, as one of the heads of passport control, she had the authority to prevent me from leaving the country. No way was that about to happen. For me, Russia had been a hellhole, and my desire to get away squelched any romantic considerations. After landing in Geneva, I checked my e-mail. Sure enough, there was a message from Katya: "You left before you said you would do so. I wanted to see you, so I was going to put a hold on your passport."

Aha, once more! As the saying goes, "Fool me once, shame on you; fool me twice, shame on me." This time, I had been on my guard and my instincts had served me well. Katya and I could stay in touch, and at some point I'd have to return to take another stab at Elbrus. However, I had no doubt that, whenever that might be—and believe me, I was in no rush—I'd hire a professional service to pick me up at the airport and take me all the way to Garabashi, where I'd also pay a little extra to stay in the Barrels. It would be worth it. I didn't have the time or the patience to go through all of the same nonsense that I'd experienced on this aborted trip.

Overconfident after conquering Denali ("We'll need only three days to climb Elbrus"), I hadn't taken into account either the local elements or the native culture. Sure, climbing there on a perfect day would be easy, but there are always numerous other factors to take into consideration. After all, as Benjamin Franklin once asserted, by failing to prepare, you are preparing to fail.

Tanzania's "Mountain of Greatness," Kilimanjaro. The first of my Seven Summits, and one of the most beautiful treks on Earth, involving a forty-five mile climb through rainforest, heath, moorland, alpine desert, and a bitterly cold arctic region. It's like walking from the equator to the North Pole. *(Photo: Richard Wiese)*

The bones of an elephant that strayed too far. The thin air at around 15,000 feet makes Kilimanjaro's alpine desert a burial ground for some and a turning-back point for others while trying to reach Africa's highest peak. *(Photo: Richard Wiese)*

Aconcagua in Argentina introduced me to the world of treacherous climbing. This included an area known as the Penatentes where, while walking into the face of high winds, my teammates and I had to navigate between the remnants of melted glacier in the form of ice stalagmites, many of them over six feet tall. *(Photo: Ed Parkin)*

A view of the sunrise from Cerro Aconcagua, South America's highest mountain, on summit day. December 30, 2003. *(Photo: Ed Parkin)*

Denali in Alaska, also known as Mount McKinley, is North America's tallest peak, and one that has a much higher vertical rise than even Mount Everest. In addition to boasting lousy weather, it afforded me my first glimpse of death on a mountain. *(Photo: Richard Thorby)*

Kneeling atop Denali with guides Ryan Campbell and Clark Fyans. By now we were all smiles, yet a few days earlier Ryan and I had nearly come to blows thanks to my impatient attitude and bullheaded behavior. *(Photo: Bo Parfet)*

On Russia's Mount Elbrus, the Garabashi "Barrels" serve as sleeping quarters and a safe haven from the stench of the mountain's repulsive latrines. Elbrus means "woman's breasts" in one of the Caucasian languages, and the left peak in this photo is the highest in all of Europe. *(Photo: Bo Parfet)*

The frozen desert of Antarctica's Vinson Massif—a vast expanse of virtual nothingness at the bottom of the world. *(Photo: Jonathan Leebow)*

The Three Amigos—Rich Birrer (center), Jonathan Leebow (right), and I ignore the sub-zero temperatures at Vinson's Patriot Hills camp. Despite the bare chests and smug expressions, we were freezing our butts off. And "Leebs" wouldn't be smiling for very long. *(Photo: Jonathan Leebow)*

Four down, three to go . . . Well, make that four. Back at Camp One after having summited Vinson (and slipped into a crevasse). *(Photo: Jonathan Leebow)*

With fellow climber Rob Milne in the village of Tengboche on the way to Everest's Base Camp during my first expedition there in April 2005. That June, Rob would tragically die during our failed attempt to reach the summit. *(Photo: Richard Birrer, Sr.)*

Even Everest's Base Camp offers some entertainment. While there, we received a snow dusting from a nearby avalanche. *(Photo: Mike Davey)*

On average, Everest's Khumbu Glacier moves about three to four feet everyday. When using a ladder to traverse a deep crevasse in the Khumbu Icefall, one of the most dangerous sections of the South Col route, you're praying that it doesn't budge an inch. *(Photo: Rob Milne)*

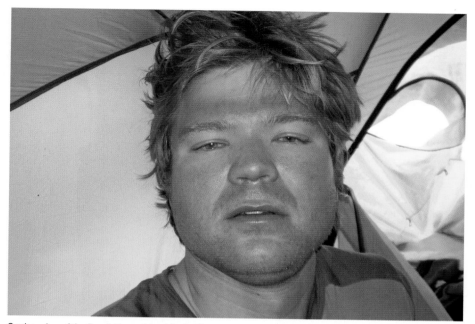

On the edge of the Death Zone. After idiotically racing to Everest's 26,000-feet Camp Four, I was exhausted, gulping for air, severely dehydrated, and vomiting whatever I drank or ate. My body was shutting down, and just sitting up for this photo required a major effort. *(Photo: Bo Parfet)*

Atop Elbrus at my second attempt, proudly displaying the flag of the Kellogg School of Management. My happiness was short-lived – Skiing down the mountain would be no easy task. *(Photo: Bo Parfet)*

Into the great unknown—Skiing Mount Elbrus was nearly as difficult as dealing with the corrupt local officials. *(Photo: Bo Parfet)*

Not your conventional food market—Fruits, veggies...and fried rat. The sight of sautéed rodent disgusted me, yet before long, starving hungry, I'd be forced to sample it en route to Indonesia's Carstensz Pyramid. *(Photo: Maxime Chaya)*

Carstensz is technically the most difficult climb of all the Seven Summits. Here, I'm ascending part of its 2,000-foot face, having nearly met my maker when blasted by high winds that caused me to dangle on a rope in mid air. *(Photo: Christine Boskoff)*

Christine Boskoff, owner of climbing company Mountain Madness, surveys the rugged granite face of Carstensz Pyramid, Australasia's highest mountain. Christine would die while climbing in China just under a year later. *(Photo: Maxime Chaya)*

With my father, Bill, in April 2007, when he and other family members joined me for the trek to Base Camp during my return trip to Everest. It was a magical experience. *(Photo: Jay Gudebski)*

Australia's Mount Kosciuszko is by far the easiest of the Seven Summits. Still, I did my best to make it as hard as possible. Standing at the top, Christmas Day, 2005. *(Photo: Chris Birrer)*

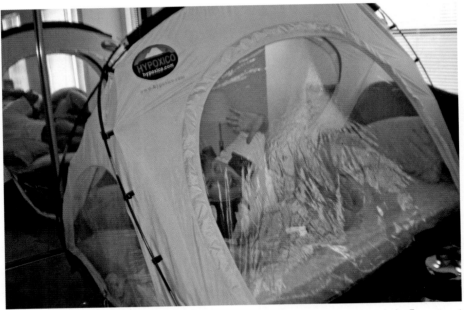

Chilling out in the high-altitude chamber that I installed in my Chicago apartment to train for Everest part two. The simulated height when I slept inside it was about 15,000 feet. *(Photo: Bo Parfet)*

April 12, 2007—Sherpas transport the body of one of their colleagues after he was killed by falling ice at the base of Everest's Lhotse Face. The corpses of people who die higher up the mountain usually remain where they fell. *(Photo: Bo Parfet)*

The world's tallest mountain casts its giant shadow toward the horizon on summit day, May 17, 2007. I was living my dream. *(Photo: Bo Parfet)*

One last look back at Everest's southeast ridge as my fellow climbers near the highest place on Earth.
(Photo: Bo Parfet)

CHAPTER 7

VINSON MASSIF

Live as if you were to die tomorrow. Learn as if you were to live forever.

—Mahatma Gandhi

UNTIL I BECAME a mountaineer, I'd always believed that, if I made a good enough plan, I could, generally speaking, stick to it. The Elbrus expedition changed all that. From start to finish, my trouble-plagued Russian debacle taught me that even the best-laid plans often need to be altered or adapted to the prevailing conditions, and that an alert and flexible mindset is essential when trying to contend with unforeseen obstacles. This lesson came into play on my next Seven Summits attempt, an ascent of Antarctica's formidable Vinson Massif, and it also loomed large during two much shorter-term escapades that immediately preceded it.

As soon as I left Moscow and arrived in Zurich, I headed for the Matterhorn, one of the best-known mountains in the European Alps. Known as Cervino in Italian and Le Cervin in French, the 14,692-foot-high Matterhorn—derived from the German words for "meadow" and "peak"—is located on the border between Switzerland and Italy, and it boasts a quartet of steep faces pointing north, south, east, and west.

The climb itself requires a rope and no small amount of skill and experience, yet it is easier than it looks. Not that this helped me at the time. After hiring a guide who had been recommended by Rich Birrer, I stayed at the Hörnli Hut, a 10,700-foot retreat located on a ridge at the base of the north face. This offered a restaurant, relatively luxurious sleeping quarters, and a close-up view of the route we'd be taking. However, after making it about a quarter of the way up the rest of the mountain, we had to turn back. Because of snow on the route, my guide and I were the only ones trying to scale the Matterhorn that day—not a good sign. And when, after about an hour and a half, he said that it was too dangerous to continue, I took his advice.

Elbrus and now the Matterhorn; both unconquered within the space of a few days, and for the same reason: bad weather. Still, I was now on a roll, bouncing from one adventure to the next without much gap in between. In addition to attempting the aforementioned mountains, I'd also spent the first days of 2004 descending from the top of Aconcagua, participated in the La Ruta Maya Belize Endurance Canoe Race back in March, and taken on Denali in June and July. Up ahead was Vinson Massif. However, immediately after giving up on the Matterhorn, and before entering business school, I took advantage of an inexpensive Internet fare and flew to Chile for a spot of heli-skiing, which entailed having a helicopter transport me and other participants to a remote and tricky ski slope.

Seven expeditions in one year. For me, this was a new way of life, and one that I assumed would continue. High mountains during extended breaks, smaller climbs on the weekends, rafting the Colorado River, skydiving—whatever the activity, I wanted to keep pushing the envelope, to do things that were harder and more dangerous. Then again, I also wanted to get into the Explorers Club, the New York–based organization where I'd first heard about the La Ruta Maya boat race. That was a big motivator for me, and not only because of the prestige. I wanted to be around people who are outstanding in their field, in all senses of the word—*out standing* in the field, by themselves. Many great leaders, from Theodore Roosevelt to Winston Churchill, have spent long periods of time on their own, exploring the Great Outdoors. I wanted to hook up with like-minded individuals: adventurous, driven, and seeking to make this a better world.

Meanwhile, there was a mixed reaction from my parents. When I climbed Kilimanjaro, they thought it was great; when I went to Aconcagua, their attitude was, "Whoa"; by the time I did Denali, I was scaring the hell out of them. They'd heard about all the fatalities that have taken place on the latter two mountains, and the deaths that occurred while I was actually on Denali only heightened their fears. They were not happy. Why did I have to do the Seven Summits?

"I respect your opinion," I told them, "but there's nothing you can say that's going to stop me. I want to do it."

"But we don't want you to die."

It would have been good had I been able to respond with something sage, perhaps quoting Shakespeare's *Julius Caesar:* "Cowards die many times before their deaths. The valiant never taste of death but once." However, nothing that profound came to mind. Still unsure as to who I really wanted to be, I was in the midst of an internal struggle that was being played out on the rooftops of the world, exploring an identity rooted in danger, action, and adventure, without being aware that I was actually embarked on a spiritual journey that would help define me as a man. I was at odds with myself, and there was no way I'd reveal this to my parents. Instead, I just told them that I'd be fine.

What could they say? My mind was made up. And as time passed, they actually came to support me in my quest and love what I accomplished. However, during the period when I segued from Elbrus to the Matterhorn to heli-skiing in Chile, they probably thought I'd lost my mind. It's lucky they weren't there with me.

After I had accepted Kellogg's offer, the school put me and numerous other new Manhattan-based students in e-mail contact with one another. This resulted in a springtime get-together at which we discussed, among other things, our pastimes and our plans for the summer break, and a short time later the skiers among us received an e-mail from a soon-to-be-classmate named Keech Combe, asking if anyone would like to join her in Valle Nevado, north of Santiago, at the start of August. This was to engage in some off-trail downhill skiing in a remote and far wilder mountain environment than what's available at regular ski resorts. The snow is thicker, the slopes are steeper, the descents are longer, natural features such as rocks and trees mean that the risks are higher, and the less accessible terrain has to be reached by helicopter rather than a ski lift.

Oh, man, I loved the sound of *that*. And I also liked the fact that, since Valle Nevado's heli-skiing program had only just started, the cost of doing it for five days was only a thousand bucks. A week of the same in Alaska would cost 10 times that amount. Thanks to all the air miles that I'd racked up while traveling on business for FASB and J. P. Morgan, I was assured of plenty of free flights. So, after returning to New York from Zurich and spending four days moving out of my apartment, I flew home to Kalamazoo, Michigan, collected my skis (which felt weird to be doing in the middle of summer), and headed down to Miami, where Keech and I boarded a plane to Santiago.

Keech was a 27-year-old granddaughter of Ivan D. Combe, the man who, in addition to creating Clearasil acne medication and Odor-Eaters insoles, launched the eponymous company that produces the Lanacane and Vagisil itch crèmes, as well as Grecian Formula hair color for men. Fresh from spending five years traveling around South America, Keech had, in addition to me, recruited three other people for the trip, and after we'd traveled by car from Santiago to Valle Nevado and been dropped off by helicopter on a slope high in the Andes, we immediately began skiing.

There were two guides, each of whom set off in a different direction, and as I followed one of them through a concave passage, he rode up on the right side and hit some lightly blanketed rocks. Almost flying out of his skis, he yelled, "Rocks!" I stopped just in time. Keech, meanwhile, was higher up the concave side of the slope, and she zoomed past me, collided with the rocks, ejected from both of her skis, hit another rock head first, and broke her neck. It was a truly horrific accident, but it happened to the one person in our group who had the good judgment to be wearing a helmet. Without it, she would have died.

"Are you okay?" I screamed.

"No, I'm not okay," came the anguished reply. The guide and I skied straight over to where she was lying.

"Can you move?"

"I can't move! I think I'm paralyzed! Am I going to die?"

As tears streamed down Keech's face, the guide said we should try to move her. I told him to leave her exactly where she was and let the rescue team decide what to do. This turned out to be one of my better decisions. A helicopter was there within 30 minutes, a stretcher was carefully slid underneath Keech's prostrate body, and I climbed on board to accompany her to Santiago's Las Condes Clinic, where she was seen by a spinal physician named Dr. Roberto Larrondo. His diagnosis: a fracture of the fifth cervical vertebra, along with bone splinters that had pierced her spinal cord. Had they gone all the way through—as they might well have done had the guide and I moved her ourselves—she would have been permanently paralyzed. As it was, saved by a matter of millimeters, she required immediate surgery, with a titanium plate being used to repair the vertebra. Thank God this resulted in a return of sensation and movement to her arms and legs, and she was assisted onto her feet within a couple of days.

Keech continued to have limited movement in her neck, but otherwise she made a full recovery. I stayed with her in the hospital for five days, after which, wearing a neck brace, she was able to fly home with her dad while I went to Buenos Aires and met the teacher whose salary had been funded by my Aconcagua trip. Having gone to Elbrus so soon after Denali, I hadn't had enough time to set up any kind of sponsorship; that would happen prior to my returning there. In the meantime, Keech found me an apartment in Chicago, and in late August I and several other Kellogg students spent five days in Panama, doing charitable work and bonding activities organized by Kellogg Adventures—Outdoor & Service (KAOS).

Designed to introduce incoming students to a core group of friends by way of various community-service activities, KAOS provides first-hand experience of the type of teamwork that's central to the Kellogg experience. We helped with food donations, home construction, and other such community efforts, and then we toured Panama. At night, we had food and drinks with our new friends. It was an invaluable form of orientation.

School itself started the first week of September, and it was amazing to be surrounded not only by some of the brightest minds in my age group, but by people from around the world. I found it fascinating to observe how, when presented with a case study, people from different cultural and economic backgrounds tackled a particular business problem. And as one of about 560 kids who were divided into seven groups—mine being called the Cash Cows—I also loved all the joking and arguing that took place in the classroom. Talented and alert, these people required more in the way of stimulation than simply having someone lecture them, and this suited me to a tee. It was rarely boring. I was in awe of how smart all these people were, and while there were provisions for my dyslexia—including a quiet room with no distractions when I took exams—being in a study group really helped me to prepare for questions in class.

Again, it was about teamwork. Yet this was a touchy subject when it came to my next climb, especially since, having been frustrated by the enforced slow pace of ascending Denali, I no longer wanted to be part of a multiguide setup. Indeed, it had been during the Denali descent—while sitting in the Camp 4 kitchen tent with Clark Fyans, Bill Bilmeier, Mike Hsu, Phil Drowley, and Alex Hoffman after Ryan

Campbell and J. P. Moorhead had set off for Base Camp with my injured friend Richard Thorby—that an expedition to Antarctica's Vinson Massif had first been proposed. As is usually the case following a climb, we were discussing, "What's next?" That's often the question, in business and in everyday life, for anyone who's just accomplished a personal or professional goal. It's the unknown challenge that drives us all.

According to Clark, Mountain Trip, the company that he, Ryan, and Bill worked for, had recently been sold by its founder, Gary Bocarde, to a couple of very experienced climbers named Todd Rutledge and Bill Allen. And now Bill Allen, who had already guided expeditions on a number of the Seven Summits, was looking for people to join him on an ascent of Vinson Massif, the highest mountain of the Earth's southernmost continent. Although a date hadn't been set, Clark was pretty sure he'd be the second guide, and he was really excited about visiting the South Pole.

Without a doubt, it would be one heck of an experience. Although smaller in area than Asia, Africa, North America, and South America, Antarctica boasts a nearly precipitation-free interior that makes it technically the world's largest desert. However, it's a frozen desert; about 98 percent of it is covered by an ice sheet that averages at least a mile in thickness, and of all the continents it has the highest average elevation, the coldest, windiest conditions (with temperatures inland ranging from –40 to –94 degrees Fahrenheit in the winter and a balmy 5 to –31 degrees Fahrenheit in the summer), about 90 percent of the world's ice, and 68 percent of its water. Should all that ice ever melt, sea levels could rise by as much as 200 feet.

On July 21, 1983, the Soviet station, Vostok, documented a record-breaking cold temperature of –128.6 degrees Fahrenheit, so it's hardly surprising that Antarctica has no permanent human residents, only plants that have adapted to the frigid temperatures and some equally adept members of the animal kingdom, such as fur seals and penguins. Still, about 2,500 people are usually to be found there during the six months of summer, when, because of the continent's latitude, there's no total darkness, and about 1,000 people during the six months of winter, when there's no sunlight.

The Ellsworth Mountains, named after Lincoln Ellsworth, who discovered and photographed them from the air during a flight in November 1935, are the highest in Antarctica, and it was within the Sentinel Range, to the north of the huge Minnesota Glacier, that Vinson Massif was first spotted by U.S. Navy aircraft in 1957. It now seems incredible to think this sighting took place so recently, in the same year that the U.S.S.R.'s *Sputnik 1* satellite became the first man-made object to orbit the Earth, but it also provides some idea of just how remote the mountain is. Indeed, the entire Sentinel Range wasn't even visited until January 1958, 23 years after its discovery.

Named in honor of Carl G. Vinson, a Democratic congressman from Georgia who, in addition to being a staunch segregationist, was a major supporter of U.S. Antarctic exploration, the appropriately titled Massif is 13 miles long and 8 miles wide. Although it is not technically difficult to climb, it presents some severe challenges because of the extreme cold, and it was only in December 1966 that a group of 10 American mountaineers and scientists, led by Nicholas Clinch (a Los Angeles attorney with two Himalayan climbs under his belt), became the first people to reach Vinson's summit. Thereafter, between 1985 and 2000, Adventure Network International helped more than 450 climbers to follow in Clinch's footsteps, and since then several other companies have also begun guiding clients up the mountain.

Still, it's a costly expedition. For example, the Kilimanjaro trip cost me about $2,500 in 2002, and in 2004 the full price for scaling the Massif would have been about $26,000. Today, it would be more than $30,000, and the flights between Punta Arenas in southern Chile and Antarctica's Patriot Hills are responsible for much of that cost. (They can't be purchased with air miles.) The seasonal Patriot Hills camp, which is utilized only between November and January, is within walking distance of a blue ice runway that, because it experiences no snow accumulation, can support aircraft landings on wheels instead of skis. This is important, since wheeled planes are capable of carrying far heavier loads than those that are ski-equipped. From Patriot Hills, 20-passenger DCH-6 Twin Otter ski planes transport people to and from Vinson Massif and the South Pole, which is about 750 miles away. It's a pricey, highly specialized operation.

Having honed my ability to sniff out a good deal, I knew that, since they were looking to establish themselves and attract customers, the unproven new owners of Mountain Trip probably wouldn't be charging top dollar. This might be a handy opportunity. What's more, Clark mentioned that a climb of Vinson would take place during the Southern Hemisphere summer, which coincides with our winter. "The best time is December/January," he said, prompting me to think that the two-week trip might tie in nicely with my Christmas break from Kellogg. The question was, would I be able to fulfill my post-Denali desire to avoid a multiguide setup?

"If I can get a team together with two of my buddies, would you guide us on your own?" I asked Clark. "That way, we could go at our own pace."

"Hell, yeah."

"Will we be able to go a lot faster than on Denali?"

"Yes, Bill Allen could have his own team, and we'd be independent of one another. Just double-check with Bill."

Which is what I did three months later, in October, several weeks after having entered Kellogg. "Yeah, I have a team, and it'll be separate from yours," Bill assured me. "You guys can go as fast as you want. We won't even be together."

What's more, Bill told me that if I could recruit two people who were willing to pay $26,000 for the expedition, he would charge me significantly less. That was quite a deal, and it was also affordable given how much I'd earned at J. P. Morgan. So, whom did I call? To start with, there was my faithful friend Jonathan Leebow, he of the Gumball 3000 and La Ruta Maya adventures. All jazzed up after the Belize trip, "Leebs" did a 360 and a double back flip when I asked him if he now wanted to follow me to the coldest place on Earth. "Oh, yeah!" he exclaimed. "I do! I've got to start training; I've got to start eating right . . ." He called me back with a whole regimen. The bottom line: Leebs was in. And having been told that he'd have to climb with crampons and an ice ax, he began training in Colorado for his first mountain expedition.

Next, I called Rich Birrer, the J. P. Morgan buddy with whom I'd attempted Elbrus. He had enough vacation time for Vinson, and he was prepared to use it. Boom, I had my own team. "These guys are in," I told Bill Allen when I called him back, and he subsequently called me to say that he himself had recruited four other people who, I assumed, would be on his team: Cheryl and Nikki Bart from Australia, attempting to become the first mother and daughter to ascend the Seven Summits, and Jeff and Justin Johnson, a father and son from Kansas City. We were all set.

Before leaving for Vinson, and in conjunction with the Explorers Club, I set up the Seven Summits Awards Program to raise $2,500 in scholarship funds for each of my remaining climbs. This meant a target of $10,000 to fund students performing health-care-related field research in Antarctica, Asia, Europe, and Australasia. The Explorers Club posted details about this on its Web site, and money was pledged not only by club members, but also by some of my old J. P. Morgan colleagues, new Kellogg classmates, family members, and friends.

At the same time, a member of Kellogg's administration who'd heard about my Seven Summits quest asked me what months are best for climbing Everest. "The spring," I replied.

"Well," she said, "we have students who take a quarter off to pursue research or other specialized activities. You should try to do the same."

Consequently, during my first quarter at business school, I was not only preparing for Antarctica and setting up the associated research grant, but also writing to the Dean to ask if I could take a leave of absence for the entire spring quarter and still obtain my MBA. That would mean graduating after completing a total of five quarters instead of six over the next two years, simply by doing five classes per quarter instead of four. It was a no-brainer.

Just before Christmas, Leebs, Rich, and I hooked up in Punta Arenas, which means "Sandy Point" in Spanish and is one of the world's southernmost cities. A popular tourist haunt as well as a Chilean center of agriculture and industry, it is one of the main jumping-off points for Antarctic expeditions, along with the smaller Argentinean city of Ushuaia, which lies even further south, and Christchurch in New Zealand. After being stranded there for three days because of bad weather, we took off for Patriot Hills at midnight on the fourth day, and the pitch darkness turned to light as we headed toward the South Pole. Looking down, we could see icebergs in the Southern Ocean, which encircles the Antarctic continent; looking into the cockpit of our old Lockheed C-130 Russian transport aircraft, I could see one of the copilots smoking a cigarette and taking a nip of vodka. For a nightmarish second, I pictured myself returning to Mineralnye Vody.

After we landed on Patriot Hills's blue ice runway, the door to the plane opened and the swirling Antarctic air enveloped us. In a split second, I felt as if I was inside a deep freeze. This was cold with a bite and an attitude like nothing that I'd ever known, slapping my face and slicing through my body to show who was now in charge. The journey to the seasonal camp was one hell of a walk, and once we were there, we struggled to pitch a tent in the gale-force conditions. Some of us actually had to lie inside the tent to ensure that it didn't blow away, and when the C-130 once more took to the skies, we all knew that there was no way back from this remotest place on Earth, located some 1,800 miles from the nearest city. It was a *long* way from home. If one of us broke a leg, we'd just have to tough it out. If there was a medical emergency, it could be fatal. Being marooned like that gave me a spooky feeling, and this was only exacerbated when, after two more weather days, we took the one-hour Twin Otter flight to Base Camp, situated at 7,000 feet on the Branscomb Glacier.

Never was the analogy between life and mountaineering clearer to me. Since inactivity bores most humans, this often results in mischief and people trying to extricate themselves from tricky situations of their own making. Now here we were, a tiny group of adventurers, isolating ourselves at the bottom of the world in order to ascend to one of its highest points. Just as most of us negotiate the ups and downs of our everyday lives, we'd traverse the mountain many times to get to the top before making our descent and returning to civilization.

When I met the four people that Bill Allen had recruited and realized that they were fairly inexperienced climbers, I was happier than ever to be on a separate team, with Clark taking the lead. But then, while we were still at Base Camp, I found out for the first time that we'd all be climbing together and that I'd be on Bill's rope team. After all, never having been to Vinson Massif before, Bill and Clark needed to coordinate with each other. If, say, one of Clark's climbers sustained a bad injury, he'd want Bill to help him out. It made sense. But I was furious.

"That's not what you told me when I first decided to come on this trip," I protested. I felt that I had been duped, yet I also knew better than to make a big deal out of it. We were in the middle of nowhere and I had to be a team player, especially since Bill and Clark had done a fine job of fueling our fears about the dangers of Antarctica. If I or one of my good friends got hurt, it would be nice to have the assistance of two guides. And since the C-130 aircraft that had returned to Punta Arenas wouldn't retrieve us for another 16 days, doing the climb in five would only mean that we'd have longer to wait around. So I bit my tongue, and we spent the next day getting ready for the climb.

By now, I finally knew how to organize my backpack. It was much, much lighter than on previous expeditions. Then again, since Vinson is like a mini version of Denali, we didn't need to bring as much food to Base Camp, while the ever-present illumination from the sun also meant that there were no head torches. On day nine, it took us around four hours to move about five miles and just over 2,000 feet from Base Camp to Camp 1. And as we advanced at a brisk pace, I just couldn't get over the vast expanses of white.

This was isolation like I'd never experienced it before, a place that is stunning for reasons totally different from those of most other locales that are afforded that description: a magnificent, monochromatic land-scape of smooth snow, jagged ice, and lurking crevasses; of barren beauty and virtual nothingness. An alternative wilderness that is as far removed from all other habitats as another planet. If anyone ever says that he'll run to the end of the Earth for you, send him here.

There are no fixed ropes on Vinson Massif. There just aren't the resources. Since Denali is situated within a national park, the park service takes care of affixing ropes on that mountain. Antarctica, with no government and no ownership—just a treaty, currently signed by 45 countries, that supports scientific research and protection of the local ecozone while prohibiting mineral mining and military activity—offers no such amenities. Indeed, it's such a pristine environment that the urine and excrement in Patriot Hills's toilets is collected in containers and flown off the continent. (Perhaps it's dumped on Mount Elbrus—the contrast between there and Vinson is like going from the ridiculous to the sublime.) On the mountain itself, we could pee into holes dug in the ice, but our team's poop had to travel with us in a lidded plastic container that would leave with us at the end of the trip. We each took turns carrying it, and as time went on, it became pretty heavy.

Meanwhile, because I was wearing so many clothes to protect me against the elements, I couldn't just unzip and go for it when I desperately needed to pee. I'd have to unpeel my way through sev-eral layers and then reach all the way in to grab hold of my freeze-shriveled manhood. Why make false boasts? It wasn't easy, and there were times when I ended up peeing down my leg. Then there was the occasion when, halfway through taking a dump, the emerging turd instantly froze. I could feel this happening, and it was freaky. All I could do was reach back, snap it off, and finish the process. There was nothing on my hand. It was like grabbing an icicle.

If all of this sounds like way too much information, my point is that the main difficulty in Antarctica wasn't the climb; it was the unbe-lievably frigid weather, along with the usual privation, exhaustion, and Neanderthal living conditions. As it happens, our team moved swiftly, and when the 24-hour sun was fully exposed, long-sleeved shirts would suffice. With less air pressure high up, as well as the reflection off the super-white snow, the powerful rays had a fast impact. However, if a –20 degrees Fahrenheit wind began to blow, even at just five miles per hour, the temperature could plunge from warm to deathly cold within a couple of seconds. It was excruciating. At night, I would disappear inside my sleeping bag, using its pull string to ensure that there was only a small circular opening directly in front of my mouth to allow me to breathe.

Be that as it may, when we reached Camp 1, everyone was in a fairly jovial mood. Leebs was keeping a journal, and he read aloud from it most nights during dinner, describing what he'd learned when doing certain things for the first time: walking on crampons, pooping outdoors in the icy conditions. It was like a daily lesson, and we all enjoyed it. Not that Leebs himself was having an easy time. From the get-go he struggled with his crampons. Reluctant to trust them and scared of falling, he would toe-point his way up a steep hill instead of using the French Technique (planting all but the front two spikes of the uphill foot solidly in the ground, then crossing the lower foot over it and planting that one solidly, too). He would also bend his legs rather than employ the rest step (locking the downhill leg and relaxing in that position). Although he'd trained beforehand, he didn't really know what he was doing, and Bill would shout at him: "Leebs, stop toe pointing! Do the rest technique! Straighten your leg! Put all your spikes on the ground!"

Despite Leebs's troubles, we still managed to move at a decent clip, and when we arrived at Camp 1, we were way ahead of Clark's team. Following a rest day, on day eleven we did a cache to the 12,500-feet High Camp, a broad col (the low point of a ridge) that forms a pass between Vinson and Mount Shinn, the third-highest mountain in Antarctica after Mount Tyree. It was on this leg of the journey that I began to get frustrated. Bill's method was to climb for an hour and then rest for 15 minutes. Being freezing cold, I wanted to rest for only 5. I didn't want to remove my backpack, which was connected to my harness and roped up to my sled, in order to take out an extra jacket. After all, once we resumed climbing, I'd become warmer, and that would entail stopping and repeating the whole process. I wanted to speed things up.

Leebs, however, was slow. Just like my friend Richard on Denali, he'd take his time methodically removing things from his pack, eating food, drinking water, and generally making the most of every 15-minute rest period. "C'mon," I'd say, "let's move!" Which is what we eventually did, by way of the lower headwall that, steepening to 40 degrees over broken terrain, represents the most technically challenging part of the climb. Without fixed ropes it's pretty intense, and while we were descending after having dropped off our equipment and supplies at High Camp, we ran into Clark's team, which was still on its way up there.

Jeff Johnson was at the end of his rope, both literally and figuratively. A Harvard Business School graduate and a real estate entrepreneur, Jeff was a tall, tanned, blonde, middle-aged bodybuilder, an outgoing alpha male who stood head and shoulders above his much quieter son, Justin, an accounting major at the University of Illinois who looked like he weighed 130 pounds dripping wet.

"I'm so goddamn pissed, Bo," Jeff told me as all of us took a short break. "These frickin' women are so slow. They don't even know how to put on their crampons."

Cheryl and Nikki Bart were well out of earshot. A lawyer and director of numerous companies, Cheryl was the chairperson of the South Australian Film Corporation, the Adelaide Film Festival, and the Adelaide Film Festival Investment Fund. Her daughter, Nikki, was attending medical school. Nevertheless, despite describing themselves as "Oz Chicks with Altitude," they were provoking plenty of attitude from Jeff.

"I want to be on *your* rope team," he continued. "At least you guys are moving fast. I'm *freezing*."

I'd been in Jeff's situation. I was that guy on Denali. And although I thought Leebs was slowing us down, we were still moving pretty fast. The fact was, even though he probably shouldn't have gone to Vinson and I shouldn't have encouraged him to do so, Leebs did a heroic thing. He had never climbed a mountain before, let alone used crampons, he'd had only three months to prepare, and he was doing the best he could. Accordingly, our team still got back to Camp 1 about two hours ahead of Clark's. Had one of his climbers got hurt, Clark would have called Bill on the radio phone to ask for help, but that didn't happen. By the time we met up, we were just tired. A round trip of some 6,800 feet had made it a long day, and Jeff was visibly disgruntled.

Following another rest day, on day thirteen we moved to High Camp. Since the headwall climb was too steep to bring our sleds, we left them at Camp 1. That meant that Rich, Bill, and I put some of Leebs's stuff in our backpacks, since his own pack was bursting at the seams. Again, never having done this before, he was making the same mistakes that I'd made when I overloaded my pack on Aconcagua. No big deal. We continued our trek across the glacial desert, and, alone with my thoughts as one crampon step followed another, I thought about how, without the modern technology of a planet that's estimated to be 4.54 billion years old, I would never have been here, in a place that had its first encounter with humanity just over a decade before my birth.

We ascended to High Camp without much problem. By the time we arrived there, the weather had taken a turn for the worse, and Rich and Leebs were so cold that they couldn't help pitch a tent. Bill and I therefore dug into the snow and set up both tents amid the freezing, howling wind. It must have taken us about 40 minutes to take care of each one, and after Rich and Leebs had dived into the first tent and Bill and I took the second, Bill complimented me on my efforts.

"I appreciate your helping with both tents," he said, "and I also know you've been carrying the heaviest pack. You're doing fine, Bo."

That made me feel good. We all make mistakes, and I'd certainly made my fair share during the Denali trip, both as a climber and as a teammate. But at least I'd acknowledged this and learned something from the experience. Others were currently learning some very similar lessons. As I curled up inside my sleeping bag, Clark's team arrived, and I could hear that Jeff was still irritated by the slow pace of his fellow climbers. Justin didn't say a thing.

Thankfully, there was no kitchen tent—it was too cold to carry one with us. Indeed, to shield us from the wind, each of our tents was enveloped with a canvas shell that was secured to the ground with metal stakes driven deep into the ice. The vestibule between the tent and its shell was where we cooked our meals. And that was also where we boiled water every night for the water bottles that we wedged under our feet while wearing down jackets and snoozing inside our sleeping bags.

On day fourteen the weather was beautiful, and with a three-mile traverse and a 3,600-foot ascent between High Camp and the summit, I was ready first thing in the morning and raring to go. But since the others were still shattered, and some were also feeling sick because of the altitude, we decided to wait until the following day. By coincidence, this matched the schedule of Vern Tejas, the charismatic Alaskan mountaineering legend who, back in 1992—when he began guiding for Alpine Ascents International—became the then-youngest person to have conquered the Seven Summits.

Vern's predilection for extreme-weather climbs has led him to make not only the first solo ascent of Vinson, but also the first winter ascent of Aconcagua, and when his group and ours set off for Vinson's summit at around the same time, the weather was cold, windy, and a little cloudy. Vern's team moved at a slower pace, so Bill, Rich, Leebs, and I took the lead, with Vern's team following behind and Clark's team bringing up the rear amid an ongoing feud between the guys from Kansas City and the gals from Down Under. "Hurry up!" Jeff was shouting. "We'll all get hypothermia! You're gonna kill me!" The Aussies were unfazed, adopting an attitude of, "Don't hassle us; just wear warmer clothes."

As we kept moving, the conditions grew worse, with the clouds dipping so low that it was hard to see more than a hundred feet ahead, and eventually Bill slowed things down so that we were overtaken by Vern's team. I was pissed. "Shit, Vern passed us!" In retrospect, Bill did the smart thing. He was scaling Vinson for the first time, and with his vision obscured, he basically had no idea where we were going. Vern, on the other hand, had reached the summit of the mountain on numerous occasions. So while my still-untamed ego stirred up the usual dose of frustration, we held back until Clark and his battling teammates caught up with us. The Barts and the Johnsons continued to do their best impression of the Montagues and the Capulets, Clark kept telling them to behave, and after a brief powwow between him and Bill, we were once more on our way, following Vern Tejas. Without Vern, we would have had to turn back and forget about the summit, underscoring how, regardless of my desire to largely go it alone without guides, it still paid for me to be around experienced people.

Eventually, our two rope teams made it to the summit headwall, and Bill advised us to put on our down suits. The weather was growing increasingly cold and windy. However, despite my having the suit that I'd needlessly bought for the Denali climb, I didn't really want to put it on. Just moving at a good pace would be sufficient to keep me warm. Unfortunately, I was in a minority of one, and the stop to remove our crampons, our harnesses, and our backpacks ended up consuming well over an hour, not least because the Aussies had difficulty putting their crampons back on. Now colder than ever, I began to share Jeff's frustration, and this intensified when, partway up the headwall, Leebs's legs locked up on him and he virtually ground to a halt. We could see the summit ridge.

Digging in with his ice ax, Leebs was moving about six inches at a time, and finally Bill said, "Leebs, you need to turn around." Then he looked at me and added, "Bo, unclip yourself and go bag the summit." I loved hearing that. Sure, unclipping would heighten the danger, but this close to the top there didn't appear to be a whole lot happening in terms of crevasses. I unclipped, but before I headed off, I went up to Leebs and spoke directly into his ear amid the raging, howling wind: "Leebs, can you hear me?"

His face totally concealed behind a balaclava and goggles, Leebs looked like Darth Vader. His breathing was loud and labored. "Do you want to go back down?" I asked. He didn't acknowledge me. "Can you hear me?" I persisted. "Leebs, you can do it. If you can hear me, just take a step."

He took a step. "That's great," I said. "Take another step."

He took another step.

"That's it! Keep doing that!"

Leebs as The Mummy—legs rigid, arms outstretched, staggering forward incrementally as I patted him on the shoulder and tried to provide encouragement. Once he appeared to have settled into some kind of robotic rhythm, I went off and traversed the summit ridge, a long path with a lengthy, deadly drop on either side. Up ahead, I could see a group of people huddled together at the summit, and when I reached them, they asked me if I could take their photo. No problem. I removed my gloves, snapped them in a variety of different poses, and then, just as they said they had to go back down because a storm was on the way, Rich arrived alone at the summit. Evidently, Bill had told him to unclip as well.

"Dude, take my picture," he said, pulling out his camera.

"Man, my hands are frozen! I've just taken a whole *bunch* of photos."

Rich ignored me. I took his picture; he took my picture. Holding the Kellogg flag, I felt so proud, both of myself and of the great institution that I was attending. While learning how to deal with people, I was also learning how to struggle. And if that sounds like a negative aspiration, it isn't. Struggling is a part of life. We struggle every day to achieve, to survive, and to be happy, and learning how to deal with that is one of the main keys to any measure of success. Again, it's about deriving help from hardships, and taking risks to do so. It's what shapes us.

While I was posing with the Kellogg flag, who should appear but Leebs, short-roped to Bill. Now *that* was an accomplishment. Talk about gutsy. Sitting down on the summit, he could hardly move, yet he was still able to put on a "Majestic Steel" T-shirt—plugging his dad's company—and smile for the camera. Next came our co-climbers from Oz and Kansas City. Everyone had made it.

"Can I meet you down by the bags?" I asked Bill. "I'd like to go down the headwall by myself."

"Yeah, you and Rich go," he replied. "I'm going to short-rope Leebs."

Rich and I walked the summit ridge, and as we descended the headwall, my right leg slipped into a crevasse that was about 18 inches wide. I was in up to just above my knee. Had I tried to step over the crevasse with my other leg, I probably would have fallen in and broken a limb. Instead, I fell forward, managed to lift my right leg out of the hole, and started sliding down the headwall head-first on my left side. This was the kind of moment I had been trained to deal with during the Aconcagua expedition. Holding my ax with one hand near the end of the shaft and the other around its arched blade, I forced the pick into some ice just above my left shoulder, pressed that shoulder and my chest down on the shaft, and executed a *self-arrest*. This was the first time I'd ever done it for real, and I did it right, with my legs stiff and spread apart, and my crampons remaining above that same snow to ensure that a spike didn't catch on something and flip me over backward. I even managed to use the axe as a pivot to swing my body the right way around, with my head facing uphill.

I looked at Rich and he looked at me. "That was close," he said.

"Damn right, it was."

So much for assuming that there weren't any crevasses close to the top. Now we were both nervous and on our guard. Thankfully, there were only a few small cracks that we had to step over as we continued down the headwall, and we made it to the bottom unscathed. There, we retrieved our bags, waited for the others to arrive, and went all the way back to High Camp in cold and windy weather that was tough to get used to.

Arriving outside his and Rich's tent, Leebs just collapsed, and I went up to him, gave him a hug, and said, "Great job, man. I'm so proud of you." He started crying like a baby, sobbing loudly while shaking all over, and he must have held onto me for a full 10 minutes. If this climb was different from any of the others that I'd previously undertaken, then it was also unlike anything that Leebs had ever known. At that moment, I began to truly comprehend the power of the mountains, the power of the challenge. Although it is capable of stretching a friendship to its limits, mountaineering can bring the parties closer together, bonding them by way of a unique, frequently gratifying, sometimes traumatic shared experience. I absolutely know that several of my fellow climbers will be friends for life. Leebs is among them. The way he cried after summiting Vinson is normally reserved for funerals. However, that whole experience had changed his life for the better, and the outpouring of emotion was due not only to his being so relieved, but also to his being so thankful.

All of us were exhausted. The next morning, after packing our belongings, we headed toward Camp 1, and as we descended the lower headwall, we spotted a large crevasse where a guide had recently broken his leg. We'd heard about this before leaving Punta Arenas, and we could now see the snapped snow bridge that he'd fallen through. After my own slip the day before, this was just another reminder of the inherent dangers. Nevertheless, a little further on, before the headwall began to flatten out, I asked Bill if our rope team could glissade down by doing a controlled slide on our butts, lifting our feet off the ground while using our ice axes as rudders. If anyone should start to catch up with the person in front, he or she could always put on the brakes. And the same would happen if the lead person (me, in this case) should slide straight into a crevasse.

Glissading is a lot of fun—you feel like a little kid on the ultimate sledding hill. And after Bill assented to my request, we cruised down the slope to Camp 1 way before the other group. What would have been a 500-foot, 20-minute descent on foot had been accomplished on butt in just over a minute. Afterward, we packed the rest of our belongings and, with the slope flattening out, just trekked down to Base Camp. By now, we were way ahead of the other group, and I was taking photos of the stunning views from outside my tent when they finally showed up, tired and bedraggled.

Early the next morning, after we'd been at Base Camp for nine hours, a Twin Otter arrived to fly Vern Tejas and his climbers back to Patriot Hills, and Clark and I grabbed the two spare seats. My buddies, Leebs and Rich, were happy to remain behind and relax for another 24 hours, but their joy faded when bad weather meant that they weren't able to leave for five full days. Running out of food, they had to survive on rations while Clark and I were eating steaks and pizzas and generally living it up. And just as my bosses at J. P. Morgan had been informed about my being stranded on Aconcagua a year earlier, they were now told the same thing about Rich in Antarctica. His eight-day leave had expanded to about three weeks. Still, a photo of us posing with the company flag atop Vinson Massif accompanied an article about the expedition in the J. P. Morgan magazine.

For me, it had been yet another landmark trip. Having crossed the halfway line in terms of the Seven Summits, I felt good about myself and my growing proficiency as a mountaineer. Kilimanjaro had been a battle. Aconcagua and Denali had been as much about luck as about skill and effort. But on Vinson, while battling the elements and still battling myself—my ego and my impatience—I had a far better idea of what I was doing. It was like my second or third year in the major leagues, making some rookie mistakes, yet increasingly aware of how to play the game. A short time earlier, inexperienced and out of shape, it would have been a very different story. These round-trip excursions to the rooftops of the different continents were forcing me not only to grow, but to do so at an accelerated pace. And in so doing, they had become a priceless part of my journey.

EVEREST, FIRST ATTEMPT

To live is to risk dying, to hope is to risk despair, to try is to risk failure. But risks must be taken because the greatest hazard in life is to risk nothing. The person who risks nothing, does nothing, has nothing, is nothing. He may avoid suffering and sorrow, but he cannot learn, feel, change, grow, or live. Chained by his servitude he is a slave who has forfeited all freedom. Only a person who risks is free. The pessimist complains about the wind; the optimist expects it to change; and the realist adjusts the sails.

—William Arthur Ward

THE "DEATH ZONE"—that region comprising altitudes above 26,000 feet, where, for most people, acclimatization is impossible, body functions fail, and a lack of supplemental oxygen leads to eternal downtime. Add high winds and low temperatures and you pretty much have the atmospheric environment for the final 3,029-foot ascent to the summit of Mount Everest, the rooftop of the world, where extreme conditions ensure that the corpses of many of the more than two hundred climbers who have died there remain to this day.

In light of these stats, why go there? Well, although I didn't really start climbing seriously until I was in my early twenties, I'd dreamt of scaling Everest ever since my teens, when I'd read about the first successful ascent in 1953 by Edmund Hillary and Tenzing Norgay.[1] During a visit to Nepal in 2000, I'd vowed to follow in their footsteps. In the spring of 2005, that dream became a reality.

K2, the second-highest mountain on Earth, also located in the Himalayas, is widely considered to be the world's most dangerous and difficult climb—it has been summited by only about a tenth as many people as have made it to the top of Everest. However, in popular terms, Everest still represents the pinnacle of mountaineering achievement—the tallest, the most prestigious, the name that everybody knows. The deaths that are reported there every year make it a high-risk/high-reward venture, comparable to the fine line between success and failure that's familiar to entrepreneurs. Since I was now attending the Kellogg School of Management alongside the crème de la crème of M.B.A. students, involved in a dogfight over grades with a bunch of alpha males and alpha females, I felt primed to raise my game to a similar level by taking on the "Goddess of the Sky" and "Mother Goddess of the Universe," the translations of Everest's official Nepali name, Sagarmatha, and its Tibetan designation, Chomolungma.

Since I'd been able to save money and invest wisely while I was working at J. P. Morgan, I could afford to indulge my passion for climbing. Nevertheless, being thrifty by nature, I still sought out the

---

1. There is an ongoing debate as to whether, 29 years before the successful climb by Hillary and Norgay, a pair of English climbers were actually the first to reach the summit of Mount Everest. George Mallory participated in the first three British expeditions to the mountain, the last of which he did with Andrew Irvine in June 1924. The pair disappeared after having last been sighted a few hundred yards from the top on June 8. While Irvine's body is still missing, Mallory's was finally discovered near the summit in 1999, and there were telltale signs that he had suffered a fatal slip while the two men were roped together. Further clues suggest that they were returning from the summit when the accident occurred, yet these are countered by the possibility that they didn't have sufficient oxygen to reach the peak. When once asked why he wanted to climb Everest, Mallory is reputed to have replied, "Because it is there," yet there's now even a debate as to whether he himself uttered these "most famous four words in mountaineering."

best deals, opting for low-budget, mac-and-cheese, pitch-your-own-tent mountaineering instead of the filet-mignon-and-legion-of-Sherpas variety. But now, as I was contemplating Everest, I was a full-time student with no job. I knew that I could be asked to fork out as much as $65,000 by a high-end mountaineering outfit that would take care of everything, including my visa, accommodation, permits, and guides, and I just couldn't rationalize that kind of expense. While descending Denali, I'd met a stout British climber named Dr. Rob Casserley who had already climbed Everest, and he'd mentioned that he knew a man who charged a very reasonable price to run logistics for independent climbers there. The guy's name: Henry Todd. His company: Himalayan Guides.

A little Internet research would have alerted me to the fact that Henry was a Scotsman with a checkered past, one that had seen him serve time behind bars for theft, fraud, and dealing LSD; face accusations of supplying faulty oxygen kits to a number of Everest climbers; and get temporarily banned from Nepal by the local government after an altercation with a liaison officer. Of course, there are two sides to every story, but I never even bothered to check Henry out, so, in typical fashion, I was blissfully unaware that there might be any sort of cause for concern. I simply contacted him before leaving for Antarctica and found him to be very charming on the phone. After revealing that one of my Elbrus colleagues, Doc Birrer, also wanted to come along, I got Henry to agree on a fee that was much lower than the price charged by the high-dollar outfits. It was a solid deal, yet one that was largely made possible by the fact that we wouldn't be using a guide, who, in return for actually leading the climb and being there every step of the way, would normally account for around $30,000 of the total costs. No way would the Sherpas be filling that role.

Whereas the high-fee companies ensure that their clients can climb with virtually empty backpacks, we'd be carrying our own food, gear, stoves, gas containers, sleeping bags, sleeping mattes, and first-aid kits. The only things the Sherpas would transport would be the tents and our oxygen. And with Henry supplying those tents and that oxygen, along with the food and permits, I could simply show up in my climbing gear and ascend the mountain with others who'd chosen to make their way without a guide.

After I wrote to the Dean asking if I could complete my M.B.A. in five quarters instead of six, it took plenty of e-mail correspondence and several meetings with the Kellogg decision makers over the course of about three months for me to receive the necessary permission. It wasn't easy, but the effort paid off, and I was even supplied with a school flag to erect atop the Everest summit—should I ever make it. Everyone—me, my Kellogg classmates, my family, and my friends—knew that this next climb was like no other that I had undertaken. I might never come back. Which is why Mom and my sisters, Jenny and Emily, wanted to visit with me before my departure for Nepal.

It was March 2005, and I was super-busy: preparing for exams, taking an extra class to ensure that I'd graduate on time, and trying to line up a summer internship. Despite this schedule, I was still anxious to connect with my family before I left, and for their part, Mom, Jenny, and Emily were happy to drive the three hours from Kalamazoo to Chicago in order to have dinner with me and hang out for a couple of hours. My brother, Teddy, didn't think he could make it, and neither did my younger sister, Emily, who was pregnant and didn't want to stay out too late. To accommodate her, we met for a quick lunch. Meanwhile, Dad gave a quick call to wish me luck. I didn't hear from anyone else. The get-together with Mom, Jenny, and Emily was a bit like the Last Supper . . . at lunchtime. Mom and Jenny cried as we said our good-byes, asking, "Why are you doing this?" They didn't understand that, regardless of the outcome, the Everest climb just had to be done.

Never for a moment did I have second thoughts about going. Climbing was my passion, my lifeblood, and, as perverse as it may sound, I actually felt more secure when I was risking my life in an extreme environment than when I was comfortably ensconced in a routine existence. It was about breaking free and going beyond the norm. The mountain-related risk and potential accomplishment not only made me feel alive, but also gave me a greater sense of my own identity, and in that regard Everest was the ultimate challenge, the peak of competing with both nature and myself. If I didn't make the summit, I was sure as hell prepared to die trying.

First established as the world's highest mountain in the mid-nineteenth century and named after Colonel Sir George Everest, a British geographer and Surveyor-General of India from 1830 to 1843, the Goddess of the Sky offers two main climbing routes: the southeast ridge from Nepal, as used by Hillary and Norgay in 1953, and the northeast ridge from Tibet, which was out of bounds to visitors after that country was invaded by China in 1950. It is important to ascend before the mid-June onset of the summer monsoon season to have a better chance of reduced wind speeds high on the mountain, since the jet stream is pushed northward as the monsoon makes its way up the Indian subcontinent. Accordingly, I was scheduled to hook up with Henry Todd and the other climbers on April 2, and I arrived in the Nepali capital of Kathmandu four days ahead of time in order to get ready. This was my first mistake.

Although the people there are very friendly, Kathmandu has to be one of the filthiest places I've ever visited. Located in the country's southeast region, in the northwest part of the Kathmandu Valley, and home to government offices, embassies, the King's Palace, Buddhist temples, Hindu shrines, and about 700,000 people, the city is full of hotels that cater to a thriving tourist industry. Yet, it has little apparent interest in adhering to the common rules of sanitation. Since the streets are without proper drainage, when it rains they're flooded with a revolting concoction of human and animal excrement. Cows, mules, monkeys, and assorted other creatures are everywhere to be seen, as are their feces, and the result is rampant disease. The sight and stench were hard to ignore.

On the first day, I met Henry, a tall, rugged-looking 60-year-old with an athletic build and weathered features, and after preparing my climbing gear, I went out that night, socialized with other climbers, drank beer, met an attractive Asian woman, and didn't get back to our spartan "Tibetan Guest House" until about 4:00 in the morning. Ditto nights two and three, when I hit several bars with my new girl-friend. By then, Doc Birrer had arrived, and we were scheduled to leave for Kathmandu's Tribhuban International Airport at 5:00 A.M. on April 2 in order to fly to the eastern Nepal town of Lukla, where we'd start our trek to climb Everest. Sitting down to dinner the night before, I knew that I was seriously ill. Every time I inhaled, I could hear phlegm fluttering in my lungs—I had the flu. When Henry pounded on my room door at five in the morning, I had perspired through my sheets and, struggling to breathe, quite literally couldn't get out of bed to let him in.

Henry finally obtained a key to enter my room, and he immediately began screaming: "You're not even fucking *packed?* What the hell, man? You Americans think someone's gonna do the packing for you?" He just freaked out.

"I don't want to go," I informed him. "I want to fly tomorrow. I'm sick, I can't get out of bed."

"Bullshit!" Henry shot back. "You don't have a choice. I've got your ticket; it's all set up."

As sick as I had ever been aside from when I'd had my appendix removed at age 14, I struggled to stand up and put things in my back-pack. Henry couldn't have cared less. "You're taking too much stuff," he growled, pushing me aside and throwing whatever he regarded as excess into my duffel bag. He then handed the bag to one of his local staff members and ordered him to have it sent directly to Base Camp. It was scary—Henry was in my face. I'd experience more of this later in the trip. And I'd also learn that, even though he was dealing with logistics and wouldn't be climbing the mountain, his thing was to bark orders. This was his show.

Feeling as sick as a dog, I nevertheless boarded the plane and arrived safely at Lukla Airport (since renamed Tenzing-Hillary Airport)—no mean feat in view of the fact that it has zero landing aids; an abbreviated, 1,730-foot-long bitumen runway with a 20 percent incline and a 2,000-foot drop at one end to the valley below; and a history of rough landings and fatal accidents. Lukla itself is 9,000 feet above sea level. Everest's Base Camp is located at 17,600 feet. So, climbing steadily and also resting in order to help us acclimatize, it would basically take us 10 days to reach our first major target.

"Don't worry about moving fast to Base Camp or up on the mountain," Henry advised us. "You have to go fast on only one day, and that's summit day, which separates the weak from the strong. If you save everything for that day, you'll make it."

Of course, thanks to my relentless ego, this well-informed suggestion went straight in one ear and out the other. You'd think I was back on Kilimanjaro. Hadn't I learned *anything* about humility?

In addition to Henry, Doc Birrer, Dr. Rob Casserley (who was making a return trip to Everest), and me, there were seven other people in our group. One of these was Rob Milne, a 49-year-old American software engineer who made his home in Edinburgh, Scotland. Having already climbed Vinson Massif, Elbrus, Kilimanjaro, Denali, Aconcagua, Australasia's Kosciuszko, and Oceania's highest mountain, Carstensz Pyramid, Rob was going to use the Everest expedition to become the first mountaineer with an IM-PAC (intelligent messaging, planning, and collaboration) system, as developed at the University of Edinburgh's Artificial Intelligence Applications Institute. During his ascent, he'd be in contact with people at Base Camp who would monitor his progress. He'd also have a laptop computer and a satellite phone that would enable details of his status to be sent via the Internet to a support team in Edinburgh. Should Rob encounter any problems, the IM-PAC technology would be used to suggest alternative courses of action or even help organize a rescue attempt.

Wiry and gray-haired, Rob was both brilliant and very likable. Meanwhile, the other teammates included David Klein, a long-maned, bearded, Budapest-based hippie-cum-philosopher who was also one of Hungary's best climbers; Claire David, an athletic French barmaid who wanted to climb Lhotse, the world's fourth-highest mountain, which is connected to Everest via the South Col; Tim Calder, a Brit who'd been stationed in Nepal while in the military and who was now a trekking guide; Mark George, a short, strong financial adviser from Melbourne, Australia, who'd once been a gym instructor and who had shaved his head in preparation for the climb; Mark's Aussie friend, Dr. Simon Holland, a geeky guy who had also shaved his head; and Mike Davey, a tall English accountant who had already teamed up with Henry to climb Cho Oyu, the world's sixth-highest mountain, located just a few miles west of Everest on the border between Tibet and Nepal. Out of the entire group, Mike was the one who was most concerned about being up to the challenge.

After a sickly, uneventful night in Monjo, the second place we encountered on our trek to Base Camp was the last proper town we'd see before getting there: Namche Bazaar, a sloped locale that commences at 11,286 feet and is the main trading center of northeast Nepal's relatively safe Khumbu region—one of the few places in this war-torn country that hasn't really been threatened by Maoist insurgents. Accordingly, Namche Bazaar is a buzzing center of Sherpa[2] activity, filled not only with mountaineering hopes and dreams, but also with plenty of tourist-oriented shops, lodges, and even Internet cafés. Indeed, the luxurious Everest View Hotel affords the first distant glimpse of the mountain, whose southern half is contained within Sagarmatha National Park.

The park's visitor center is situated near the top end of Namche Bazaar, adjacent to the barracks of a Nepalese Army company whose primary purpose is to protect this place of stunning natural beauty. Rising sharply from an elevation of 9,335 feet at its southern entrance to the 29,029-foot summit of Mount Everest, Sagarmatha National Park actually boasts four different climatic zones and widely

---

2. Although the term "sherpa" is commonly applied to the local people who are employed as porters on mountain expeditions, the Sherpa ethnic group refers specifically to the descendants of Tibetan migrants who reside in the most mountainous region of Nepal. They speak their own Sherpa language and are valued not only as porters on Himalayan climbs, but also as expert guides who are superacclimatized to high altitudes and know all about the local terrain. As a result of his and Edmund Hillary's 1953 ascent of Everest, Tenzing Norgay was celebrated as the most famous of all Sherpa citizens.

varying terrain: a forested zone that is home to more than a hundred species of birds, as well as yaks, snow leopards, foxes, wolves, monkeys, deer, black bears, red pandas, and Himalayan ibex; the alpine scrub and upper alpine zones that contain dwarf trees and shrubs; and the Arctic zone that commences at around 18,700 feet and has no vegetation whatsoever.

We spent a couple of days acclimatizing at Namche Bazaar, and throughout that time I was sweating through my sleeping bag, suffering from diarrhea, and generally feeling so sick that I wore a surgical mask and quarantined myself from the rest of the group within our guest-lodge dining area. Barely able to get up, I'd eat some soup, drink some water, and go straight back to bed, having been told by all three docs (Birrer, Casserley, and Holland) that I couldn't take any medicine for the flu. I'd just have to suck it up. What's more, I also had to listen to plenty of good-natured banter among my teammates. With discussion topics such as which country has the best athletes, the Aussies were giving the Brits a hard time, and ditto the Brits toward the Americans—especially Henry Todd, who made no bones about his disdain for "you bloody Yanks." Not that anyone was spared his sharp comments.

Doc Birrer, whom some may kindly describe as being financially cautious, was wearing trekking boots that he'd had for the past 15 years. I have no idea how many times they'd been resoled, but at Namche Bazaar their bottoms blew out and his feet were sticking out the front. "Buy some new boots!" Henry told him. "You can get them here in Namche."

"No," the Doc replied. "I've found someone to fix them for two bucks."

That was all it took. "You cheap fucking Americans!" Henry yelled. "Why don't you part with some money?"

It was becoming clear that Henry always chose someone to target. Right now it was the Doc, but the Doc wasn't going to rise to the bait. Neither was I. Sure, he was my good friend and Henry was giving him a hard time, but I had bigger concerns. I somehow had to make it to

Base Camp. The next day, we passed by Tengboche (home to the Khumbu region's largest Sherpa monastery) en route to Pangboche, and once we were there, I decided to rest for another day and give myself a chance to recuperate. Being in no hurry to get to Base Camp, the Doc said that he'd remain behind with me. Henry wasn't happy.

"You need to keep going," he told me.

"No, I'm sick," I insisted. "I'm staying here."

That made Henry mad, but not so mad that he didn't ask me to loan him 10 bucks because he was a little low on cash. I lent him the money.

After a day's rest, the Doc and I continued our journey; one of the most beautiful treks anywhere in the world. Walking across suspended bridges high above the Dudh Kosi River and amid lush, colorful, picture-postcard-type scenery while herds of yaks transported people's expedition gear, we arrived in a small settlement named Orsho. After a night's stay, we then passed through Dingboche on our way to Lobuche, located 16,108 feet above sea level. There we caught up with Mike Davey, the British accountant who was intimidated by the Everest climb.

"I had to stay here because I have a major headache," he informed us. "Of course, Henry got all pissed off at me for not going to Base Camp, but I knew you guys would be arriving soon, and I'm glad you're here."

I was feeling a little better by the time I eventually did arrive at Base Camp on April 12, ahead of both Mike and the Doc. This is located on the two-and-a-half-mile Khumbu Glacier, in the Western Cwm (pronounced "coom"—*cwm* is Welsh for "valley") at the foot of the Khumbu Icefall. Henry chose to set up our tents as far as possible from the icefall entrance in order to help us avoid contracting illnesses from other climbers. Even though it necessitated a 30-minute trek to the entrance, this was a good idea because, while Everest climbers are justifiably concerned about accidents, avalanches, rock falls, crevasses, edemas, and extreme weather preventing them from reaching the summit, they often overlook other things that can hamper their success: blisters on their feet, ice on their extremities, dehydration, lack of sleep, and the common cold.

Aware that if one person got sick, everyone might get sick, Henry didn't want us to even mingle with the other groups. When I first saw him at Base Camp, he was angry because he had a sniffle and was convinced that I'd given it to him. That's why he wouldn't talk to me.

"Hey, Henry, how're you doing?"

Silence.

"Do you have that 10 bucks you owe me?"

More silence. I then went into the kitchen tent and was told by Rob Casserley that Henry was really pissed at me.

"What?"

"Yeah, well, for one thing, he's mad at you because you drove such a hard bargain when it came to the cost of this trip. Then you got him sick. And then he heard that, having been a Wall Street investment banker, you could actually have afforded to pay the full price."

Whether I could or couldn't was beside the point. Given what Rob Casserley had just told me, I was amazed that Henry had managed to contain himself when I'd asked for my 10 dollars. So much for dispelling his notion of "cheap fucking Americans."

Within 10 days we'd ascended a little under 9,000 feet. Up ahead was a daunting 11,429-foot climb by way of the Death Zone to the highest place on Earth. All of us would need plenty of time to acclimatize, and to that end we spent the next few weeks moving between Base Camp and various elevations. The camp itself was a rudimentary site with hundreds of tents, and although nighttimes there can be incredibly cold, the daytime sun, reflecting off the brilliantly white snow, occasionally turns conditions so unbearably hot that inexperienced climbers, walking slack-jawed while breathing really hard, suffer burns on their tongues and the roofs of their mouths.

Still, while most people lose weight (the higher the altitude, the more the body consumes itself in order to conserve energy), I amassed the pounds by eating as much as I could for breakfast, lunch, afternoon tea, and dinner. The fact is, I love food, and so does most of my family, following the credo, "We eat until we're sleepy and then sleep until we're hungry." Sure, those of us who'd booked our trip through Henry Todd's Himalayan Guides had to ingest local fare rather than the pricier western cuisine laid on by some of the high-end outfits, but that didn't bother me. Neither did the knowledge that some of the more pampered climbers were also provided with showers and electric generators.

My teammates and I simply made do with an extended rest after arriving at Base Camp, and on our fifth day there we familiarized ourselves with the Khumbu Icefall by doing a cache to the 19,900-foot Camp 1. This entailed donning our ice axes as well as the harnesses that, with the use of attached ascenders and carabiners, would enable us to clip ourselves to the mountain's fixed ropes. Everest is much more of a mental and physical challenge than a technical ascent, yet the labyrinthine icefall is undoubtedly one of the most dangerous sections of the South Col route. On average, the glacier moves about three to four feet every day, and this causes large crevasses to open without warning and, on occasion, blocks of ice the size of a six-story building to come tumbling down. The path through there is constantly changing. As I quickly discovered, and as evidenced by all of the fatalities that have taken place there, traversing the Khumbu Icefall is a treacherous business.

"I could die here." This occurred to me for the first time as I walked on ladders that had been placed horizontally across huge crevasses. I was clipped to ropes that, like the ladders, had been screwed into the massive ice blocks that make up the icefall. However, not only could an avalanche snap the ropes and crush the ladders, but I also didn't feel totally confident that, in the event that I fell, the ropes would come to my rescue. Only in theory would I be safe. The reality was that many crevasses represented a drop into eternity, and as I walked along those ladders, I could feel my heart beating out of my chest. I was really scared. Since I'm not the kind of person who scares easily, this actually made me feel truly alive and in the moment. It's what climbing is all about. Everything gets quiet, and I don't even feel the wind or the cold as I focus on the task at hand, placing one foot in front of the other while telling myself, "Don't fall, don't fall."

In some cases, two ladders had been placed end-to-end and tied together with rope in order to span an opening, and if the point where they were joined was sagging, there'd be plenty of sway. Talk about an unnerving sensation. Aware that a steady stream of pedestrian traffic probably caused movement, I'd test the ropes to ensure that they were strong and also check the anchors in the ice before traversing a crevasse. Not that this served as any sort of guarantee, especially when I had to wobble my way up and down a vertical stretch of five attached ladders near the top of the icefall.

Avalanches are a common occurrence there. About halfway through my first negotiation of the icefall, I heard a huge pop, followed by a sliding sound. Immediately ahead of me was a massive 40-foot-high wall of ice. "Oh, my God," I remember thinking, "that thing's going to crush me." Running for my life, I slid feet-first past the end of the wall and lay flat on the ground, my hands protecting my head (as if that would help), only to hear a huge rumble and a Sherpa laughing at me.

That particular avalanche was on a different part of the mountain, and although some debris reached the icefall, the wall didn't come down. I realized that fear is a constant element on Everest, different in its duration and power from that experienced on any of the other Seven Summits. Once again, I was scared out of my mind. We ended up making it to Camp 1, using jumars for the final part of the climb, and then returning to Base Camp, but I never felt safe in the Icefall. People die there every year (that's a fact), and who's to say when your number's up? It's a constant thought, and every step up and down the steep terrain is taken gingerly. About a half-hour into my second time there, I saw a dead body about 10 feet away from where I was standing, wrapped and on a sled. That must have been the guy I'd heard about the day before. He'd suffered a fatal slip, but his body wouldn't be removed until the weather cleared and a helicopter was able to fly into Base Camp, recover it, and transport it back to the United States.

Just seeing that corpse really drove home the message of how dangerous this mountain could be. So did the grisly sight of skeletal remains between Camp 4 and the summit. Climbing Everest was like moving through a battlefield, and before long I was observing the Sherpa custom of burning juniper branches for protection before heading up the Icefall, having already taken part in a Puja ceremony at the start of the expedition. Uniting people of all races and religious denominations, the Puja involves a Lama chanting sacred verses while everyone else prays to the Chomolungma gods for permission to climb, as well as safe passage when doing so. Again, it's about having respect for the mountain.

Back at Base Camp, Henry persisted in giving me the silent treatment until I tried to reach out to him.

"Hey, I hear you're pissed off with me because I brokered a hard deal," I commented. Since he had accepted that deal, I wasn't sure why I had to explain myself, yet I also knew that I was relying on his expertise to get me to the top of the mountain.

"I'm paying for this trip myself," I continued. "Even though I worked on Wall Street, I have business school expenses and other overheads, and I'm not drawing a salary for two years. Still, if you want me to pay you more money, I'll pay you more money."

"No, no, no, it's fine, it's fine," Henry replied. "Forget about it."

At least we were talking again. Now I could expend my energy on the climb rather than waste some worrying about Henry.

After a couple of rest days, the climbers moved to Camp 1, and then on April 21 the Doc and I ventured up the Western Cwm, a broad glacial valley that's transected by massive lateral crevasses. These necessitate yet more horizontal ladders, as well as crossing over to the base of the adjacent Nuptse mountain and a small passageway known as the Nuptse Corner, from which there are stunning views of the ultimate prize, the summit of Mount Everest.

The high altitude and lack of crosswinds on the Western Cwm made it excruciatingly hot. Had I climbed it naked, I still would have felt uncomfortable. (Never mind the discomfort that this would have caused for anyone who saw me.) Camp 2, located at the top of the Cwm and the base of the Lhotse Face—where Claire David was headed—stands at an elevation of 21,300 feet, and after reaching it, the Doc and I turned around and returned to Base Camp. We'd never sleep at Camp 1 again.

After four more rest days, we ascended all the way from Base Camp to Camp 2, and I made it there in just under four hours. Hauling butt in this way made me feel good about myself, but in a climbing group that was largely driven by ego, mine was veering off the rails and I was in danger of burning myself out. Now, if you're wondering why I still hadn't learned to pace myself, all I can say is that I've repeatedly asked myself this and other pertinent questions: How can one be the best, yet not have a sizable ego? What does being the best really mean? Why am I looking for external validation of my supposed worth—the fastest, the strongest—instead of learning the ultimate lesson of the mountain, which is my *internal* value? Why am I willing to die trying instead of live trying?

Racing everyone all the time, trying to prove how capable I was of climbing the mountain—it was ridiculous. My previous climbs had humbled me, and by the time of the Antarctic expedition I'd felt like I had figured things out. Yet, here I now was, on mountaineering's main stage, and without realizing it I was having to relearn some valuable old lessons. "The mountaineer returns to his hills because he remembers always that he has forgotten so much." (Geoffrey Winthrop Young)

After a rest day at Camp 2, the plan was to start ascending the Lhotse Face on fixed ropes, navigating a 45-degree wall of blue ice until we reached the 24,500-foot Camp 3, which is perched on a small ledge about halfway up the Face. We'd spend the night there, then go all the way back down to Base Camp, rest once more, and wait for weather clearance to summit by way of stops at Camp 2, Camp 3, and, for the first time, Camp 4, located on the South Col at 26,000 feet, just below the Death Zone. If we got there at four in the afternoon, we'd rest for four hours and have a couple of hours to prepare before embarking on the final 3,000-foot climb at 10:00

that night. Effectively, therefore, we'd depart from Camp 3 on the summit day, which would end with us going back down to Camp 4 after hopefully having reached the top. There would then be rest days on either side of a stop at Camp 2, and by the time we returned to Lukla, the whole trip should have taken around 40 days. That, as I've said, was the plan.

When we set off for Camp 3 on April 28, the ground was covered with four to five inches of fresh snow from the night before, and as we approached the Lhotse Face, we could see another group of climbers on their way down. Tim Calder, the trekking guide and ex-military man, was adamant. "I'm not going up there," he said.

"Why not?"

"Those people coming down right now are going to die. There's going to be a huge avalanche."

"Tim," I said, "I've never seen the Lhotse Face before and I don't know if it's going to slide, but I've skied on slopes as steep as that, and I don't think a few inches of snow is going to cause an avalanche. And if it does, how far can it slide?"

"I'm not going up," Tim reiterated.

"We need to get to Camp 3," I countered, impatient as ever. At that moment, the group coming down turned a corner and kick-started a tiny avalanche that was more like falling dust. Although this wouldn't endanger lives, it confirmed Tim's worst suspicions. "See?" he exclaimed. "If we were up there, we could have gotten killed."

I didn't agree, but why take an unnecessary risk? We all returned to Base Camp and spent four more days there before moving to Camp 2. Henry, who never left Base Camp, wanted us to depart at 6:00 A.M., but I figured that would place us on the Western Cwm just as the sun was hitting it. We'd bake there. Accordingly, Hungary's premier climber, David Klein, was setting out at 4:00 A.M., and since I was a little faster than he, I told Henry that I was going to leave at 4:30.

"You can't go alone," Henry remarked as all of us ate breakfast in the kitchen tent the day before departure, prompting the Doc to say, "I'll go with you, Bo. I don't like the heat either."

"Good," said Henry. "Make sure you tell Kame that you'll be leaving then, and he'll have the portage done for you." Kame was our *Sirdar* (the Nepalese lead guide in charge of the Sherpas), and he served as a conduit between them and Henry.

That day, I went for a walk and had lunch, and everything seemed to be fine. However, when I walked into the kitchen tent at dinnertime, Henry was there and the conversation stopped immediately. It resumed after I sat down and started to eat, but after Henry left, a couple of people told me that he was mad at me again because I wanted to leave at 4:30 in the morning to go through the Icefall, whereas most of the other group members would be leaving at 6:00. "But he was okay with this so long as I didn't go alone," I pointed out.

At 10:30 that night, I was asleep in my tent when a Sherpa woke me up: "Henry wants to speak with you."

Walking into the kitchen tent, I saw that it was filled with Kame, the three kitchen staff, and all of the Sherpas. Henry was there, too. "Sit down," he remarked casually, motioning me toward a seat that was directly next to him. Then, as soon as my butt hit the chair, he came straight to the point: "You listen here, you sonofabitch! I don't bloody like you! You've been trying to sabotage my expedition since day one, and if you fuck up one more time, I'm gonna throw you off the expedition!"

Jabbing a finger in my face while showering me with spit, Henry was furious. And when I pursed my lips to ask what I'd done wrong, he put a forefinger to his mouth and hissed, "Shhhh!" I felt like I was being roasted by the principal back in elementary school. "Get out of my sight!" Henry continued. "I don't want to talk to you!"

The silent treatment resumed. The next day, May 3, everyone other than Henry moved to Camp 2, and then on May 6 David Klein and I left early for another attempt to climb the Lhotse Face as far as Camp 3. However, when we were about halfway there, we again had to turn around because of snow flurries, high winds, and increasingly cloudy conditions. The others in our group, following an hour behind, gave up at the base of the Face. For the next four days we were stuck at Camp 2, and when the weather didn't clear, we went back down to Base Camp, where it was easier to breathe, but the air was thick with frustration and—thanks to an unexpected announcement by Henry—tension.

On the night of May 15, following four days at Base Camp and more than a week since any of us had moved in an upward direction, our logistics guy told us that we were being split into an "A Team" and a "B Team." After all, he was running things on such a tight budget that there were only a half-dozen Sherpas to transport gear for the 10 climbers. Team A would therefore be afforded the first crack at the summit; Team B would comprise the Doc, Mike Davey, Claire David, and me.

"I've consistently been the fastest climber," I protested.

"Yeah, but you and Richard Birrer are the only ones who haven't been above 8,000 meters before," Henry explained. "You have to go on the second team."

I was really pissed, especially since there was little way of knowing when there'd be a seven-day weather window that would enable Team A to reach the summit and return to Base Camp. So far, because of the lousy conditions, no other group on the mountain had been able to achieve this. Henry actually paid a hefty fee to subscribe to several daily weather forecasting services, but since it would take a minimum of five days to reach the summit and a five-day forecast isn't totally reliable, the whole enterprise was something of a gamble. Still, that's the name of the game. And it was certainly a large part of the reason for the May 11, 1996, Everest disaster, when eight people died during a single day of summiting attempts.[3]

On May 16, 2005, while Team A temporarily relocated from Base Camp to the more comfortable Sherpa village of Orsho, the rest of us took advantage of a break in the bad weather and headed for Camp 2.

---

3. A total of 15 people died on Everest in 1996, making it the most lethal year in the mountain's history. The May 11 disaster, described by firsthand witnesses in several books, resulted from a surplus of climbers, delays at the Balcony and the Hillary Step caused by Sherpas and guides failing to set fixed ropes, alleged misuse of bottled oxygen, and a full-scale blizzard. As with the Titanic, a convergence of mishaps and mistakes led to tragedy.

In this case, "us" included Henry, who for some reason decided to come out of retirement and actually move up the mountain. But about 20 steps from Base Camp, he fell through some ice that was covering a small pond and tore a calf muscle. That marked the end of his climb. With Drs. Casserley and Holland down in Orsho, it fell to Doc Birrer to remain behind and take care of him.

Claire, Mike, and I made it to Camp 2, and on May 18, while Mike was still resting, Claire and I left early to avoid the incredibly hot sun on the Lhotse Face and, en route to Camp 3, successfully traversed the glacial blue ice. Because of fresh snow, the fixed ropes on the Face itself were iced over and buried, and I therefore had to dislodge them and make sure the jumar teeth were unencumbered. Not that this slowed me down. Whereas Claire arrived at Camp 3 a couple of hours after I did and then spent the night there, I returned to Camp 2 after having idiotically raced from 21,300 feet to a new personal high of 24,500 feet in about two and a half hours. Even though I'd practiced pressure breathing every few seconds—forcefully exhaling as much air as possible through pursed lips in order to counter the effects of low atmospheric pressure reducing my lungs' intake capacity—I felt nauseous. Ego, ego, ego. It's lucky I didn't end up with a cerebral or pulmonary edema.

Claire joined me the next day, and on May 21, with the weather again taking a turn for the worse and no imminent sign of it improving, we reunited with Henry and everyone else back at Base Camp. Henry, who was constantly monitoring the five-day forecasts, told us on the 24th that companies such as Mountain Madness and International Mountain Guides were aiming for a May 29 summit day. "You watch," he said, pointing to the predicted high wind speeds. "On May 29, people are going to die."

Consequently, while a number of other teams at Base Camp were setting off for the summit, he sent our own A Team members further down the mountain to the village of Orsho, where they could rest, eat, and put on some weight before aiming for the top. In the early hours of May 27, Henry then recalled them and sent the rest of us down to Orsho, explaining that Team A would hopefully now head for the summit and reach it on May 31, with Team B following a couple of days later. The only climber who remained at Base Camp the entire time was the Doc. No way was he going to spend money to eat and sleep in the village.

With high winds forecast for June 1 and 2 and the monsoon season rapidly approaching, I was concerned that our team might never get the chance to summit. However, no sooner had we gone down the mountain than Henry radioed for us to return to Base Camp. More bad weather had delayed Team A's departure, and with time running out he wanted all 10 climbers to reassemble as a single group, share Sherpas, and leave as soon as possible. It was now May 29.

By the next day, we were hearing other climbers' radio messages: "Woo-hoo! We're on the summit, and it's beautiful!" Did that ever bug us. We should have left on the 24th. More people summited on May 31. Still, we were stranded at Base Camp. And when some who had summited began coming back down through the Khumbu Icefall, we were practically climbing the walls of our kitchen tent. Part of everyone's Everest permit fees helps pay three Sherpas to maintain the Icefall, yet now those Icefall doctors were saying that they were going to shut it down. The monsoon was nearly upon us, and the climbing season was over. When Henry heard this, he entered the tent just as we were finishing dinner and said, "You're heading for the summit tomorrow."

The Doc was so pumped up by this latest announcement that, after taking a couple of shots of whiskey, he went absolutely bananas and, without saying a word, stormed out of the tent. Emotions were running high. We'd been in or around Base Camp for precisely 50 days, and during the past week we had understood the meaning of stir-crazy. However, Henry knew that if we quickly ascended through the Icefall to Camp 2, the Icefall couldn't be closed until we came back down. So we set off on June 1 and, bypassing Camp 1, went straight to Camp 2. Then, following a rest day, we ascended to Camp 3.

The Doc arrived there ahead of me, but when I saw him emerge from his tent onto the steep slope wearing inner booties without crampons, I wondered what the hell he could be thinking. One slip might have been fatal. "Hey, Bo, do you need any help?" he called out. Here was a highly disciplined ex-military man and experienced climber displaying the effects of subsisting on 35 percent of the oxygen that's available at sea level because of the reduced atmospheric pressure. It was freaky. But then, a deficiency in the amount of oxygen reaching the brain can result in some pretty abnormal symptoms, ranging from slow reaction times and skewed logic to slurred speech, nonsensical comments, and full-scale hallucinations.

While the clients of high-end mountaineering outfits all have supplemental oxygen when they sleep at Camp 3, we had no such luxury. And although this didn't concern David Klein, who intended to summit Everest without relying on bottles of O_2, we were on the verge of entering that zone where, without them, most of us couldn't survive.

Only about 5 percent of the nearly 2,000 summits of Everest since 1953 have been accomplished without supplemental oxygen. In 1978, Reinhold Messner and Peter Habeler were the first to do so, disproving the scientific theory that if anyone were to even survive at the summit, he would basically be immobile. This was based on the fact that, while the resting heart rate increases with higher altitudes, the maximum heart rate decreases, and when the two become equal, the body is capable only of resting. In 1980, Messner summited without oxygen on his own, and since then a select few have followed in his footsteps. But these individuals, whether they are superacclimatized Sherpas or unbelievably resilient climbers, have to be regarded as the Michael Jordans and Wayne Gretskys of mountaineering: a select few who defy the odds, confound the experts, and achieve the seemingly impossible.

The vast majority of those who reach the top of Everest (or get within 3,000 feet of it) cannot survive on about a third of the oxygen that they're normally accustomed to. Without a supplementary O_2 supply, their bodies will often drown in their own fluids after those fluids seep into the brain and lungs, or else they'll succumb to other vital organs shutting down. That's why, after we left Camp 3, the bottles with which Henry supplied us were an absolute must. We'd managed without them before, yet I had certainly experienced some headaches. And Rob Milne, the American-born, Scottish-based software engineer whose progress was being monitored by an Edinburgh support team, had also contracted the *Khumbu cough*, or *high-altitude hack*, which is sometimes triggered by overexertion amid the low humidity and subzero temperatures of extreme elevations. Persistent and irritating, the cough can become so violent that the sufferer experiences torn chest muscles or even broken ribs. Fortunately, Rob wasn't at that stage yet.

Getting to Camp 4 involved a 1,500-foot ascent using fixed ropes to traverse a rugged expanse of interlayered metamorphic rocks known as the Yellow Band, and then scrambling across a snow-covered section of anvil-shaped black rock that a 1952 Swiss expedition had named the Geneva Spur. Thanks to my ongoing need to race everyone, including myself, I was the second member of our team to reach the South Col. Instead of seeing several tents already set up there, I saw just David Klein and a single Sherpa attempting to pitch a tent in high winds. The Sherpa that I was sharing with the Doc hadn't arrived yet, and I had no clue when either of them would show up. So, being in need of shelter, David, his Sherpa, and I set up another couple of tents.

Totally exhausted and gulping for air on the threshold of the Death Zone, we each crawled into our own sleeping quarters. Then, feeling thirsty and realizing that I had no water, I went back outside, cut up some huge chunks of ice, and proceeded to warm them on the stove that I'd been carrying. Just as they began to melt, Rob Casserley entered the tent, collapsed on the floor, and asked me to help him remove his crampons and boots, which I did before getting back to my boiling water. I was so thirsty. However, just as Rob settled inside his sleeping bag, Mark George, the Aussie financial adviser, fell into the tent, and I had to help him with *his* boots. My throat was bone dry and I was literally gasping, and when I did eventually pour myself a liter of water, I guzzled half of it so fast that I immediately puked it back up. Now I was more dehydrated than ever.

Upon arriving at the South Col and settling into our tents, we each removed our oxygen mask. There weren't enough bottles to keep us supplied around the clock, but every hour we'd reattach them for five minutes in order to feel a little better while using a pulse oximeter to measure our heart rate and blood oxygen saturation levels. My saturation level is usually 98 to 99 percent at sea level, but it had fluctuated between 84 and 88 percent at Base Camp and was 78 percent at Camp 4. This was better than some of my teammates, yet it still resulted in my breathing about three times faster than usual, making it really difficult to just sip water. When I did try to drink, I felt like I was drowning, and the same applied when I ate food. Gobbling it far too quickly, I vomited yet again, underscoring just how much my system was out of whack. Focusing on keeping the vital organs working in order to stay alive, my body no longer perceived digestion as a major priority. Instead, it was eating itself, and I could feel it wasting away.

Racing to the South Col, setting up the tents, chopping the ice, removing Rob's and Mark's boots, boiling the water, throwing up, eating some food, throwing that up, too—I was physically wrecked. However, it was 9:00 P.M. and we'd soon be heading for the summit. This was what I'd dreamed about for so long, especially during the past few weeks of hard slogging and sometimes mind-numbing boredom. I just had to dredge up whatever resources I had left for the final assault, as did everyone else. Thirsty, hungry, underweight, suffering from muscle wasting, and deprived of sleep for the past few nights because a pounding heart makes dozing difficult at high altitudes, many of us spent nearly two hours dressing, putting on our boots and crampons, and loading our backpacks. One part of me didn't want to climb or even go back down—I just wanted to stay where I was and have a good snooze. And then there was the other part that couldn't wait to venture out into the dark, cold, windy night wearing a face mask and head torch while relying on two bottles of oxygen. Inevitably, that's the part that won.

Communication in such adverse conditions can be really hard, and with talk time on radio phones being kept to a minimum in order to preserve batteries and the wind making it difficult to hear when people *do* talk, it's not surprising that some climbers get lost. Mental and emotional toughness are all-important, especially since some individuals get incredibly lonely. This has never been an issue for me, even if my mental approach has needed improving. The truth is, when I'm on the side of a mountain, I just relish the tranquility, the struggle, and the joy of climbing, as well as the opportunity to be away from everyday noises and concerns while focusing on the summit and getting down safely. I mean, here I was, attempting to scale the highest mountain on Earth, and although I'd already achieved a personal best in terms of elevation, that wasn't enough. Some people may be happy completing three-quarters of a marathon; I'd come here to secure the ultimate prize, and accepting anything less would amount to selling my goals short.

Rob Milne left Camp 4 before I did, but after about 45 minutes I caught up with him. Although it's often impossible to recognize people at night when they're wearing goggles and face masks, I could tell it was him because of his down suit.

"Hey, Rob, how are you doing?" I asked.

"I'm doing good," he replied. "Just slow and steady."

"Good job," I remarked, slapping his butt with the flat end of my ice ax as I overtook him. "We're climbing Everest, man."

Since my Sherpa, Tindu, was behind me and the Doc was behind him, I was climbing by myself, unsure of where I was going, but just following the fixed rope. At one point I needed to scurry up a small section on all fours, and about halfway up my head torch died. It was pitch black, there was low cloud cover, and when I tried to keep climbing, I couldn't find the holes in the rocks where I could insert my crampons. I therefore went back down the rope and waited, and after about 20 minutes—during which I discovered that my torch was broken, since neither my spare bulb nor my spare battery worked—I saw a light coming toward me. It was Tindu. The Doc followed close behind.

At this point, it was decided that Tindu would take the lead, I'd follow his light, and the Doc would follow me. At least I could now navigate in the dark. However, as we moved a little higher, the wind really started to pick up and the quintessential Everest plodding began. "I've got to force myself to take another step . . . Now, one more . . ." Step, step, step. In between the eternity of one step and another amid the icy blasts, chatter was coming from Tindu's radio, all in Nepalese, punctuated by bursts of wind and snow. Finally, Tindu stopped on a small rock outcrop. I stopped on one just below and the Doc climbed to one slightly above me. We all had our hoods pulled over our faces to protect us from the frigid air. From my vantage point I couldn't hear the Sherpas yelling at one another, but I knew that something serious had occurred. Just seeing Tindu's body language, silhouetted in the dark, told me that he was agitated and starting to panic.

"Bo, do you know what just happened?" the Doc screamed down to me through the howling wind.

"What?" I screamed back.

"Do you know what just happened?"

"No, I have no idea."

"Rob Milne just died!"

Now I, too, was filled with panic. "But I saw him a little over an hour ago!"

"Well, the Sherpas are saying he's dead."

I couldn't believe it. Fifteen minutes of waiting and patchy radio communication followed while we huddled on the side of the mountain. The Sherpas spoke little English, and our Nepalese vocabulary was limited to simple phrases about speed, weather, and avoiding obstacles. Needing to contact Henry for instructions, they commenced a complex procedure of high-altitude "radio talk" that resulted in Kame waking him up and relaying information from 9,000 feet above. All the while, conflicting accounts of the situation filled the frozen nighttime air, ranging from Rob's just requiring oxygen or being gravely ill to his actually having died. The only thing we knew for sure at this point was that he was surrounded by highly experienced Sherpas and was with Mike Davey. And so, taking Tindu's advice, we waited for more information before making a move.

More than an hour passed. I felt the kind of shock and disbelief that I'd previously experienced when hearing about terrorist events and natural disasters. Sorrow, fear, head shaking, heart racing—*panic*. When I'd passed him, Rob had seemed fine, and he certainly didn't appear to be in any kind of trouble. Doc and Tindu had also passed him, followed shortly thereafter by Mark George and Drs. Simon Holland and Rob Casserley, and none of them had seen anything wrong, either. Cloud cover kept obstructing our view of what was going on further down the mountain. We were just below the Balcony, the small platform at 27,600 feet that serves as a sort of halfway point between Camp 4 and the summit, and so we waited there for more information. Soon, others decided to join us, and eventually the entire group was together, except for Mike Davey. He was still with Rob Milne.

All the while, the wind was blowing so hard that, even at close quarters, we still had to scream in order to hear one another speak. And with concealed faces it was impossible to determine anyone's expression. "What actually happened to Rob?" we were yelling. "Did he just collapse? Has anyone given him CPR?" Back at Base Camp, we'd all discussed what should happen if any of us were to die suddenly. Each of us had agreed that we'd want the others to continue with the expedition. True, we were independent climbers who were just using Henry for logistics, but we were now also a team, and Rob would undoubtedly want us to carry on. He had said so. The problem was, it was June 5, the end of the season, and we were running low on O₂ amid increasingly lousy weather. No one else was doing the climb. No one else was that crazy.

Despite our pact to keep moving onward and upward, the present reality and uncertainty now made me question that agreement. I'd once read a quote by author and screenwriter Mark Spragg in his book *Where Rivers Change Direction:* "I lose my belief that anything changes gradually. I realize that there is only the flash of accident and the level time afterward where we are allowed to gather our strength for the next." Over the course of my summiting ventures, I had acquired experience gradually, and as a result, I had become a better mountaineer. But in truth, nothing about me had changed. Now, in an instant, my world reeled and I changed forever. That's not to say that I gained some sort of mystical mountain enlightenment. I just took the first true step toward connecting with a higher form of myself.

Of course, my "flash of accident" was fleeting. When it was finally confirmed that Rob had died, we felt powerless, and the Sherpas were spooked. Despite the fact that we'd participated in a Puja, we had evidently angered the mountain gods, and the Sherpas didn't want to hang around. While we remained below the Balcony, some of them began turning around, and we were now left to figure out whether we should keep going or return to the South Col and not summit until the following day. At this point we were still waiting for advice regarding our oxygen, and since radio communication with people who spoke only Nepali didn't help in this regard, we spent a couple of hours trying to decide what to do. It was the common mountaineer's conundrum: observing a pact to continue the climb versus the ultimate value of a human life. This was complicated by the fact that the Sherpas who'd gone back down were carrying the extra bottles of oxygen for the team. Regardless of the elevation, right now it was as if we were underwater and they'd taken our tanks.

While we were strategizing I was having trouble breathing through my mask. I felt like my energy had been zapped, and when I took off my backpack and looked at my oxygen tank, I could see that it was empty. I grabbed hold of the second tank and tried to hook it up, only to discover that the connecting nozzle had somehow snapped off and the tank couldn't be used. Terrific. Never before had I been at this altitude, and now I had no oxygen. At sea level, I might survive weeks without food and days without water, but things would end for me far more quickly without supplemental O_2 at this altitude. When an aircraft loses cabin pressure, the "Time of Useful Consciousness" at 28,000 feet is between two-and-a-half and three minutes. Having acclimatized up to 26,000 feet, I'd last longer than that, but no doubt about it—I was in big trouble.

Right then, everybody started to climb toward the Balcony. What could I do? Go back down by myself? Then and there, I decided to climb with them. It was absolute torture. Panting like a dog between every painful step as the cold air scorched my lungs, I struggled to move just a few inches. Falling asleep would have been so much easier. So would slipping into a coma. But I knew that I didn't want to die. I was in pure survival mode, and although I was in no way the Michael Jordan of mountaineering—hell, I wasn't even his trainer— I somehow managed to stagger and drag myself another couple of hundred feet until we were just shy of the Balcony.

I had actually survived about two hours without supplemental oxygen, but I couldn't last much longer. Stacking up all that had happened to me, I reached a major decision: This was not my time to summit. I was heading back down. Then, while I sat on the ground and planned my next move, a Sherpa appeared out of nowhere with four spare bottles of oxygen in his backpack. It was like a miracle. Or a hypoxia-induced hallucination. Within minutes I was once more hooked up to oxygen, and almost immediately I felt better. Nevertheless, my mind was made up. "I'm going back down," I told the Sherpa and the Doc.

By now the sun was up, and within about 10 minutes of my heading down our entire team was doing the same. Not only did none of us have enough oxygen to summit and spend a couple of days descending to Base Camp, but just after I'd turned around, Henry had also radioed to say that a storm was approaching and everyone should abort the climb immediately. Had we continued, it might well have proved fatal. This was brought into sharp focus when we eventually reached Rob Milne's body. The doctors on our team hypothesized that he'd suffered a heart attack or stroke or died from exposure.

Mike Davey had headed down to Camp 4, the Sherpas were gone, and Rob was all by himself, his body already frozen, with one arm across his mid-section, the other outstretched in the frigid air, and his eyes still open. Simon Holland tried to close Rob's eyelids but they wouldn't budge, and neither would his outstretched arm. It was a gruesome, tragic sight, and when several of us struggled to shift his body off the trail and place it face down to lessen the effect, it felt like a solid lump of ice. Standing around him, we all observed a moment's silence. Then we prayed for a higher power to take care of Rob, a former chief scientist at the Pentagon's Artificial Intelligence Center; a successful entrepreneur who had co-founded Intelligent Applications, a company specializing in expert systems technology; an accomplished mountaineer; and a wonderful guy whose departure from this world was hopefully devoid of the trauma that it left behind.

Taking his watch, photos of his kids, and other paraphernalia that would be returned to his family, we continued heading down toward the South Col. "This could have been me," I thought. "It could have been any of us." Surviving for two hours without oxygen, I had known that I was close to the edge. Now, breathing through my mask and planning to bypass Camps 4 and 3 before navigating down the rest of the Lhotse Face to Camp 2, I was physically and emotionally beyond the barrier of exhaustion. All I wanted was to return to Camp 2—a nonstop descent of about 6,000 feet.

As it happened, locating Camp 2 wasn't easy. The last time I'd seen it, there had been loads of tents. Now there were just a few. We were the only climbers left on the mountain, and when the other team members arrived in the dark, many of them went straight past and ended up all over the Western Cwm. Either delirious because of the altitude or just plain disoriented, they kept radioing to say they were lost. The Sherpas had to go out and rescue them before they wandered into a crevasse.

Claire David, meanwhile, had been guided in the wrong direction up Lhotse and never even got a shot at that summit. She and I helped to carry some of the Doc's gear when we departed from Camp 2 on

June 6, and we couldn't help noticing that he never clipped in when we descended through the Khumbu Icefall. The altitude was still affecting him. At the very edge of the Icefall, where the fixed ropes stop, he stood about two inches from a lump of ice and stared at it, his head tilted like a dog that doesn't understand what's going on. "Doc, what are you doing?" I asked.

"I swear this is an ancient Aztec symbol," came the confusing reply.

"Doc, let the symbols go," I told him. "Let's continue down."

That is what we did. And by the time everybody helped to pack all the equipment and we were ready to leave Base Camp, it was June 9. It was unbelievably late to be ending an Everest expedition, and in order to get away as quickly as possible, we paid $800 per person for a helicopter flight from Lobuche to Kathmandu that would save us a three-day trek.

Unfortunately, on the flight from Kathmandu back to Chicago I suffered food poisoning—*again*—and I was in such a bad state that a wheelchair had to be used to get me off the plane and take me through customs. You can only imagine the expressions on the faces of my mom and my sister Jenny when they greeted me at the airport. Since they'd last seen me, I had lost 20 pounds, suffered muscle atrophy, and turned into a disheveled wreck. Taken straight to the hospital, I was pumped with antibiotics and four liters of water before I went home and slept for 24 hours straight. Afterward, I was so strung out that it took me half an hour to write a five-line e-mail. Dyslexia? Forget it. While my brain may have swelled at high altitude, it was presently shrinking, yet I could still figure out that I'd now have to return to Nepal for a second attempt at Everest.

If there was one thing that the expedition finally taught me, it was to rein in my rampant ego. Where had all the rushing got me? Part way to the hospital rather than anywhere near the summit. And what was the point? I wasn't impressing anybody, and I didn't need to prove myself. My primary concern in such a hazardous undertaking should always be safety, for without it there can be no achievement, not even another shot. We can climb tomorrow.

In order for you to change, something inside you has to die. For two long months, I had been inexorably connected to Mount Everest, looking up at it every day and picturing myself on the summit, only for that vision to be superseded by a stark recognition of everyone's mortality. Conquering it, I now realized, wouldn't be a sprint or a marathon, but an out-and-out endurance test involving all facets of mountaineering: the physical, the mental, the emotional, and the spiritual. I would be pushed—and would have to push myself—to the outer limits of my ability and understanding. However, in so doing, I might also be reborn through truly bonding with the natural wonder that was also my potential killer.

ELBRUS, SECOND ATTEMPT...
PLUS EXPLOITS

One's destination is never a place but rather a new way of looking at things.

—Henry Miller

OKAY, SO I'D be going back to Everest. However, on either side of my first time there I also made return visits to a couple of other mountains on my Seven Summits list; one of them already conquered, the other still waiting to be crossed off.

The former was Kilimanjaro, which I had climbed as an overweight investment banker in January 2003, at the very start of this odyssey. In February 2005, still requiring a scientific research project to gain me membership in the Explorers Club, I participated in a "flag expedition" (a one-of-a-kind trip) to Africa's highest peak, organized by the

Club's President, Richard Wiese, and sponsored by a California-based biotechnology company named Diversa (now the Verenium Corporation) that specialized in prospecting for extremophiles— organisms that thrive in extreme environments—whose physiology might help to develop or improve any number of applications.

In other words, whatever it is that enables these microbes to survive in conditions that are detrimental to most other life forms could lead to, say, a medical cure or the enhancement of a commercial product. And it was hoped that on top of Kilimanjaro, within the 1.5-mile-wide crater of the Kibo volcano, our Explorers Club team of members and wannabe members—including Keech Combe (recovered from her Chilean heli-skiing accident), Jonathan "Leebs" Leebow (who had partnered Richard Wiese and me in the La Ruta Maya boat race and also climbed Vinson Massif), and Dan Bennett (who'd later succeed Richard as the club's President)—would make just such a find.

In off-trail areas on the way up the mountain, we were taught how to take soil samples and GPS (satellite-based global positioning system) readings, while also compiling photographic evidence and documenting the depth and temperature of the soil from which the samples were taken. Although the Kibo volcano is dormant, it still emits gases, and when I measured the ground temperature at various points inside the rim of the crater, using a needle that is submerged about six inches below the surface, it ranged from 180 to 220 degrees Fahrenheit. If I stood around too long, my boots would start melting. Nevertheless, within a thin layer of air between the hot soil and the cold air just above, we discovered 29 new species that were thriving in the rarefied atmosphere of a 19,340-foot elevation that's bathed in ultraviolet sunlight. This sunlight kills bacteria and other microorganisms, and it was determined that whatever protects these little guys could also aid commercial endeavors, preventing car paint and house paint from fading as a result of the effects of similar light. (Not, of course, that anyone would drive a car on top of a dormant volcano at above 19,000 feet.)

The trip itself was pretty straightforward—a 12-day trek that had been designed for explorers who were mainly in their fifties and sixties. Although I was excited about carrying out scientific research and keen to use the climb as a means of training for Everest, I'd planned to take only a week off from Kellogg, and so by using car transportation and then hiking by myself, I met up with everyone else at the 12,700-foot Barranco Camp. I was younger than they and in far better shape than I'd been when climbing here a couple of years earlier, and I still wanted to move at a fast pace in preparation for my next trip to Nepal. So after jogging to the next camp, I then took a full load of four tents in my backpack and hauled ass with the porters the rest of the way up.

Near the very top of the crater, where it was cold but sunny, a porter and I set up the kitchen tent and smaller tents for sleeping, before walking around to the other side and taking about 20 soil samples. Then we returned to our makeshift camp. No one else had arrived yet. Lying down outside, I fell asleep in my hiking pants and puff jacket, and by the time I woke up a couple of hours later my body temperature had plummeted. Darkness was starting to fall, the other team members were now arriving, and when I climbed into my sleeping bag, I was really shaking. Then I puked. What the hell was happening? Richard was called to my tent, and as soon as he took a look at me and put a hand on my back, he said, "You've got hypothermia. You're ice cold."

It would have made a great headline: "Man Survives Everest and Then Freezes to Death in Africa." And if you're thinking, "Doesn't this guy ever learn?" all I can say is, "Slowly and obstinately."

In the kitchen tent some people were boiling water, and by inhaling the steam I was immediately able to start warming myself up from the inside. At the same time, a couple of hot water bottles were placed on my chest and my back, and after half an hour of trembling and chattering, I felt better, if a bit foolish. The next day, I was able to complete the 45-minute ascent to the Kili summit, which, thanks to Vodacom, used to be the highest place in the world with cell-phone service. (That honor now goes to Everest, courtesy of the coverage provided by China Mobile.)

Our bioprospecting expedition was an *Outdoors Magazine* cover story, and shortly after the trip I became a member of the Explorers Club. Missions accomplished. Following the failed Everest climb, however, I was feeling kind of down about still having conquered only four of the Seven Summits, so that June I e-mailed Christine Boskoff, whom I'd met on Vinson Massif, and asked her to help me take care of some unfinished business: making it to the top of Russia's Mount Elbrus. The only American woman to have successfully ascended six 8,000-meter peaks, as well as the first to have reached the summit of Lhotse, Christine ran the climbing company Mountain Madness. Although she guided climbs of Elbrus, after everything I had learned there on my previous visit and all of my past mistakes, I was more confident that I could do this on my own, and this time I also intended to ski back down. All I wanted her to do was take care of the logistics: my accommodations, ground transportation, and, most importantly, visa, permits, environmental fees, and ski-lift passes. I had no intention of dealing with the kind of baloney I'd encountered during my previous visit.

The trip was scheduled for the last week of July. Before that, and immediately after returning from Nepal, I had a summer internship in Beijing, China, handling mergers and acquisitions for a company named Bridge Laboratories that (like my dad's firm, which I hoped to work for eventually) carries out scientific research for the pharmaceutical/biotech industry. The internship was scheduled to start June 1, so it had to be delayed by about 10 days because of the extended Everest sojourn. Yet, once I was there, I had an extremely productive time, working in cities such as Taipei, Shanghai, Guangzhou, Shenzhen, and Hong Kong in order to value different companies, while memorizing a vocabulary of about two hundred Mandarin words that helped me get around. It was exciting. And it was also an incredibly rewarding experience that taught me a lot about business on the international stage.

A day after returning to Kalamazoo from Beijing to collect my skis, I was on a plane headed for Moscow, followed by another one that delivered me to good old Mineralnye Vody Airport in Stavropol Krai. There I saw the burly, bloody-knuckled guard with whom I'd tangoed the last time around, but he didn't recognize me in my Panama hat and dark glasses. (If I was going to be a suspect, I might as well look the part.) It was July 28, and thanks to Christine Boskoff everything ran smoothly all the way to the mountain. In Terskol, the small town at the foot of Elbrus, I met the team of rookie climbers that she was guiding, and they were all really nice people: Susan Houby, Steve Cameron, Tony Optican, Billy Blann, and Guiherme Bertani.

After a night in a hotel, all of us relocated to the Garabashi "Barrels" at 12,500 feet, near the upper station of the ski-lift system. This meant no sleeping in tents next to the 14,000-foot Diesel Hut, just a visit, when nature inconveniently came calling, to that poop-plastered Priut 11 hole-in-the-floor latrine. From the Barrels, I climbed on my own for about three hours to the 15,840-feet Pastukhov Rocks and then skied back down. The next couple of days I rested, and then at about two in the morning on August 1 we all paid for a Sno-Cat—a huge, tracked snowmobile—to transport us up to the Rocks, from which we departed at 3:00 A.M. for the 18,510-foot summit.

Heading east toward the 17,800-foot saddle that's situated between the mountain's two breastlike peaks, I climbed much faster than Christine and the rest of her team, wearing lightweight alpine touring skis that had synthetic skins attached at the base. The surface grip of these skins, together with open rear bindings that enable climbing with heels raised, facilitates the ascent of steep slopes, and I skinned to the saddle in time to see the sun rise at around 6:00 A.M. Because of sheer ice, I had to switch from skis to crampons for the remaining steep ascent to the 18,510-foot west summit, yet by 7:30 that morning I had achieved my goal. Standing atop Europe's high point, enjoying the warmth of the sun, I savored the moment and thought, "This puts me at five." There were now only a few mountains—and just over 52,000 vertical feet—to go.

Everest had been a hard expedition—mentally, physically, emotionally, spiritually, and even intellectually—and Elbrus helped to relight the fire in me. I had learned how to climb this mountain. The previous attempt had been partly killed by a half-assed plan, whereas this time, properly trained and having paid someone to handle the logistics, I'd been able to focus on the task at hand and capitalize on better weather by not only climbing in great time but even using my skis. As I stared out from the summit toward the horizon, I felt more than ever like I actually knew what I was doing. Nevertheless, my satisfaction was soon tempered by thoughts of the journey back down the mountain.

As I'd discovered on the way up, the stretch between the top and the saddle was pure ice. As happy as I was, I knew that I had my work cut out for me skiing all the way from the summit to the Barrels. Not only was the vertical descent far longer than that of a regular ski run, but it started at a much higher altitude, and when I got going, I could immediately feel the effects. My legs were burning, and although the edges of my skis were sharp, the sheer ice meant that I couldn't stop. It was basically a controlled slide, and it was frightening, especially when I had to steer around some rocks near the saddle.

While sitting at the saddle and eating a Snickers bar, I began gagging because of the active volcano gases that are prevalent there. The smell of sulfur served as a flashback to my recent Kilimanjaro trip. The Elbrus guidebooks advise visitors to avoid hanging around at the saddle for too long, yet while I was getting ready to leave, I saw Christine arriving with the other climbers as they made their way toward the summit. It was now around 8:30 in the morning and they were in pretty good spirits, so I gave Christine a hug and she immediately threw up. Maybe that's the effect I have on women, but I swear it was due to the volcanic gases. (They must reach all the way to Kalamazoo.)

"It's real gassy here," she remarked. I didn't need to fake innocence. She was referring to the mountain. And when some of the other climbers started gagging, we decided that it was time to go. They headed up; I got ready to head down. Having already seen crevasses not very far from the main trail, I knew that I'd have to hug that trail to avoid a potential disaster. Fortunately, an experienced Russian climber with whom I began talking told me that he was skiing down and that I could follow him. That was a stroke of luck. The 5,300 feet from the saddle to the Barrels was one hell of a descent, but I hung in there and made it back safely.

This wasn't graceful stuff, it was about battling gravity at every turn, yet it kick-started my passion for high-altitude skiing, and after reaching the bottom I set my sights on Cho Oyu, about 12 miles west of Everest. Although it is the world's sixth-highest mountain, I'd read that the moderate slopes of the northwest ridge make it one of the easiest 8,000-meter climbs and a top contender for skiing back down. That was definitely something to look forward to. In the meantime, after a couple of rest days, I flew out of Moscow on August 4 and, continuing with the theme of winning the rematch, landed in Geneva, Switzerland, enjoyed a four-hour train ride to Zermatt, and once more took on the Matterhorn. As in Russia, this time there were no problems with the weather, and as with Elbrus, the mountain was transformed from victor to vanquished.

That put two defeats behind me and served as yet another much-needed tonic after my Everest experience. It felt good to start a winning streak, and now that I was on a roll and had a few more days to spare, I decided, on a whim, to hitch a ride to Chamonix in France so that I could test myself on another of the world's most famous mountains: Mont Blanc, the highest point in the Alps, boasting a 15,781-foot peak that, because of its location on the border between Italy and France, is placed within their respective boundaries on their respective maps. Suffice it to say that the "White Lady," as she is known in France, is close to both Chamonix and the Italian town of Courmayeur, and conquering her requires stamina, endurance, and a knowledge of high-altitude mountaineering. Being in pretty good shape after all the climbing I'd been doing, I felt that I had the necessary qualifications.

Starting the climb at 5:30 in the afternoon after riding a tram partway up the mountain, I followed the popular Voie des Cristalliers route, which took me through the Gôuter Corridor, notorious for its frequent rockfalls, and then on to the Gôuter cabin, where most people spend the night. Although this is supposed to be a two-day climb, I just kept going in the pitch dark all the way to the Vallot cabin, where I rested for an hour before continuing to the summit. Arriving there at around 10:00 in the morning, I posed for the obligatory photo and then started back down after just a couple of minutes. From the top, I could clearly see a snowstorm approaching, and I ended up jogging through clouds in crampons amid total whiteout conditions. This was the antithesis of my well-planned return to Elbrus, and I suffered the consequences in terms of both the lousy weather and the excruciating 22-hour trip (with only an hour's break) up and down the mountain. But I made it.

Aside from a day back in Kalamazoo following the Everest trip and another to collect my skis before leaving for Elbrus, I hadn't been home in several months. I've since asked myself if, in maintaining such a frantic pace, I was running away from anything, substituting adventure for feeling connected. Certainly, all the travel was placing distance between me and my roots, as well as from those who could in no way relate to what I'd been experiencing. If somebody asked, "How was Everest?" how could I answer that? "Oh, it was *amazing.*" That might be the standard response, but it would hardly convey what I'd seen or how I felt. Still, I really don't think I was traveling to escape anyone or anything. I was just having a great, *great* time. It was my time in the wilderness—climbing mountains and exploring the world while taking the opportunity to read, learn about myself, and reflect on whom and what I wanted to be. It was magical. And if I live to be a hundred and hopefully have other equally incredible years, I'll still look back on 2005 in this way.

Not that it was over by any means. After completing my mini-tour of three European mountains, I returned to Michigan in mid-August and spent a couple of weeks relaxing and preparing for a quarter on my M.B.A. course that would take place far away from Northwestern's Evanston, Illinois, campus. Back in February, while still applying for time off from Kellogg in order to participate in the Everest expedition, I had taken advantage of the opportunity to spend a quarter studying abroad by arranging to do this in Bangkok, where Sasin—a joint venture between Kellogg, the University of Pennsylvania's Wharton Business School, and Thailand's renowned Chulalongkorn University—provides English-language MBA programs.

Since my dad was thinking of expanding his company, MPI Research, into southeast Asia, and I wanted to assist him in that venture, it made perfect sense for me to go there, get to know the culture, and network with others in my field. The course began in early September, and I had a great time, studying alongside kids from some of Thailand's wealthiest and most powerful dynasties while sampling the Bangkok nightlife, enhancing my knowledge of international business, and familiarizing myself with a culture in which the lack of punctuality makes *me* look like a stickler for time, while anger is perceived as a sign of weakness. It was a fascinating experience. And it ended by segueing straight into my next mountaineering challenge: the *eighth* summit on my Seven Summits list.

The list postulated by mountaineer Richard Bass in the 1980s includes Australia's Mount Kosciuszko as the highest peak of the Australian continent. However, Reinhold Messner—he of the first solo ascent of Everest without supplemental oxygen—came up with his own list, which replaces Kosciuszko with Indonesia's far taller and technically more difficult Carstensz Pyramid, which is the tallest peak in Oceania and Australasia, both of which incorporate Australia, New Zealand, and the Pacific island of New Guinea, where Carstensz is situated. I'd known about this since I had first set my sights on the Seven Summits, but it had been a moot point after the Indonesian government stopped issuing permits to climb the mountain because of security problems relating to an adjacent gold and copper mine.

That was in 2002. One night in July 2005, while playing cards with Christine Boskoff at the Garabashi Barrels during our climb of

Elbrus, I learned that Carstensz had been reopened to climbers. According to Christine, Mountain Madness was trying to arrange an expedition there. I immediately told her, "Hey, listen, I'll be in the Far East for school. My Christmas break is the whole month of December. If you can do a trip then, count me in!"

She did.

What an unbelievable calendar year this had turned out to be— Vinson Massif, Everest, Kilimanjaro, Beijing, Elbrus, the Matterhorn, Mont Blanc, Bangkok, and then, just when I thought I'd seen it all, I was off to one of the most far-flung places on the planet to undertake one of its most difficult climbs. It's just a pity that I didn't realize this was only partly due to the mountain itself.

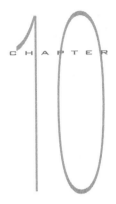

CARSTENSZ PYRAMID

The climber is not in love with the idea of getting himself killed . . . .
He is in love with the idea of embracing life and living it to its fullest.
It is for this reason that we as climbers embrace the mountains and climb
in the first place. For on the other side of fear . . . is freedom.

—Italian climber Walter Bonatti

IT WAS FOLLOWING my stint as an exchange student in Bangkok that, eager to capitalize on the recent reopening of Carstensz Pyramid, I flew to the "Wild East" Indonesian province of Papua on December 1, 2005, and found myself in the rudimentary, dilapidated facilities of Timika Airport. While I was habitually guilty of not researching the places I'd be visiting, I actually had read that back in November 1961, Michael Rockefeller, the youngest son of billionaire New York governor and future U.S. Vice President Nelson Rockefeller, had disappeared during an expedition in the Asmat region of southwestern New Guinea. His body had never been found, and there was plenty of suspicion that he'd been killed and eaten by cannibals. Now here I was, waiting for my luggage, being eyeballed by a forty-something guy wearing baggy pants, a thread-bare T-shirt, and a dogs-teeth necklace, and wondering whether he thought I might make a tasty snack.

Initially we got into a staring contest. The bags still hadn't arrived, so peering into his eyes helped me pass the time. The expression on his face remained stone cold and heartless, but since there were other people all around, I wasn't overly concerned. After a couple of min-utes I looked away, and pretty soon I forgot all about him. Still, when I looked in his direction a good half-hour later while waiting for that goddamn luggage to find its way onto the conveyor belt, the guy was still staring at me. He hadn't moved one inch. Now I was spooked.

Being sized up like a slab of beef by a man who probably moon-lights in nothing but a penis gourd wasn't my idea of fun. He was like a lion sizing up its prey, ready to pounce. You can wave your hands and whistle all you want, but that lion's got an agenda. It's operating on pure instinct and nothing's going to stop it. This guy was the same. If I'd thrown a baseball at his forehead, he probably wouldn't have budged. People had certainly stared at me before, and I'd also got into my fair share of fistfights, but I'd never, ever had anyone fix me with a lockdown laser stare like this. It was scary and bizarre, and for the first time in my life I slouched around with a sickly expression, doing my best to look . . . well, let's just say unappetizing. Still, in no way was this about to overshadow my preoccupation with Carstensz, the 16,023-foot colossus, also known as Puncak Jaya ("Peak of Glory"), that not only is Oceania's highest mountain, the highest point between the Andes and the Himalayas, and the world's highest island summit, but is also located in one of its remotest places.

Part of Dutch New Guinea before Indonesia declared its inde-pendence in 1945, Papua is the largest province of the world's fourth most populated country (and most populated Muslim-majority nation). Between 1969 and 1973, it was variously known as West Irian and Irian Barat, before being renamed Irian Jaya ("Glorious Irian") by the administration of military leader Suharto, who ruled Indonesia for three decades after being elected president in 1968.

Puncak Jaya, meanwhile, was given the Pyramid name still favored by mountaineers in honor of the Dutch explorer Jan Carstensz, who first sighted its glaciers in 1623 and was then ridiculed for asserting that he'd seen snow near the equator. The mountain is situated within terrain that is still a big unknown to most people, including geologists and anthropologists. One reason for Everest and Kilimanjaro being more famous is that they're considerably easier to reach. Just making it as far as the Base Camp on Carstensz by way of mud tracks and dense jungle on the world's second-largest island, New Guinea, is a feat in itself.

Power struggles, political corruption, and widespread unrest have characterized much of Indonesia's history. And had I broken with convention by doing my homework, I would have known that a visit to Papua meant diving head-first into a ton of sociopolitical nonsense involving big business, shady government officials, terrorist groups, cannibalistic tribesmen wearing nothing but penis gourds, and double-dealing military personnel with a long record of human rights violations. These Indonesian soldiers are seemingly in everyone's face and on everyone's payroll. They're fighting guerrillas who are either seeking independence for this former Dutch colony, attempting to seize control of local resources, or trying to establish Muslim fundamentalism in a mainly Christian region of the world's largest Islamic country. The troops are also protecting the interests of the world's biggest gold and third-biggest copper reserve, the 1.25-million-acre Freeport-McMoRan mine that stretches from the small coastal town of Timika to the base of Carstensz Pyramid.

Boasting an 18,000-plus workforce and output that provided Indonesia with $33 billion in direct and indirect benefits between 1992 and 2004 (nearly 2 percent of the country's gross domestic product), Freeport holds plenty of sway over the government, which in turn has a 20 percent stake in the mine. However, since it's part-owned by a

Louisiana-based financier and has dumped several billion tons of waste all over the adjacent mountains, as well as into the rivers that feed the island's low-lying wetlands, Freeport isn't nearly as popular with environmentalists or the local residents, whose 1996 riot prompted the mine's owners to hire soldiers to keep trespassers off their property. This makes things highly inconvenient for climbers.

The mine, you see, owns a long gravel road that runs from Timika to the pit and goes up, over, and even through the mountain. Although it is by far the easiest and most direct way of reaching Carstensz Pyramid, it's now off limits to the possibly troublesome general public, and the more circuitous alternatives are less than savory. These include a five-day jungle trek that requires hard-to-obtain permits from the police, the military, and assorted others who might or might not help you navigate the various war zones. In this part of the world, bribes are a way of life, as are the inherent risks, which is why in 2002, amid travel warnings by the U.S. government, all means of accessing the Pyramid were shut down.

It was only thanks to the efforts of a local jack-of-all-trades whom I'll refer to as "Frankie" that the mountain was reopened to climbers in July 2005. Assigned to guide me there by Mountain Madness, the Seattle-based climbing outfit that I'd used to book the trip, Frankie was a swarthy, rotund little guy, usually dressed in a grubby T-shirt and jeans, and it was he who initially devised a novel method of avoiding the mine altogether by bribing officials to get special climbing permits and chartering equally crucial helicopter flights to and from the Zebra Wall. This 12,800-foot, black-and-white stretch of rock, located just beyond the Freeport-owned land, can present altitude problems for those who aren't properly acclimatized. But at least it helps circumvent the often far more serious difficulties of traversing the mine.

Frankie played a major part in facilitating an expedition that, time and again, had me asking what I'd gotten myself into. During the Everest, Elbrus, Aconcagua, Denali, and Vinson Massif trips, there hadn't been a day when I didn't think, "What the hell am I doing? I hate this. It's so stupid." Low self-esteem was often part of the equation, and despite all the hard, hard work, I'd still keep telling myself to quit. Then I'd finish the climb and move on to the next one. Yet, in the case of Carstensz Pyramid, I was unnerved from the moment I arrived in Timika and was ogled by the guy at the airport. It didn't take long for me to figure out that worse was to come.

To start with, there were armed security guards checking people into and out of the hotel where I and the other climbers were staying. This, believe it or not, was a Sheraton, located in a jungle village where the buildings were mainly shacks and mud huts; it was funded by the Freeport mine and used to house visiting engineers after they touched down on a runway that the mine also helped pay for. The guards were constantly combing the hotel grounds for looters and kidnappers, and it quickly became clear that neither I nor the other guests would want to walk down one of the surrounding dirt roads by ourselves. If we did that, there'd be a good chance of our being whisked off into the forest by a bunch of tribal warriors with spears at our throats.

After we'd been stuck at the hotel for five days while waiting for rain and freezing sleet to clear, an unfavorable weather forecast inspired Frankie to finally announce that, instead of hanging around any longer and taking a chopper past the Zebra Wall to the Base Camp, we'd simply have to bribe our way across the mine. Frankie would take care of the bribes, since we'd already taken care of Frankie.

Each of us had paid Mountain Madness about $15,000 for the trip, and Frankie was handed a sizable chunk of that, as attested to by the two-story home that he owned in the city of Manado, along with several four-wheel-drive cars. Having guided people up and down the mountain before it had been closed, he'd forged plenty of invaluable relationships with soft-palmed members of the military and the police, as well as government officials in Timika and the Indonesian capital of Jakarta. Now he was cashing in those chips.

This became clear on the second day of our hotel hiatus when members of another mountaineering group, who'd booked with

International Mountain Guides, informed us that they were using an American guide to take them up the mountain, and that he was $5,000 cheaper than Frankie. Word of this soon found its way back to our man, and he quickly arranged a meeting in the lobby.

"I guarantee you those guys are not going up the mountain," Frankie told us in good English. "They don't have the connections I have. They're not going to make it. But please do not say a thing, because if you do, they're going to ask me to help them, and that will take my energy away from you. Just believe me—they will not climb that mountain."

Whenever we met people from the other team at lunch or dinner, they'd tell us, "We're setting off tomorrow." Then, after another 24 hours of rain and sleet, they'd say, "We're definitely leaving tomorrow." They were really optimistic. Their guide would take care of them, and they hadn't used Frankie because he was too expensive. They were basically rubbing this in our faces. However, on the fifth night, while they were still cooling their heels, Frankie came to each of our rooms at around 10 o'clock and said, "Be very quiet. We are leaving at midnight. You must be packed and ready. Don't say a word. I'm going to tell everyone on our team. We will meet at the back entrance of the hotel, where a van will be waiting, and you must get into that van as quietly as possible."

After five days of wondering whether we would ever see the Pyramid, it was go time, and we all felt good about it because at that point Frankie hadn't told us of his little change in plans. As far as we were concerned, the van would take us to the helicopter, and we'd then fly to the Base Camp. Sure enough, at around midnight, we all met outside the rear entrance of the hotel and were driven to a military outpost located just a short distance from the mine. It was there that Frankie threw us a major curve.

"Look," he announced, "the weather could stay like this for another month. No one is flying, and that other group back at the hotel is not going anywhere. We're going to have to sneak through the mine."

Before anyone had a chance to react, he tossed us some military fatigues—camouflage hats, shirts, and pants—told us to put them on, and then instructed us to climb into the back of a truck that would hopefully evade the attention of eagle-eyed soldiers as well as Freeport's security guards.

Now I was nervous. "Holy shit," I recall thinking. "What is this guy getting us into?"

Within seconds, and without any say in the matter, I'd been transformed from a wannabe Sir Edmund Hillary into a budding Che Guevara. Still, there was no turning back. Where could I go? And besides, my anticipation of the climb, now augmented by the intrigue of negotiating forbidden territory under the cover of darkness, actually fueled an adrenaline rush that underscored my love for adventure: Why have a dull moment? Along for the ride were Christine Boskoff, owner of the now appropriately named Mountain Madness; "Wayne" (name changed), a 60-year-old former junkie from Kentucky who'd apparently found himself late in life; a levelheaded ex-naval officer named Chuck Raup; and the irrepressibly high-spirited Max Chaya, one of Lebanon's foremost climbers. The notion that, along with Frankie, the militia, and the tribesmen, this cross-section-of-society cast of characters could have been straight out of a disaster movie wasn't lost on me—the only ones missing were the young newlyweds, the precocious kid, and the scruffy dog.

Wayne was the first to say that he felt uneasy about traversing the mine, and Chuck had reservations as well. "Are you sure this is going to be safe?" Christine kept asking Frankie. As our vigilant leader, Chris was constantly mindful of our well-being, whereas I, already in go mode, was mainly preoccupied with what to expect once we were in the truck. "Are we going to face any problems?"

"We have to go through five military checkpoints," Frankie told us. "What will they be like?"

Frankie was noncommittal. We'd basically have to wait and see. Max, who was also concerned about what we were letting ourselves in for, listened intently, while the others were now mumbling under their breath. Tension filled the air, but there was little time for hesitation, and Frankie had been canny in this regard when he sprung everything on us at the last minute.

"We will head for the mine in 15 minutes," he said. "Go through your bags and get rid of everything you don't really need. We must lighten the load or else the truck could overheat and we'll have to spend the night in the jungle."

It's doubtful that any group of travelers has lightened its load more quickly than we did. For me, this initially included getting rid of my water bottles, before thoughts of a sweltering truck made me reconsider. While taking one last leak, I retrieved the three bottles, filled them out of a dirty tap, and threw in a few tablets to clean the water. This meant that while everyone else was going through their own bottles pretty quickly, I'd have one for my personal use and the others to share with the team members. This turned out to be a wise move.

Before we knew it, the back of the truck was opened and we were shoved in, faces down, arms outstretched, wedged in alongside the climbing gear and assorted ammunition, and then covered by several huge military blankets for a six-hour drive through the Wild East that would see us ascend from sea level to 11,850 feet. It must have been 110 degrees Fahrenheit.

The only person who was visible in the back of the vehicle was a gruff, no-nonsense military captain who was on Frankie's payroll. Everyone, it seemed, could be bought, and this cold, unfriendly guy, a chain smoker with a dark, chiseled face, would cover for us should the truck be searched at any of the checkpoints where squads of soldiers, armed with machine guns, kept the area clear of trespassers. We passed through the first two without incident,while our hired captain whispered sharply for us to "stay down, no sound." Then there was a honk of the horn from our driver, a brief exchange of words, and we were on our way. However, when we rolled up beneath the floodlights of the third checkpoint, the truck's rear gate was thrust open and I could immediately sense the nervous tension. Our vehicle was probably surrounded, with rifles pointing at its windows, while the beams from several flashlights penetrated our blanket.

"Oh, Christ," I thought. "We're busted." Could the soldiers hear my heartbeat? In this kind of situation it didn't matter how we matched up. They were armed and we were in no position to bargain. I silently cursed Wayne when I heard our eldest climber's sharp intake of breath, but it went unnoticed. And I cursed myself every time I heard myself swallow. We were now in the heart of the mine, and there was plenty of shouting as our hired captain was, presumably, being grilled about the purpose of his trip. Short, sharp, increasingly aggressive exchanges of dialogue were punctuated by even more scary moments of silence when I wondered what the hell might be going on. Had a guard spotted something? Was one of them about to look under the blankets? It was an eerie, terrifying feeling.

The interrogation went on for several minutes. If, as I presumed, the guards weren't buying whatever our captain was telling them, then why weren't they searching the back of the truck? Were they just bartering over the price of not doing so? All of us inside that truck were, to say the least, sweating bullets. But then the doors suddenly closed, our captain hopped back into the vehicle, and we moved beyond the range of the floodlights toward the next checkpoint, ascending a road so cripplingly steep that drivers need a special license to navigate it.

No one was surprised when the engine overheated. We each donated a water bottle and the truck recovered, but the next to overheat at high altitude was Wayne, who began hyperventilating and gasping for air while attempting to turn onto his back. His panic attack concerned everyone. Fortunately, I hadn't donated my second water bottle, so I gave him my reserve and, once hydrated, he calmed down.

"I miss home," he murmured. At that point, I think we all did. Without warning, we were informed that, instead of continuing to drive through the tunnels, we were to switch to a Swiss-made cable car that would transport us more speedily from about 8,000 to 10,500 feet. Our captain didn't speak much English, but as the truck backed up toward the car, he had the following lines down pat: "When this door opens in the next few seconds, on my command you dive out of here, chest-down with all your gear, and slam yourself against the foot of the wall of the gondola. The surveillance camera won't detect you down there."

As he finished talking, the truck hit the side of the cable car. This, apparently, was standard procedure when food and supplies were being delivered to the mine. "Jump!" the captain shouted. Terrified, we did as we were told, with Frankie and me taking care of Wayne's backpack to make things easier for our elder partner. The whole process was so quick it was amazing, and once the cable car was on its way, the captain told us that we could get up and take a look at the sight below. What we saw was incredible: one of the most massive mines imaginable, so heavily lit that it looked like midday at 4:30 in the morning, with tons of oversized equipment that contributed to the process of making huge, seemingly bottomless holes in the earth. Even the tires on the specially made two-story dump trucks must have been about 20 feet tall.

As the cable car neared the end of its journey, the captain told us to once again move out of camera range, forcing us to virtually lie on top of one another against the wall and close to the door. Then, as soon as that door opened, he ordered us to jump back into the truck the same way we got out, diving chest-down to avoid detection. It was a different truck, but we were covered in the same old blankets, and soon we were back on the road while the captain yelled at our driver and shouted into his walkie-talkie. Apparently, the sun was coming up and there was no way we could make it to the end of the mine without risking being spotted by mineworkers. We'd have to stop and finish our trip after dark.

Tired and hungry, all of us were ready to take a break despite our eagerness to get the subterfuge over and done with. What we weren't prepared for was the standard of food and accommodation that had been laid on for us. No Sheraton this time around. Instead, we were dropped off at an army barracks where I and the four other climbers huddled on three twin mattresses inside a cramped, filthy room covered with graffiti and black holes the size of tennis balls. And it was there, within minutes of our requesting a snack, since our main supplies were still en route, that room service delivered a plateful of deep-fried bat, followed by the specialty of the house—a hefty serving of sautéed rat.

Now before you cry, "Gross!" consider whom you're dealing with. Sure, Wayne and Chuck both balked and dug into their power bars, but for the rest of us do-or-die adventurers it was a case of "when in Rome . . ." We just had to try the local delicacies and live like the natives while pushing the envelope and facing adversity like we'd never done before. Then again, I also have to admit that, as I pulled the flesh from my feast (still covered with patches of fur) and considered the fact that human flesh is said to taste much like pig, even I began wondering whether the cannibals were on to something.

Free to speak for the first time since our departure from the hotel, some members of our party began to openly question why they'd traveled to a region known to the rest of the world as a hotbed of police brutality, killing, torture, hostage taking, and ethnic cleansing. They questioned, but we all knew. Less than 200 people had successfully climbed Carstensz Pyramid, and the goal of climbing the Seven Summits had been branded into my head. Having crossed the Rubicon, I wasn't about to let some armed guards and fried rodents put me off my game plan. On the contrary, the excitement filled me with optimism. The hard part was being forced to wait in this dump for the next 18 or so hours.

Eventually I dozed off, only to be awakened by some creature crawling across my left cheek. As I swiped it with the side of my hand, I could hear its scaly flesh rip in two. Startled, I opened my eyes and saw its tail fall to the floor, enabling the head and front legs to scurry even faster across my face. Indiana Jones, eat your heart out. It suddenly dawned on me that the tennis-ball-sized holes in the wall were not holes at all. Get me out of here!

Having smuggled us in, our hired captain had to wait for the right time to smuggle us out, and the 24-hour surveillance of the entire mine meant that this wasn't going to be easy. Take, for example, the huge 60-mile pipes that are used to funnel the excavated raw minerals directly to the ocean, where freighters transport the goods to Japan for processing. If you knock one of those pipes with your hand, you can expect a helicopter to be circling overhead within minutes, and to have a gun at your head shortly thereafter. There's no messing around, and the captain knew it. After the sun went down, he kept delaying the time of departure, until at about one in the morning he finally told us to dive back into the truck for the hourlong drive to the Zebra Wall and the start of our three-hour hike to Base Camp.

After our arrival at Base Camp, we waited several hours for the six soldiers who'd been commissioned to act as porters and carry our excess gear. When they still didn't show, a couple of us volunteered to retrace our path. As it turned out, they had succumbed to overloading and exhaustion, and we discovered that each of them had collapsed at a different point. Without the energy to even pitch a tent, they'd burrowed beneath the canvas to protect themselves from the elements while awaiting our arrival. So it was that we retrieved our food and other necessities, and then returned to Base Camp. For three days there was no respite from the rain, sleet, and snow. Again, we were forced to wait it out.

Our intention was to do a round trip between Base Camp and the summit in one day. Finally the weather cleared, and it was after we'd hastily geared up that I found myself staring at a 2,000-foot-high granite wall, reflecting on what I'd already endured to make it this far and contemplating the seven-hour ascent, which would follow a route up the north face that had been pioneered in 1962 by Heinrich Harrer, the Austrian mountaineer and author of *Seven Years in Tibet* (later made into a feature film starring Brad Pitt). Far from feeling exhausted, I now experienced an adrenaline rush that revitalized my muscles and filled my head with a steely determination.

Everest, as I had already discovered, requires more mental and physical strength. You can climb it with one ice ax and not even use the ax that much. And while the Hillary Step is basically a 40-foot, near-vertical snow, ice, or rock climb, depending on the season, I'd been told that you really can just hike or scramble your way to the top. You're on a rope, you're clipped in, and that expedition is obviously a big deal—for me, the biggest deal until I'd manage to complete it. Both Carstensz and K2 are more technical climbs; they're more vertical, and you're using all four limbs. It's about scaling a wall instead of climbing a snow slope.

Some parts of the rock wall had safety ropes that had been affixed by previous climbers, and our group was able to use those. Elsewhere, we used the ropes that we'd brought with us, and in still other places we free-climbed without ropes but with our hands and feet. The problem was, given the ongoing cycle of freezing and thawing that was taking place as a result of the weather conditions, the rocks themselves were constantly expanding and contracting, so who knew whether it was safe to cling to the ropes that were already wrapped around or wedged between those rocks?

Groping around with head torches in the pitch dark of the early morning hours, Max and I took the lead, making our way up a chute full of cracks, many of which we could wedge our hands and feet into, while the less experienced Wayne and Chuck followed way behind, along with Christine, who was serving as their guide. Tragically, just under a year later, Christine and her partner, Charlie Fowler, would die while climbing Mount Genyen in southwest China, an avalanche the presumed cause. When we were climbing the rock wall, there was no such threat. Everything appeared to be going fine until Max and I tested the ropes and a couple of them broke free. This was serious, not least because I could see Wayne down below actually pulling on a rope to winch himself past one of the tougher spots. Left to his own devices, he could go for quite a ride.

Max and I therefore began securing the ropes as we went up, replacing some of them while fixing most of the anchors and installing extra protection until the two of us reached a plateau that gave way to a steep and slippery scree slope. What with all the tiny little pebbles, it was tricky hiking up there because if one of us were to fall, it was possible to slide all the way back to the start. Fortunately, we didn't, and about 45 minutes later, after having also made our way through frozen waterfalls and small tunnels, we rested and waited for Chris, Chuck, and Wayne to arrive.

By now the sun was starting to come up, and the view of the mine down below was breathtaking. It looked like a metropolis in the middle of nowhere. Eventually, the other members of the group joined us, and after we exchanged notes on the climb up to this point, as well as our expectations of what lay ahead, Max and I set off on the second phase. This again involved some free climbing, as well as reinforcing the loose anchors of preattached ropes for those following in our footsteps, until we found ourselves atop an exposed, knife-edge ridge with a 2,000-foot drop on either side. The ridge itself was often only about two feet wide, and given the high altitude and strong gusts of wind, it honestly felt like a high wire as I initially tried to walk along it. Quickly I decided to crawl on all fours. This was definitely heart-in-the-mouth time.

Midway through our three-hour traverse of the ridge, there was a V-shaped notch, or gap, that was the most dangerous part of the climb. Max and I would have to descend a 40-foot slope on one side and climb up a steep inverted wall on the other in order to get back to the ridge. Rappelling down the slope was easy enough, but making our way up the inverted wall was a different matter altogether. With a 2,000-foot vertical drop staring us in the face, all we had was one old fixed rope to pull ourselves up with the assistance of jumars. The problem was, we had no idea how long the rope had been there or the condition of its anchor up top. And all this was amid a sudden onslaught of sleet and hail. It was scary as hell.

After everything we'd been through, we weren't about to turn back, yet on Max's initial attempts to scale the wall, he made it only about five feet off the ground because his jumars were badly adjusted.

Unable to hoist himself up any further, he struggled to loosen the jumars' grip for about 20 minutes, and I was laughing out loud (partly cackling with nerves) because here was one of the best climbers in Lebanon wiggling around like a helpless chicken. "What are you laughing at?" he asked, after having returned to where I was standing. "It's your turn." My cackling turned to terror. At 185 pounds, I weighed probably 20 pounds more than Max. What was I going to do?

For the past few hours we'd taken turns leading the way, but now all of the momentum had switched to me. This was a big moment. Taking hold of the rope, I shook it really, really hard, trying to break up some of the snow and ice, and then, after attaching my jumars, I took a deep breath and looked up at the wall. "Man," I thought. "Forty feet!" Normally that would be nothing. Now it looked like half a mile. "C'mon," Max said, "hurry up!" This was pretty rich coming from him after his failed attempt. However, while I considered this a good point at which to turn back, he was only trying to encourage me.

Slowly I began making my way up the rope, using my gloved hands to clear the part just above me of snow and ice before trying to grip it with the jumars. This seemed to work, and soon I was about halfway up. Then I heard a massive sound, much like a freight train coming straight at me, and the wind came up fast and furious and whipped both me and the rope about 20 feet to the right. Before this, given how the rope was suspended from the top, I still couldn't touch the inverted wall. Now, dangling in midair, sustained there by the huge gust of wind, I was looking up at the rope sliding across the razor-sharp jagged rock and—since I was no longer above the ledge on which Max was standing—down at a sheer drop of 2,000 feet. Picture Wyle E. Coyote as he runs off a cliff and defies gravity for a moment before plummeting to earth.

"This is it," I thought. I should have left climbing to those seeking a religious experience or trying to rescue mountain goats. I missed my mom, my dad, my friends. I wanted to go home. Unable to breathe, I had to squeeze my butt cheeks together to prevent myself from pooping my pants. Somehow the rocks didn't slice the rope, and after about 30 seconds that felt like an eternity, the wind subsided and I swung back above the ledge. I was on my own. Yet, faced with the choice to either get busy living or get busy dying, I instinctively decided to push on. No way would I go back to Jakarta without reaching the summit.

Scared that the rope might snap at any minute, I nevertheless resumed climbing, one inch at a time, trying to put as little stress on it as possible. All the while I was growing more and more exhausted, yet conversely there was also an inner momentum and a growing hope that I was, indeed, going to live, and by the time I was about four feet from the top of that inverted wall I could, at last, touch the rock.

As I scrambled atop the flat surface, I lay down, closed my eyes, and breathed out, thanking a higher power while my legs dangled precariously over the edge. Normally, I'd never do that—I'm afraid of heights. Right now, though, I was totally wasted. In our lives, in an assortment of ways, many of us strive to reach the highest peaks. I knew I wasn't doing this just for the pure adventure.

"All clear," I shouted down to Max. "C'mon up." I felt like I'd already made the summit, and with the accompanying sense of relief came the conviction that this was my last climb. I wasn't going to put myself through such an ordeal ever again. Then I looked up, expecting to see the summit of Carstensz Pyramid, and realized that I wasn't even close. "Holy shit." That was my mantra. The peak still had to be at least an hour and a half away.

After 10 minutes of daydreaming, I set off once more, negotiating another ridge and a couple more notches while dealing with some pretty sketchy exposure in near-blinding snow. Nothing about this climb was particularly easy, and in the end that's what made it the most gratifying of all. I'd quite literally navigated jungle terrain, gone through a war zone, battled the elements, and scaled a 2,000-foot wall en route to summiting the highest mountain in Oceania.

I waited at the top for about 30 minutes before Max joined me, and by then it was full-on snowing. "We've got to go," I told him. "Let's get the hell out of here. It's gonna be dark soon."

"What time do you think it is, Bo?"

"I don't know. Four P.M.?"

"It's 10:00 in the morning."

KOSCIUSZKO
(AND SOME MAJOR SIDE ADVENTURES)

All men dream: but not equally. Those who dream by night in the dusty recesses of their minds wake in the day to find that it was vanity: but the dreamers of the day are dangerous men, for they may act their dream with open eyes, to make it possible.

—T. E. Lawrence

TO CLOSE OUT 2005, I returned to Bangkok following my Carstensz adventure. Then, after hanging out with my Thai buddies, I flew to New Zealand just before Christmas, at the height of the Australasian summer.

While climbing Everest, Simon Holland and Mark George had told me that Aussies train for that mountain by going to New Zealand's South Island and climbing Mount Cook. At 12,316 feet, this is taller and far more challenging than New South Wales's Mount Kosciuszko, the one place I hadn't yet visited as part of my Seven

Summits quest. Kosciuszko and Carstensz contend with each other on the Bass and Messner lists, yet Cook somehow gets squeezed out of the picture because New Zealand isn't on the Australian continent. Instead, it is part of the Oceania geopolitical region, which is home to the even loftier Carstensz. *Whatever.* I decided to cover all bases.

Named in honor of the famed eighteenth-century British explorer Captain James Cook, Mount Cook is known as Aoraki ("Cloud Piercer") in the language of the native Maoris, who call New Zealand Aotearoa ("Land of the Long White Cloud"), and boasts no less than three peaks, the north one being the highest (although it lost 33 feet in elevation following a 1991 rock avalanche). This is flanked by a couple of glaciers: the Tasman to the east, which is the longest in New Zealand, and Hooker to the west. All this adds up to a pretty tricky ascent up steep slopes covered in ice and snow, as quickly became apparent after I began climbing on a three-man rope team with a couple of local guides—one of them an apprentice—at 2:00 in the morning.

At around 3:45, in the first part of the Hochstetter Icefall, which reminded me of the Khumbu on Everest, I was walking across a snow bridge, unaware that there was a hidden crevasse, when—boom!—it collapsed. I must have fallen about 10 feet. The smaller, lighter main guide in front of me was ripped off his feet and flew backward, yet he immediately performed a self-arrest, leaving me dangling inside this chasm in the pitch dark, susceptible to the hypothermia that's an immediate threat because of the far colder temperature there. Looking up at the stars via the small hole through which I'd slipped, I felt my heart pumping out of my chest. I had dropped in over my head instead of just up to my waist, and I therefore knew that the main guide must have fallen and slid toward the opening. Might he suddenly land on top of me? There was no time to waste. It was up to me to get out of there quickly.

As I had been trained to do, I removed my backpack, attached it to the rope behind me, undid the top zipper, took out an extra jacket, put it on, and then set about getting myself out of the hole by means of two *Prusiks* attached to my harness. Each of these was made up of a length of rope with a foot loop at one end and, at the other, a smaller Prusik loop that, when pulled by hand with an attached carabiner, would tighten a Prusik knot that slid up and down the vertical rope connecting me to the guide. In effect, the Prusik loop serves as a lightweight version of a jumar, clamping onto the vertical rope when pulled. Holding one in each hand while my feet were in the foot loops, I could haul myself up that rope. Having recently used jumars to ascend vertical ropes on Carstensz, I certainly knew how to do this, and so I climbed out of the crevasse, shaken and more than a little stirred.

The assistant guide looked shocked and scared. "Holy smoke," he remarked. "That happened fast!"

"You're telling *me*!" I replied.

The mazelike icefall in which I fell had huge slopes on either side, and at one point during our ascent in the increasingly warm early morning hours, the path took us really close to one of these, prompting us to run in case there were falling chunks of ice. Just a spot of bad luck and/or bad timing could prove fatal. On the other side of the icefall, as the technical climb was about to begin, the main guide told me, "I've been guiding Mount Cook for 20 years and I have never seen it this bad. I'm afraid that by the time we summit and come back down, it's going to be so warm that we won't be able to cross any of the zigzagging crevasses in the icefall. We could be stuck, so my recommendation is that we turn around right now."

That's what we did, and to compensate, we then hopped on a helicopter that had dropped off some other climbers and flew to Mount Aspiring, which we summited the next day. Known as Tititea, which means "the Shining One" in the Maori language, and at 9,950 feet New Zealand's highest mountain outside the Mount Cook region, Aspiring is nicknamed the "Matterhorn of the South" because of its pointy, pyramid-shaped peak. Given the balmy conditions, it turned out to be a much safer option. Next stop: Australia.

On Christmas Day, I flew to Sydney and hooked up with Rich Birrer's twin brother, Chris, whom I'd last seen on the first, fruitless

Elbrus trip. We had e-mailed one another while I was studying in Thailand and planned to climb Kosciuszko together. And since Rich—who'd been there a few weeks before—had told us that this would involve a walk of just a few miles up a dirt path to the extremely modest 7,310-foot summit, I'd booked a flight to Bangkok for 2:00 P.M. on December 26, only 28 hours after my arrival in the New South Wales capital. That left little room for delays. But how much time would we need to complete a fast and easy trek that probably could be done in shorts and flip-flops? The answer: Enough time to secure transportation for the 220-mile southwesterly drive to Kosciuszko National Park, since none had been arranged. Well, guess what? No more rental cars were available during the holiday season.

Dumb, dumb, dumb. My return to Bangkok couldn't be rescheduled because flights out of Sydney were as fully booked as the aforementioned cars. The Aussies love Indonesia and Thailand, and evidently that's where many of them were going just before the New Year. This meant that, having traveled all the way from New Zealand, I might not even glimpse the highest point Down Under, let alone scale it . . . unless we could come up with a quick solution. Walking around Sydney Airport, I saw a limo driver holding a sign with a client's name. "Do you have a car?" I asked.

"My limo's outside."

"No, do you have your own *personal* car?"

"Sure."

"Well, we could give each other a Christmas gift."

"Huh?"

"I'm a mountain climber, I've flown in to climb Mount Kosciuszko, I'm here for just 28 hours, and there are no cars. I'll give you $300 U.S. if I can borrow your car, drive it to the mountain, and meet you back here tomorrow at noon."

"Oh, no, mate. I'm not sure about *that*."

"Please, sir, it's Christmas. Here's my climbing gear. I'm trying to complete the Seven Summits . . ."

After I told this total stranger to take my passport as security, he called his wife and asked her to bring the family car. A half-hour later, she showed up in a crappy blue Chevy Nova that came with a baby seat and a bad smell. Apparently, their dog had had a litter in there the day before. Still, beggars could hardly be choosers, and after we'd documented the dents and scratches on the vehicle and posed for photos, Chris and I were on our way. Neither he nor the owners knew of my Gumball Rally pedigree, and I planned to drive like Indy racer A. J. Foyt.

While my climbing partner dug his fingernails into the sides of his seat, we bombed our way toward our destination, named in honor of Polish hero General Tadeusz Kosciuszko by his fellow countryman Count Paul Edmund Strzelecki. This was after the latter, the first to discover gold in Australia, had climbed its highest peak in 1840. As it happens, the mountain that he summited (and which was Anglicized as the more simply spelled "Kosciusko" until 1997) is, in fact, now known as Mount Townsend. When surveys of the neighboring peaks proved that the original Mount Townsend was slightly higher, the New South Wales Lands Department switched their names so that Kosciuszko would remain Australia's tallest mountain.

If all of this sounds complicated, the climb itself certainly isn't. Until 1974, it was possible to drive a car to the top, and today an annual average of 30,000 people make the trek on foot. The two most popular routes are the Summit Walk, which commences at Charlotte Pass, continues for five-and-a-half miles, and takes about three-and-a-half hours each way; and the shorter and easier Kosciuszko Walk, which starts with a chairlift ride from the alpine ski village of Thredbo, continues for four miles, and takes about two-and-a-half hours each way . . . if the chairlift is in operation. Given that it was midafternoon when Chris and I neared the end of our drive to Kosciuszko National Park, and that the sun would be going down at around 7:30, we drove straight to Thredbo and arrived just after 4:00, only to learn from a guide that the chairlift had shut down at 4:00. There would be no chairlift.

While I was aware this meant a much longer walk and that we wouldn't reach the summit until after dark, I also figured out that there was no way that I could climb the following day and return to Sydney in time for my flight. "Forget the chairlift," I told Chris. "We've got to go *right now*."

"But it's going to take longer."

"Let's just do it!"

"All right, let's do it."

We did it.

Running like crazy up the grassy, snowless ski hill was tiring, but at least we didn't have to deal with high altitudes, and by the time we got to the top of the chairlift, we thought we were close to the summit. We weren't. We also didn't know which way to go. There were roads pointing left and right as well as a couple of paths going straight ahead, so we took one of the paths and naturally made the wrong choice. After doubling back, we then took the other path and, without knowing if this would be any better, fortunately commenced the Kosciuszko Walk—or, in our case, running for two minutes and then walking for thirty seconds. We were really moving. Then we saw a sign: "Kosciuszko 3 miles."

"Oh, man," I exclaimed, "we should turn around." It was already getting dark. However, Chris thought we should press on. "Okay," I agreed, "let's do it!" Continuing the routine, we jogged for 30 seconds, walked for 15, jogged for two minutes, walked for one. After crossing the Snowy River and passing the Kosciuszko Lookout, we reached an outhouse not far from the summit and saw a guy in a stationary truck. "Can you wait for us and then drive us back down?" Chris asked him. "Yeah, sure," came the reply. "I'll wait 20 minutes, but you'd better hurry."

Although we could have made a beeline for the top, there were signs stating that, since this was an environmental zone, we had to stick to the trail, which now wound in a huge semicircle. Despite driving to—and presumably from—the mountain without insurance, for some reason we didn't want to break the rules. So we jogged all the way around to the peak, snapped our photos by the little summit sign, and then looked down to see the guy driving away. Merry Christmas!

The only climbers there right from the get-go, we stood atop Kosciuszko for less than five minutes. This was all business—get to the top, go back down—and there was no time for savoring the moment or feeling a sense of achievement, especially since it was not only dark but also cold and windy. We thus began our return journey, and it was unsettling to jog around rocks and bushes that, in the black of night, looked like undercover kangaroos. Chris had a head torch, but I didn't, and it was only when we finally reached the top of the chairlift system that we could see lights down below. The grassy ski slopes were slippery and we hit the deck a few times, but we made it all the way to the parking lot and, at around 11:00 P.M., headed straight for a hotel.

Note that I said *a* hotel, not *the* hotel. Of course, we hadn't booked. And just as obviously, nothing was available. After feasting on a couple of granola bars for Christmas dinner because all the restaurants were closed, we slept in the car and then woke at 6:00 the next morning to drive back to Sydney. At noon, we met the limo driver and his wife, and after we'd exchanged their vehicle for my passport, they drove Chris to the home of Cheryl and Nikki Bart, with whom his brother Rich and I had climbed in Antarctica. Chris had arranged to stay with them for a few days. I was returning to Bangkok to celebrate New Year's Eve and then using more air miles for a flight to Chicago in order to be at Kellogg by January 3.

Thus, 2005 had been one hell of a year—*eleven* mountains, or an average of just under one a month, including five of the Seven/Eight Summits. No way could 2006 match that, and it didn't. Instead, the first six months had to be largely dedicated to obtaining my M.B.A. This, remember, was a two-year program, and I hadn't seen my classmates for just under nine months. During that period, my life had moved in a totally different direction from theirs, and while we were glad to get reacquainted, I was also aware that they'd forged their own memories that I wasn't privy to. It was a weird feeling, especially since all this had happened within such a relatively short space of time. Initially, I felt like an outsider, yet it didn't take long for me to readapt to the Kellogg community. After working hard to obtain five credits during each of the last two quarters, I graduated on June 17, my twenty-ninth birthday.

The very next day, using the last of my air miles, I flew to South Africa to meet with Dr. Tendani Mutambi and chemical engineer Lungile Dlodlo, both of whom had benefited from my Kilimanjaro-related sponsorship of college students. And while I was there, I also took the time to go on safari and—heaven knows why—get up close and personal with a bunch of great white sharks. My La Ruta Maya experience had already put me off the idea of any more aquatic adventures, yet when someone told me about observing the world's largest-known predatory fish in the waters around Seal Island, this sounded like a once-in-a-lifetime opportunity that was impossible to resist. I should have resisted.

Located in the Atlantic Ocean, a short powerboat ride from Cape Town, Seal Island is populated by fur seals that serve as a tasty attraction for the great whites. However, when I and four other foolhardy folks were lowered a few feet below the surface inside a cage whose two-inch-thick galvanized steel bars were spaced a couple of feet apart, there was a consensus that we might also be on the menu. Wearing goggles and wet suits and breathing through tubes connected to a ventilator on the adjacent boat, we all waited with deer-in-headlights expressions for our hosts to appear in the cold and cloudy water. Ten minutes went by, and when nothing happened, someone on the boat decided to liven things up by dangling a huge, decapitated marlin's head in front of our cage. Which one of us was being used as the bait?

The answer arrived about a minute later. As I turned my head, I found myself face-to-face with a great white shark, around 15 feet long and probably weighing 2,000 pounds, its eyes as cold and expressionless as those of a contract killer (at least, those that I'd seen on TV). Cue the music from *Jaws*. I wanted to get the hell out of there.

Still, even though any one of us could have pulled on our breathing tubes to signal that we'd had enough, on a subconscious level we were probably still clinging to the idiotic notion that this was fun. So, the show continued.

The shark swam around the bait but didn't touch it. Then a couple of others decided to check it out. Looking below me, I saw yet another shark about 10 feet away, staring straight back at us. *Whoa!* We were on high alert, looking up, down, and all around, and when one of the boat guys then upped the ante by wiggling the marlin's head from side to side, a huge great white appeared out of nowhere and ripped off a chunk. Still doing the tourist thing, we were busy snapping photos with our underwater cameras, looking at each other as if to say, "Did you see those *teeth?*"

Whenever the marlin's head moved, the sharks would get feisty. When it stayed still, they wouldn't mess with it. Eventually, one of them ripped the entire head off the rope. Then another head appeared, and an absolute monster shark that had missed out on the earlier meal darted toward it at what appeared to be full speed, bit it, and slammed into the cage. We all went flying, and when the shark's conical snout entered our cage and everyone went bananas, my right foot momentarily slipped out between the bars. At that point, the nose was about three inches from my chest, and when I instinctively grabbed it, the shark just peeled away.

That was enough. All of us were tugging on our breathing tubes, and within a few seconds we were lifted out of the water. Cage or no cage, we had been at the mercy of those killers, and while Everest had challenged my humanity and been psychologically very difficult, seeing that great white come straight at me was, without a doubt, the more viscerally scary experience. Admittedly, it was one hell of a rush, and I probably enjoyed it in a twisted sort of way, yet I'd sooner jump out of a plane without a parachute than do shark cage diving again.

Being anxious to do some climbing, in late August I flew from South Africa to Kathmandu in order to ascend and ski down Cho Oyu, which I'd planned to do ever since I'd descended Elbrus. Shortly before I left, I abandoned my plans to work for MPI Research. This was a complicated and, in part, emotionally difficult decision, but in the end I accepted the Nature Conservancy's offer of a job in Beijing. This would start November 1, giving me more than enough time to take on the world's sixth-highest mountain.

Situated on the border between China and Nepal, with a Tibetan name that means "Turquoise Goddess" because of the color of its peak in the afternoon sun, Cho Oyu is 2,118 feet shorter than its near neighbor, Mount Everest. My logistics man on Everest, Henry Todd, was handling the trip. Sure, we'd had our run-ins, but I also knew that Henry didn't take chances. When a couple of weather reports had indicated that it was okay to climb Everest and two others had indicated that it wasn't, he had erred on the side of safety. And when he had ordered us to retreat on summit day, it wasn't because of the weather forecasts, but because he had seen a storm coming up the Khumbu Valley. He had used judgment based on experience, and I trusted and respected him for that.

By the end of the Everest trip, Henry and I had been really getting along, and it was because I trusted him, as well as because he provided plenty of bang for the buck, that I used him for logistics on Cho Oyu. Others who were along for the climb included Rob Casserley, who had introduced me to Henry; Ward Supplee, a carpenter and Stanford M.B.A. with whom I shared a tent and, on summit day, a Sherpa; Nick Farr, who intended to become the first Australian to ski an 8,000-meter peak; Tom Avery, an outstanding English explorer and author; and his fellow London-born mountaineer Kenton Cool, who in addition to guiding both Tom and Nick, also wanted to become the youngest Brit to ski an 8,000-meter peak. For my part, I intended to be the youngest American to accomplish the same feat.

Following a car drive to the Chinese Base Camp at 16,076 feet, our route commenced via two other Base Camps: the Chinese at 17,388 feet and the Advanced (ABC) at 18,372 feet, which is near the Nangpa La pass that traders use to cross between Tibet and Nepal. We were at ABC on September 30 when, at around 10:30 in the morning, we heard the unmistakable sound of machine-gun fire. As we hit the ground, we could see Tibetans running for their lives across the open glacier and hiding behind rocks as Chinese Border Security guards tried to mow them down. It would later be reported that these people were followers of the Dalai Lama who wanted to join him in Dharamsala, India, the capital of the Tibetan government in exile. The Chinese authorities claimed that their guards were defending themselves, which was a total lie. Those poor men, women, and children were unarmed, and while a number of them were injured or went "missing," several others were killed, among them a 25-year-old nun and a little girl. The child's body lay there for a day, next to her knapsack and stuffed animal—an image that is burned into my memory. I saw this with my own eyes, and to this day it sparks rage at this terrible injustice and loss. Indeed, as other eyewitness accounts leaked out, there was outrage among the international community.

After leaving ABC as quickly as possible, we stayed at the 20,997-foot Camp 1, located in a saddle at the foot of the northwest ridge, and then at Camp 2 (22,965 feet), at the base of the northwest face, where Rob, Ward, and I spent a night before going straight to the summit. Kenton, Nick, and Tom, wanting a shorter summiting distance so that they could save their legs for the ski down, went there from the 22,442-feet Camp 3, located below a rock band that cuts into the snow slopes of the upper face.

From Camp 3, the route consists of an ascent through the rock band and up a slope to the plateau, which, although flat, requires a long, pain-in-the-ass walk to the tiny elevation that marks the summit. Having carried my skis all the way from Camp 2, I was really struggling by the time I approached the plateau. Those high-altitude skis are relatively light, but on my back at that elevation they felt really heavy, as did my heart after witnessing the earlier violence, and I was gagging as I struggled to keep going. Every step of the way, I repeated to myself: "I'm going to quit; this is too hard. I'm going to quit; this is too hard," nonstop, for four hours. It was torture. This concerned me. Weather-wise it was a perfect day, and if I couldn't even summit Cho Oyu, then what chance would I have on Everest?

Finally, unable to go on, I sat down. This time I *was* going to quit. However, the Sherpa whom Ward and I shared was a powerful guy, and I gratefully accepted his offer to carry my skis, while asking him to park them at the plateau so that I could retrieve them and ski back down following my trek to the top. My climbing boots also served as my ski boots. This wasn't the case for Nick Farr, who was carrying one of his ski boots in his backpack while his Sherpa carried the other. When Nick tried to put them on at the summit, they were frozen solid, and he was so mad that he just threw away his skis and left them up there.

Kenton Cool, meanwhile, had put on his own skis, and he asked if I wanted to descend the mountain with him. Since I had summited from Camp 2, my legs were like Jell-O, and I knew that I'd die if I fell in a place with a sheer drop, such as the rock band. Kenton wasn't nearly as tired, and he was also a better athlete, so I told him that I'd climb down with Ward and then ski to Camp 2 from just above Camp 3, which is what I did. At long last, my ego was receding. I wasn't racing anybody. But if I'd thought that skiing Elbrus was difficult, the higher altitude ensured that it was 10 times worse on Cho Oyu, requiring me to navigate crevasses and *sustrugi* (steep and bumpy waves of ice, like hard-packed snow dunes) while wearing an oxygen mask and a tank on my back. This, in a nutshell, was survival skiing. And after a night's rest at Camp 2, I alternately skied and rappelled to Camp 1. I was told by a fellow explorer that I became the youngest American to ski the mountain. (Yeah, this and a bag of chocolate would take me places.)

As on Elbrus, my happiness upon summiting was diminished by thoughts of the challenge on the way back down: "I'm only halfway." And when I skied, I really didn't enjoy it until I arrived safely at my destination. Nonetheless, I did it because I wanted the challenge to be tougher. I wanted to raise the bar, and in that regard Cho Oyu was yet another invaluable experience, while its summit afforded me a glimpse of Everest. I knew I'd return there sometime soon. Yet, before that happened, I had still another mountain to climb.

The spectacularly beautiful Ama Dablam, the "Matterhorn of the Himalayas," had called my name as soon as I'd seen it when I was looking east while climbing Everest. Extended armlike ridges on either side of a hanging glacier are what inspired the mountain's name, which translates as "Mother and Pearl Necklace," yet it's the exposure while climbing and the incredible views from the summit that make this ascent like no other. It is, in a word, breathtaking . . . according to the photos. I never quite made it there.

Ama Dablam is a full-on technical climb, like Carstensz Pyramid, only taller, with a classically pointed main peak that stands at 22,349 feet. Nevertheless, already acclimatized after having climbed Cho Oyu just a few days earlier, I intended to do the round trip between Pangboche (one of the villages I'd passed through during the Everest expedition) and the summit in three days instead of the usual three weeks. While most people were getting used to the altitude at the 14,700-foot Base Camp, I was 1,500 feet lower in Pangboche, watching movies at the guesthouse of my Sherpa on Cho Oyu. The only problem was, when he and I climbed to the Base Camp, we discovered that ropes hadn't been fixed all the way up.

Each of the expedition teams climbing this mountain was supposed to donate a Sherpa and some rope to ensure that this wasn't an issue. Unfortunately, most people were unwilling to contribute either Sherpas or resources and hadn't helped out, so the ropes had been fixed only up to halfway between Camp 1 (19,360 feet) and Camp 2 (20,000 feet). This meant that we'd have to hang around for "a few days." And when it became clear these few days might stretch beyond the date of my dad's sixtieth birthday party in Kalamazoo (which I was supposed to emcee), I decided to leave and fly back to the States.

It was the end of October. After I left Ama Dablam, ropes were indeed fixed all the way to the top. But in the early hours of November 14 the collapse of a massive column of ice from the hanging glacier caused an avalanche that wiped out several tents at Camp 3, killing six climbers. Noting when the ropes had been fixed and doing the math, I realized that I would most likely have been at Camp 3 that night. Going to my dad's birthday party had saved my life.

I really wanted to spend more time with my family, so that's what I did through the end of the year. At the same time, intent on exploring my entrepreneurial abilities, I ended up passing on the job with the Nature Conservancy, moved to Chicago in January 2007, and, while training for Everest, cofounded my own company. Business had always been in my blood—*five generations* of entrepreneurs—and with the M.B.A. under my belt and no remaining obligations, this felt like the right time. My partner was Bill Bennett, an engineer and ex-classmate of mine who had been voted "most likely to succeed" by our business school classmates, and the company we started was Iconic Development LLC, a green (environmentally friendly) real estate development firm.

That March, our first piece of property went under contract. And at the same time, I was closing in on my final Summit.

CHAPTER 12

EVEREST, SECOND ATTEMPT—
ON TOP OF THE WORLD

Come to the edge. We might fall. Come to the edge. It's too high! Come to the edge! And they came, and we pushed, and they flew.

— Christopher Logue

EVER SINCE MY first attempt to climb Everest in 2005, which had been preceded by a hasty lunchtime get-together with my mom and two sisters after years of discord among the various family members, I had been making a concerted effort for my family to reconnect—to talk, meet, and generally interact with one another more than we'd done in a long, long time. In the spring of 2007, this culminated in my asking my parents and siblings if they'd like to join me on the spectacular trek from Lukla in Nepal to the Everest Base Camp, giving us an opportunity to bond and me the perfect send-off as I once again tried to climb to the highest point on Earth.

Only some of them were able to join me, but I was really grateful—and in some cases pleasantly surprised—that those who did included my dad, who had recently celebrated his sixtieth birthday; my stepmom Barbara; her brother, Danny; my stepbrother, Ryan, together with his fiancée, Martina; and my brother-in-law, Jay, who's married to my sister Jenny. On March 31, we flew to Kathmandu together, and then on to Lukla, where everyone met Henry Todd. As on my prior trips to Everest and Cho Oyu, he would be handling the logistics while not moving beyond Base Camp.

Henry, as you may recall, is not averse to speaking his mind or snapping somebody's head off whenever he sees fit. So I was a little apprehensive when Barbara began plying him with some pretty basic questions about the climb. I need not have worried. Throwing me yet another curveball in terms of his behavior, Henry was all sweetness and light as he patiently listened to Barbara's concerns and assuaged her fears, while also having a couple of beers with us the night before we set off on our 30-mile, 8,600-foot ascent to the 17,600-foot Base Camp.

Barbara and Dad had trained beforehand by dieting and walking at least an hour almost every day in Kalamazoo. (Now you know where my "fly by night" training comes from.) The others in our party had also prepared for the trip. Yet Dad amply demonstrated the blood tie that he and I share by saying that he wanted to complete the journey in just eight days. "No, Dad," I told him when he insisted that he had other commitments and had to return quickly to Michigan. "If climbers need 9 or 10 days to get to Base Camp, you need at least 12."

The two-day, 10-mile trek from Lukla to the town of Namche Bazaar is pretty heavy going, especially since its 2,286-foot ascent from a 9,000-foot elevation has everyone experiencing shortness of breath due to the thin air. That's why the rest of us advised Dad and Barbara to spend an extra day in Lukla so that they could acclimatize while we walked halfway to Namche. The following day, they met us in Namche after flying there in a helicopter, and after that, we all hoped, things would get a little easier, with a less hilly trek to the village of Pangboche (13,123 feet) while porters carried the bags of Dad and Barbara, whom they appropriately called Big Papa and Big Mama.

Feeling less than great, Big Mama actually rode a donkey up the huge hill on the way to Tengboche. Then, suffering from altitude sickness, Danny unfortunately had to turn around at the village of Pheriche (14,340 feet) and head back to Lukla. Indeed, every day represented new elevation highs for everyone in our group except me and Jay, who had been to Pangboche before. Dad's daily mantra was, "Barbara's going to quit. She doesn't like it here; it's too dirty for her." Meanwhile, she would say, "Bo, your dad doesn't like it here. He wants to leave." In other words, with the mountain already taking a physical toll, they were behaving like a normal married couple, each using the other as the excuse for what he or she wanted to do. And this meant that Ryan, Martina, Jay, and I had to behave like any normal set of kids, scheming together to keep them going.

It was great that everybody got to see the magnificent scenery while traversing suspended bridges high above the Dudh Kosi River. But by the time we reached the village of Lobuche, 16,108 feet above sea level, Big Papa and Big Mama had hit their personal wall. On the way there, they barely made it up the intensely steep Dugla Hill, and having regularly used a pulse oximeter to monitor their heart rate and blood oxygen saturation levels, we agreed that that they shouldn't go any further. Doing so would have risked their health. Besides, there isn't a whole lot to see at Base Camp aside from the Khumbu Icefall and a bunch of tents. For really stunning views of Everest all the way up to its peak, people need to do the nontechnical climb to the top of Kala Patthar at 18,500 feet. There was no way that Dad and Barbara would make it that far, and there was no need for them to do so. They could take pride in what they had already done.

Accordingly, they decided to get up early the next morning and hike to Gorak Shep (17,000 feet), the final acclimatization stop for many people on their way to Base Camp. "Okay, just walk there, but don't push it," I advised them. Jay, Ryan, and Martina went with me to Kala Patthar, and although they found the high-altitude trek really difficult, they did a good job of pushing themselves all the way to our destination. There, Jay placed a Nepali prayer flag in honor of his brother, Jordan, who was battling cancer. The hope was that the winds would transport the prayers to the mountain gods, and evidently this worked. Jordan underwent chemo and made a full recovery.

At about 11:00 that morning, we arrived back in Lobuche, from which everyone except me would fly by helicopter to Kathmandu and, along with Barbara's brother, Danny, return to America that same day. They were cutting it pretty close. When the helicopter showed up, I handed Dad the watch that he'd given me after I'd graduated from business school, wrapped inside a Nepali prayer flag along with a handwritten note for him to read in the event of my dying on Everest. It basically told him how much I loved him and that, despite the conflicts between us during my formative years, we had come a long way. Hugging each other, we both cried. Then he and the others boarded the helicopter, and as they flew off, I could see him waving to me for what might be the last time. Their expedition was ending. Mine was just beginning. And for the next few hours, unsure as to whether I'd ever see Michigan or my folks again, I felt a little homesick.

Once the climb began, I focused on the mountain. My last time here, I had largely subsisted on a Nepali diet of *daal bhaat*—lentils and rice. I don't like either, however, and force feeding myself really sucked, so this time around I spent a few hundred bucks to ship my kind of food from the United States to Kathmandu and then straight to Base Camp: air-sealed bags of meat and cheese, dipping sauces, and my personal favorite, macaroni and cheese. Why should I care if my fellow climbers teased me? While they were tucking into their *daal bhaat*, I'd be living high on the hog.

My teammates were Rob Casserley, the 32-year-old English doctor with whom I'd already climbed Everest and Cho Oyu; Mike Davey, his 41-year-old fellow Brit who had stayed with the body of

Rob Milne after he'd died during that former expedition; Rob Casserley's 27-year-old girlfriend, Dr. Anna Shekhdar; Ward Supplee, the 43-year-old San Franciscan who had been my tent partner on Cho Oyu; Jean Clemenson, a 69-year-old guide who had been the first Frenchman to summit that mountain; Bob Jen, a 53-year-old marathon man from New York who had already summited Everest and was now headed for Lhotse; Mike Allsop, a 37-year-old pilot for Air New Zealand; and University of South Carolina nursing professor Pat Hickey, a.k.a. Prof, for whom Everest also represented the final installment of a quest to conquer the Seven Summits. In addition, there were three other teams that were concurrently using Henry Todd for logistics: one with Kenton Cool, the London-born mountaineer who had guided a couple of climbers during my Cho Oyu expedition; another with British guide Victor Saunders; and a British military team.

On April 13, we set off from Base Camp, and this time around I felt far less encumbered than during the first Everest expedition, thanks largely to my new sponsorship deal with Gordini, a Vermont-based winter sports outfitter that was providing me with climbing gear and funding for the trip. This made things much easier, and there were no real incidents until we were at the 21,300-foot Camp 2, atop the Western Cwm, at the base of the Lhotse Face. The day before heading to Camp 3 (24,500 feet), we learned that a Sherpa had been killed by a chunk of falling ice at the base of the Face, and even though his body had been removed, we saw his blood all over the ground when we continued our climb. None of us was unaware of how dangerous this environment could be, but it seemed to go out of its way to keep issuing reminders.

On the upside, the weather was far better than during my first Everest trip, and this enabled us to make swift and steady progress, which I did as part of Henry's A Team alongside Rob and Ward. Preparing for the summit, we spent a night acclimatizing at Camp 3 and then returned to Base Camp. On May 14, we were back at Camp 2, and while I was checking my gear, the zipper on my right climbing boot broke halfway. It couldn't be repaired, so I began asking the other climbers if they had an extra pair of boots. One after the other told me that they didn't, and after a couple of hours I was getting desperate—until Rob informed me that he had a second pair.

"They're raggedy and they've got holes in them," he said, "but I've sealed those with some old duct tape. What size are you?"

"Ten."

"These are size twelve."

What the hell? When I tried on the right boot, it felt pretty good. I just wore an extra sock on that foot (three instead of two) and, with one size ten and one size twelve boot, continued my drive toward the summit. (Award yourself a *daal bhaat* if you've already noticed that I'm wearing different-colored boots there on the front cover of this book.)

On May 15, we reached Camp 3. On May 16, we were at Camp 4, located at the 26,000-foot South Col. The year before, I'd vomited there when I tried to eat and drink. This time, by staying relaxed and taking small sips and little bites, I easily kept everything down, and I even managed to doze off before spending two hours getting ready and venturing into the Death Zone. It was a little windy and really cold when I left the tent at 10:10 that night, followed by Ward and then Rob. And since I had a Sherpa named Top-Jin all to myself for this final part of the climb, I had to carry only one bottle of oxygen while he carried two in addition to his own.

Kenton and another guy had set off about 30 minutes before I did, and I started out at a good pace, hoping to catch them up. I had been calm in the tent, but I was now feeling anxious as I approached my ultimate goal, and for the first hour my heart was pumping and I was gagging while I climbed. What was happening? Could I be getting altitude sickness? I pressed on regardless, unaware that, even though I thought I was speeding up, I was actually slowing down. When Doug Beal, one of Victor's team members, overtook me, I was pretty shocked. At that precise moment, just like on Cho Oyu, I told myself, "Slow down. It's okay to let people pass you. Just focus on your breathing and enjoy this, Bo. You're *climbing*. *Enjoy it*."

Ever since I was a kid, I had always been a repetitive self-talker. Something about being dyslexic and bad with words made me want to repeat them to myself over and over. "Shoot the ball, shoot the ball, shoot the ball," I'd mutter while hovering around the basketball hoop in our driveway for hours on end, and as a climber I'd indulge in a similarly meditative solo conversation, with a constant refrain of "Faster, faster, faster," or perhaps "That *?%@$! guy is *not* going to pass me." Although the nature of this internal dialogue changed over time, the annoying repetition didn't, and by constantly talking to myself on this second Everest summit attempt, I started to get into a rhythm: "Find your rhythm, Bo. You've done this before. Remember how you did it that first time on Kilimanjaro."

Climbing is all about finding a rhythm. A lot of people have told me that when they climb, they hear classical music. Even without music in my head I found my rhythm, my space, and my zone, and before I knew it, two hours had passed and I was on somebody's heels. When I looked up, I saw Kenton Cool. I had actually moved faster by going slow and steady instead of trying to race. Now going at the same pace, I followed Kenton as we headed toward the Balcony. The fact that Rob Milne's body remained where I'd last seen it, buried in the snow, filled me with an indescribable sadness. But then I was shaken back to the present when, shouting through his breathing apparatus, Kenton told me that his oxygen wasn't working properly and that he was feeling really tired.

When we reached the Balcony—a small platform at 27,600 feet, higher than I'd ever been before—he stood near the edge, looked toward the horizon, and yelled, "Does anyone have any oxygen?" Uh-oh. Who was he talking to? Doug Beal, Doug's Sherpa, a Sherpa on Kenton's team, my Sherpa Top-Jin, and I were all standing behind Kenton, and none of us replied. "I've had a really hard time getting up here," he continued to yell in the direction of an invisible audience, his body silhouetted against the stars. "It's the hardest time I've ever had, and I think it's because my oxygen's not working. So, I'd really appreciate it if anyone can help . . ."

It was a weird, amusing little monologue. And although his O_2 wasn't flowing properly, it was still flowing sufficiently to ensure that he wasn't in any danger. I, meanwhile, switched over to my second tank and stashed the first one right there at the Balcony. As it was half full, I was saving it for the descent. Hopefully, no one would steal it.

It's funny how, when you're climbing, you often switch so quickly from the personal to the profound, the physical to the ephemeral. One second, I was furtively protecting my remaining oxygen and focusing solely on my physical needs, and the next, looking up and to either side, I saw thousands of stars. Gazing down ever so slightly toward the horizon, I saw thousands more. It was as if I'd climbed into outer space—a magnificently surreal, otherworldly sight. I stayed at the Balcony for about 10 minutes, drinking water and eating half of a Snickers bar. Then I resumed climbing with Top-Jin immediately behind me, encountering some pretty difficult rock steps en route to the tiny dome of snow and ice that is known as the South Summit.

With every stride my body screamed at me to turn around. This was too hard. Nevertheless, I forced myself to keep going, again trying to get into a rhythm, and although Top-Jin and I rarely spoke, he'd smack me on the butt with the flat end of his ice ax whenever he wanted me to pass someone. On and on we plodded. Then, just as I began thinking, "Am I ever going to get there?" the sun came up. Seeing it rise was yet another magical experience, not least because of the immense black triangle that now stretched from behind a range of neighboring mountains to my right across a blood-red sky toward the horizon. That triangle was the shadow of Mount Everest. I couldn't see my own miniscule outline, but I knew it was on there, near the very top. I was living my dream.

There was absolutely no wind as we approached the South Summit. Once we were there, standing at 28,700 feet, with just over 300 vertical feet to go and a slope that was not nearly as steep as some that I'd negotiated on other climbs, I was sure for the first time that I'd reach my goal. There it was, at the far end of a four-foot-wide ridge that, even though I was clipped to a fixed rope, I'd have to approach as if I were traversing a knife edge—one with a sheer drop of about 10,000 feet down the eastern Kangshung Face to the right and another drop of about 8,000 feet down the southwest face to the left, which a couple of South Koreans had been trying to climb when they were killed by falling rocks the previous day.

Dramatically cast against a vast backdrop of increasingly blue sky, the skinny, snow-covered southeast ridge certainly looked frail enough to snap or crumble at any moment. However, it was my only means of reaching the Earth's apex, and with this plainly in sight, I now had full-blown summit fever. Forget any feelings of tiredness. Unperturbed by the overt danger—while simultaneously being motivated and inspired by it—I set off on the most exposed part of the climb, known as the Cornice Traverse.

My right foot was in Tibet, my left foot was in Nepal, and it was to the left, down the aforementioned southwest face, that at one point a climber in front of me slid head-first. Fortunately, he was clipped into a fixed rope (that's what saved his life), but for me it was another wake-up call, like witnessing the immediate aftereffects of a horrific accident while speeding down the highway. "Take it *real easy*," I kept telling myself as I passed him by while a couple of Sherpas helped him climb back up.

Near the end of the ridge, a left turn led me to a 40-foot rock wall known as the Hillary Step, named in honor of Edmund Hillary, who, together with Tenzing Norgay, was the first to ascend it. Unlike them, I had the benefit of doing so with a fixed rope. And unlike many other people who climb Everest via the southeast ridge, I didn't have to wait. The narrow passage to the Step, combined with the popularity of this route, often results in its being a huge bottleneck. This was the case during the deadly disaster of May 11, 1996. When I reached it, however, I was the only one there.

Having done plenty of rock climbing to prepare for this moment, I was surprised to discover that the Step is somewhat sloped rather than straight-up vertical. This certainly made things easier. Looking at a selection of about 15 fixed ropes, some of them clearly quite old,

I tested what looked like the newest one by pulling it hard. Then I clipped into it, grabbed several of the other ropes with my left hand, used my right hand to hold onto some rocks, and within about 30 seconds I had climbed the Hillary Step. It really wasn't that difficult. Still, it was special to me. Over the years, numerous climbers had reached the base of the Step and then turned back without summiting Everest. The fact that Hillary and Norgay free-climbed this monolith underscores just how outstanding their achievement was.

I actually traversed the last few hundred yards of superexposed ridge without fixed ropes. None were there. Sure, this was risky, but if I couldn't walk that final section, I didn't deserve to be there. Instead, I just kept trudging along the loose, rocky, more horizontal ground, and as I neared the sign identifying the summit, I could see a couple of people who had reached it from Tibet's northeast ridge. *I had made it.*

The last 10 steps were ones that I savored. I didn't want them to end. My joy at conquering the other mountains had always been tempered by the knowledge that I still had to deal with the biggest one of all. Now I had dealt with it, and the sense of achievement was as sweet as it gets. I strode up to the summit—an elevated point about six feet high and six feet in diameter—sat down, looked around, and cried my eyes out. The words of all those naysayers who had doubted me as a kid no longer meant a thing. Having proved to myself what I was capable of doing and how much I could change, I wasn't shackled anymore by other people's observations, judgments, and opinions. All that mattered was that I truly believed in *me*, and this, in turn, set me free.

It was 6:30 in the morning of May 17, 2007. When I asked Top-Jin if I could radio down to tell Henry I had made it, he told me that he didn't have a radio phone. Wow, what would have happened if I had been injured? I pulled out my satellite phone, and the first person I called was my dad. He said he was very proud, and the two of us cried. His acknowledgment meant so much to me. Then I called my mom and left her a message, telling her how much I loved her. Next I called my sister Jenny and told her the same thing. Finally, having borrowed a radio phone from another climber, I contacted Henry Todd at Base Camp and said, "Hey, I've got a problem. I've run out of road—I'm at the summit."

"Congratulations," Henry replied. "Take it in, enjoy it, but hurry back." Because it was such a beautiful day, I'd spent long periods of the past hour wearing neither my gloves nor my oxygen mask—at 29,029 feet. However, I was living on borrowed time.

I had achieved my greatest ambition, summiting the highest peak on each of the continents—a vertical climb of 149,425 feet. Within those feet I had undergone immeasurable personal growth. It was a growth immersed in some basic truths.

The Burmese pro-democracy activist and Nobel Peace Prize recipient Aung San Suu Kyi famously asserted, "Fear is a habit." I would take that a step further by stating that fear is a habit that we have to break over and over again. It surfaces not only at times of great adversity but also in everyday life. And while it's okay to feel fear on the side of a mountain—healthy doses of it help keep you alive—it can also lead to life-threatening paralysis and inactivity.

When I was at Everest's Base Camp, readying myself for the final move to Camp 1, I spent an afternoon preparing my gear with Top-Jin. At one point, I asked him if he had any words of advice, fully expecting him to tell me to sharpen my ice ax, eat plenty of food, and get enough sleep. Instead, he remarked, "Be humble."

For the longest time I had thought that, in order to climb, I needed stubborn confidence. (Or confident stubbornness—take your choice.) After all, how could I make it to the top if I didn't have something to prove while relying on my ego to keep me motivated? Now, staring blankly at Top-Jin, I heard him say, "When you are humble, you know your surroundings; you respect them. I am sure that, when you left for Everest, you felt pressure from yourself, from your family, and from your community to accomplish the goal of the summit. Don't think about this. Just save your energy." In other words, if you climb this mountain thinking you have something to prove, you will waste precious energy, and you don't have any energy to waste.

Wasted energy can be the difference between life and death. When you are humble, you experience each moment, you focus on each step, and you discard thoughts of what others—and you, too—think about the process.

These words stayed with me, and therefore during the climb I stopped wondering, "What will people think if I don't make it?" Instead, I asked, "Who am I now? How do I survive now? How do I take the next step?"

The possibility of accomplishing more than I ever could in my daily American existence was largely what motivated me to keep moving forward on the mountain. And while I was risking my life, I was also making a statement—that I could grow, that people can change, that it is within everyone's grasp to write his own destiny. Knowing that not only helps us to understand the here and now, but also engenders in us the belief in what we can achieve tomorrow.

While climbing to the top of the world, I learned that, if fear is a habit, then so is humility. The first habit is hard to break; the other is hard to initiate. In life, everyone has his or her own Everest to climb, whether it relates to a tragedy, a hardship, or a personal limitation, and surmounting it is not about the grand gesture but about finding grace in the everyday challenge.

To summit a mountain takes many steps. To begin climbing it takes only one. And while scaling the peak is the ultimate prize, that first step holds the key to life-affirming change.

The Seven Summits Gear List

Having the proper equipment is very important to the success, enjoyment, comfort, and safety of your expedition. Many items are staples of any climbing trip; others are specific to a particular mountain and, in some cases, the chosen route. Here's what I recommend if you want to follow in my footsteps on the Seven Summits (while skipping the canned tuna). Please note: This is meant to be a guide. Each person is different and will have to tweak this list according to his or her personal preferences.

Kilimanjaro

Clothing

HEAD

▲ Warm hat

▲ Sun hat

▲ Scarf or bandana

▲ Glacier glasses (category 4)

UPPER BODY

▲ Quick-dry T-shirts

▲ Long, thick, medium-weight undershirt

▲ Gore-Tex jacket (waterproof is a must)

▲ Down jacket

HANDS

▲ Gloves: light, medium, and heavy weight (all waterproof)

LOWER BODY

▲ Quick-dry underwear

▲ Hiking shorts

▲ Long underwear

▲ Soft-shell pants

▲ Gore-Tex pants

FEET

▲ Socks, three pairs each of thin and thick

▲ Light to medium weight hiking boots, large enough to wear one thin and one heavy sock

▲ Gaiters or Crocs

▲ Tennis shoes or flip-flops

Sleeping Gear

▲ 0 degree Fahrenheit sleeping bag

▲ Sleeping pads (cell foam and Therma-a-Rest)

▲ Compression stuff sacks

Carrying Gear

▲ Day pack (40–50 liters)

▲ Large duffel bag

Miscellaneous Equipment

▲ Toiletries: the bare minimum (plan on using two or three wetnaps per day)

▲ Sunscreen

▲ Lip balm

- Earplugs
- Headlamp
- Adjustable ski poles
- Basic personal first-aid and drug kit
- Towel
- Spare eyewear
- Snacks: bring a few of your favorite treats
- Dry bags: all sizes
- Paperback books, cards, Walkman or iPod, journal, etc.
- Camera
- Two water bottles
- Water treatment tablets
- Powerade or Gatorade

Aconcagua
Clothing
HEAD
- Warm hat
- Sun hat
- Balaclava
- Face mask
- Glacier glasses (category 4)
- Ski goggles

UPPER BODY
- Polypropylene T-shirts
- Lightweight, long-sleeved polypropylene shirts
- Soft-shell shirts
- Down sweater

▲ Hard-shell jacket

▲ Expedition down parka with hood. Must be 800+ fill

HANDS

▲ Liner gloves

▲ Fleece gloves

▲ Expedition shell gloves

▲ Modular expedition shell mitts

LOWER BODY

▲ Shorts

▲ Nylon pants

▲ Lightweight long underwear

▲ Fleece pants

▲ Soft-shell pants

▲ Hard-shell pants

FEET

▲ Four pairs of liner socks

▲ Three pairs of lightweight socks

▲ Four pairs of medium-to-heavy warm socks

▲ Trail shoes

▲ Flip-flops

Sleeping Gear

▲ –10 to –20 degrees Fahrenheit down sleeping bag

▲ Sleeping pads (cell foam and Therma-a-Rest)

▲ Compression stuff sacks

Carrying Gear

▲ Large-capacity pack

▲ Daypack

▲ Two large duffle bags

▲ Small padlocks for duffel bags

Climbing Gear

▲ Alpine climbing harness

▲ Locking carabiner

▲ Ice ax

▲ Plastic expedition boots

▲ Insulated super-gaiters

▲ Crampons

▲ Adjustable trekking poles

Miscellaneous Equipment

▲ Toiletries: the bare minimum (plan on using two or three wetnaps per day)

▲ First-aid kit

▲ Lip balm

▲ Sunscreen, at least SPF 40

▲ Headlamp

▲ Two water bottles

▲ Pee bottle

▲ Two water-bottle insulators

▲ Plastic mug

▲ Plastic bowl and spoon

▲ Pocketknife

▲ Water purification tablets

▲ Three or four large plastic bags for keeping miscellaneous gear dry

▲ Nylon stuff sacks for food and gear storage

▲ Bandana

▲ Camp towel

▲ Earplugs

▲ Small stainless steel thermos

▲ Favorite snack foods

▲ Paperback books, cards, Walkman or iPod, journal, etc.

▲ Camera

Denali

Clothing

HEAD

▲ Warm hat

▲ Face mask or balaclava

▲ Sun hat or scarf/bandana

▲ Glacier glasses (category 4)

▲ Ski goggles

UPPER BODY

▲ Polypropylene T-shirt

▲ Lightweight long-sleeved polypropylene shirt

▲ Expedition-weight long-sleeved polypropylene shirt

▲ Soft-shell expedition jacket

▲ Down sweater

▲ Hard-shell waterproof jacket

HANDS

▲ Light- or medium-weight gloves

▲ Summit mittens

▲ Hand and foot warmers

LOWER BODY

▲ Lightweight long underwear

▲ Expedition-weight long underwear

▲ Expedition-weight fleece pants

▲ Fleece or insulated pants

▲ Waterproof/quick-dry underwear

▲ Waterproof shell pants

FEET

▲ Liner socks

▲ Heavy warm socks

▲ Gaiters or Crocs

▲ Down booties

Sleeping Gear

▲ Sleeping bag, rated to –30 degrees Fahrenheit

▲ Sleeping pads (cell foam and Therma-a-Rest)

▲ Compression stuff sack

Carrying Gear

▲ Expedition pack

▲ Large zip duffel

Climbing Gear

▲ Alpine climbing harness

▲ Two locking carabiners

▲ Eight regular carabiners

▲ Ascenders with one leg and waist loop and a second ascender

▲ Ice ax

▲ Plastic mountaineering boots

▲ Forty feet of five- or six-millimeter perlon cord for sled and pack tie-off

▲ Snowshoes

▲ Adjustable trekking poles

Miscellaneous Equipment

▲ Personal first-aid kit

▲ Lip balm

▲ Sunscreen

▲ Two wide-mouth, one-liter water bottles and insulated covers

▲ Pee bottle

▲ Plastic mug

▲ Plastic bowl and spoon

▲ Pocketknife

▲ Water purification tablets

▲ Toiletry kit

▲ Nylon stuff sacks for food and gear storage

▲ Disposable lighters

▲ Snacks

▲ Camera

▲ Paperback books, cards, Walkman or iPod, journal, etc.

Elbrus

Clothing

HEAD

▲ Ski goggles

▲ Warm hat

▲ Balaclava

▲ Baseball hat

▲ Glacier glasses (category 4)

▲ Bandanas

UPPER BODY

▲ T-shirts

▲ Long-sleeved polypropylene shirts

▲ Soft-shell jacket

▲ Down sweater

▲ Hard-shell jacket

▲ Down jacket

HANDS

▲ Liner gloves

▲ Warm gloves

▲ Nylon shell gloves

▲ Insulated over mitts

LOWER BODY

▲ Light/midweight long underwear pants

▲ Soft-shell pants

▲ Nylon shorts

▲ Waterproof shell pants

FEET

▲ Liner socks

▲ Heavy warm socks

▲ Gaiters or Crocs

▲ Light hiking boots

▲ Plastic mountaineering boots

Sleeping Gear

▲ Sleeping bag rated to 10 degree Fahrenheit

▲ Sleeping pads (cell foam and Therma-a-Rest)

▲ Compression stuff sacks

Carrying Gear

▲ Medium/large backpack

Climbing Gear

▲ Alpine climbing harness

▲ Locking carabiners

▲ Regular carabiners

▲ Ice ax

▲ Crampons

▲ Adjustable trekking poles

▲ Skis and mountaineering ski boots if you want to ski down (a dangerous but enjoyable option)

Miscellaneous Equipment

▲ Lip balm

▲ Sunscreen

▲ Headlamp

▲ Two water bottles

▲ Pee bottle

▲ Pocketknife

▲ Water purification tablets

▲ Toiletry kit

▲ Nylon stuff sacks for food and gear storage

▲ Snacks

▲ Camera

▲ Small padlock for duffel bag

▲ Earplugs

▲ Paperback books, cards, Walkman or iPod, journal, etc.

▲ Hand wipes

Vinson Massif
Clothing
HEAD

▲ Warm hat

▲ Balaclava

▲ Ski goggles with UV protection

▲ Sun hat

▲ Nose protector

▲ Glacier glasses (category 4)

▲ Bandanas

UPPER BODY

▲ Long-sleeved shirts

▲ Long underwear shirt (expedition weight)

▲ Soft-shell jacket

▲ Expedition down jacket

▲ Down sweater

▲ Waterproof hard-shell jacket

HANDS

▲ Thin liner gloves

▲ Warm gloves

▲ Shell mitts and down mittens

LOWER BODY

▲ Lightweight long underwear pants

▲ Lightweight-medium weight fleece pants

▲ Down pants

▲ Waterproof shell pants

FEET

▲ Liner socks

▲ Medium socks

▲ Down booties

▲ Plastic mountaineering boots

▲ Overboots

Sleeping Gear

▲ Down sleeping bag rated to –40 degrees Fahrenheit or below

▲ Sleeping pads (cell foam and Therma-a-Rest)

▲ Compression stuff sacks

Carrying Gear

▲ Large backpack

Climbing Gear

▲ Alpine climbing harness

▲ Locking carabiners

▲ Five regular carabiners

▲ Ice ax

▲ T-block

▲ Crampons

▲ Thirty feet of six-millimeter perlon cord for prussik material

Miscellaneous Equipment

▲ Lip balm

▲ Sunscreen

▲ Headlamp

▲ Two water bottles

▲ Pee bottle

▲ Pocketknife

▲ Water purification

▲ Toiletry kit

▲ Nylon stuff sacks for food and gear storage

▲ Snacks

▲ Camera

▲ Small padlock for duffel bag

▲ Earplugs

▲ Paperback books, cards, Walkman or iPod, journal, etc.

▲ Hand wipes

Carstensz Pyramid
Clothing
HEAD

▲ Warm hat

▲ Balaclava

▲ Sun hat

▲ Glacier glasses (category 4)

▲ Bandanas

UPPER BODY

▲ Long-sleeved shirt

▲ Expedition-weight long underwear shirt or medium-weight fleece shirt

- ▲ Soft-shell or fleece jacket
- ▲ Down jacket
- ▲ Hard-shell waterproof jacket
- ▲ Medium-weight down parka

HANDS
- ▲ Liner gloves
- ▲ Medium-weight gloves
- ▲ Mittens
- ▲ Shell gloves

LOWER BODY
- ▲ Light or medium weight long underwear
- ▲ Soft-shell pants
- ▲ Quick-dry nylon shorts
- ▲ Lightweight pants
- ▲ Waterproof shell pants

FEET
- ▲ Liner socks
- ▲ Medium weight warm socks
- ▲ Gaiters or Crocs
- ▲ Flip-flops

Sleeping Gear
- ▲ Sleeping bag rated to at least 10 to 20 degrees Fahrenheit
- ▲ Sleeping pads (cell foam and Therma-a-Rest)
- ▲ Compression stuff sacks

Carrying Gear
- ▲ Large backpack that can convert to medium size
- ▲ Two large duffel bags

Climbing Gear

▲ Alpine climbing harness

▲ Four locking carabiners

▲ Four regular carabiners

▲ Belay/rappel device

▲ Mechanical left- and right-hand ascenders with handles

▲ Climbing helmet

▲ Adjustable trekking poles

▲ One shoulder-length and double-length sling

▲ Rappel gloves

Miscellaneous Equipment

▲ Lip balm

▲ Sunscreen

▲ Headlamp

▲ Two water bottles

▲ Pee bottle

▲ Pocketknife

▲ Water purification

▲ Toiletry kit

▲ Nylon stuff sacks for food and gear storage

▲ Snacks

▲ Camera

▲ Small padlock for duffel bag

▲ Earplugs

▲ Paperback books, cards, Walkman or iPod, journal, etc.

▲ Hand wipes

Kosciuszko

- ▲ Six-pack of beer
- ▲ Flip-flops
- ▲ Basic sunglasses
- ▲ Sunscreen
- ▲ Camera

Everest

Clothing

HEAD

- ▲ Warm hat
- ▲ Balaclava
- ▲ Face mask
- ▲ Sunhat
- ▲ Glacier glasses (category 4)
- ▲ Ski goggles

UPPER BODY

- ▲ Cotton T-shirts
- ▲ Polypropylene T-shirts
- ▲ Long-sleeved polypropylene shirts
- ▲ Soft-shell jacket
- ▲ Down sweater
- ▲ Waterproof hard-shell jacket with hood
- ▲ Expedition down jacket
- ▲ Expedition down suite

HANDS

- ▲ Thin warm liner gloves

▲ Warm gloves

▲ Expedition shell gloves

▲ Modular expedition shell mitts

LOWER BODY

▲ Nylon shorts

▲ Nylon pants for trekking and around camp

▲ Lightweight long underwear bottoms

▲ Fleece pants

▲ Soft-shell pants

▲ Hard-shell pants

FEET

▲ Liner socks

▲ Lightweight trekking socks

▲ Medium/heavy warm socks

▲ Plastic mountaineering boots

▲ Gaiters or Crocs

▲ Trail shoes

▲ Flip-flops

Sleeping Gear

▲ Two down sleeping bags rated to –40 degrees Fahrenheit

▲ Sleeping pads (cell foam and Therma-a-Rest)

▲ Compression stuff sacks

Carrying Gear

▲ Small duffel bag for luggage storage in Kathmandu

▲ Large backpack that can convert to medium size

▲ Two large duffel bags

Climbing Gear

- ▲ Alpine climbing harness
- ▲ Two locking carabiners
- ▲ Three regular carabiners
- ▲ Ice ax
- ▲ Crampons
- ▲ Adjustable trekking poles
- ▲ Belay/rappel device

Miscellaneous Equipment

- ▲ Small padlock for duffel bag
- ▲ Lip balm
- ▲ Sunscreen
- ▲ Headlamp
- ▲ Two water bottles
- ▲ Pee bottle
- ▲ Pocketknife
- ▲ Water purification
- ▲ Toiletry kit
- ▲ Nylon stuff sacks for food and gear storage
- ▲ Snacks
- ▲ Camera
- ▲ Earplugs
- ▲ Paperback books, cards, Walkman or iPod, journal, etc.
- ▲ Hand wipes

A C K N O W L E D G M E N T S

I would like to thank all of the people who, in one way or another, have helped this project come to life. Some have been directly involved with it; others have had a positive effect that has helped me get to this point. Unfortunately, I don't remember the names of all the porters and sherpas who have worked so tirelessly during my mountaineering expeditions, but I am eternally grateful to them, my assorted climbing partners, and to the following wonderful people:

My dearest grandma, Martha Parfet, who didn't retire until she was well into her eighties, and showed me the value of hard work and helping people. Thank you for informing the entire family about the significance of my Seven Summits odyssey.

My terrific parents Bill Parfet and Maury Reed, who have supported me throughout this fulfilling journey. I know you'd like me to stop climbing, but you know I'm not going to! Thanks for always being there. And I also greatly appreciate the support of my sister, Emily Lennen, and brother, Ted Parfet.

Next, there's my sister, Jen Gudebski, without whom I would never have been able to complete this project. Jen, you've done so much for me while I've been away on my various trips—communicating with my college professors, updating family and friends on a daily basis, quelling people's concerns, paying my bills, and dealing with the media. Most of all, however, it has been your belief in me that has given me strength and kept me going. I will never forget your love and support.

Other family members to whom I wish to extend my heartfelt appreciation in this regard are my stepdad, Dick Reed; stepmom, Barbara Parfet; brother-in-law, Jay Gudebski; half sister, Sarah Parfet; step brother, Ryan Johnson, and his wife, Martina; stepbrother, Kevin Reed, and his wife, Justine; and stepbrother, Brad Reed.

Among the mentors are my good friend and expedition comrade, Richard Wiese, who I wish to thank for writing the foreword and for always pushing me to be the best I can be; Larry Winokur, my dear friend, who actually came up with the phrase that became the title of this book, and who has a masterful way of lifting my spirits and putting me back on track when something overwhelms me or gets me down; Brian Greene, whose ongoing support and guidance have been a true comfort in my life; Tom Claytor, who taught me that a little turbulence, with healthy doses of adrenaline and self-belief, is necessary to take flight; and Wayne Safro, whose advice over the years—combined with optimism and sprinkles of pessimism—have been nothing less than refreshing and inspiring. Thank you, guys.

My business partner and co-founder of Iconic Dvelopment, Bill Bennett, has always encouraged me to fulfill my dreams. Thanks, Bill, for holding down the fort while I was away, resolutely keeping an eye out for investors, partners, employees, and clients, and for also helping me to become better in terms of who I am and what I do.

The list of friends to whom I'd like to express my love and appreciation goes on and on, but among them (and please forgive me if I've left you out) are the following stars: Tom Avery, Doug Beal, Chris Birrer, Richard "Doc" Birrer, Rich Birrer, Jr., Rob Casserley, Max Chaya, Kenton Cool, Mike Davey, Yale Dieckmann, Cara Doran, Mike Dudas, Simon Galed, Mark George, Andy Giraldo, Al Hanna, Pat Hickey, Mark Holland, Tori James, Bob Jen, Ken Kamler, Darren Klein, Dave Larson, Samantha Larson, Jonathan Leebow, Craig MacFarlane, Joe Medved, Jason Munoz, Omar Samra, Victor Saunders, Anna Shekhdar, Will Smets, Ben Stephens, Ward Supplee, Richard Thorby, Henry Todd, Mead Treadwell, Jason Van Buren, and Bill and Judy Wahlberg.

It gives me great pleasure to acknowledge the immense contribution of our editor, Bob Nirkind, who believed in this project right from the start. All it takes is to have someone believe in you. Thanks, Bob, I am forever grateful.

At the same time, I also want to thank Meredith Wilson, whose insights, editorial suggestions, and ability to draw that extra anecdote out of me helped make this book so much better. Meredith, you did a spectacular job. You are a wonderful partner and friend.

Finally, there's my co-author, Richard Buskin, with whom I've spent hundreds of hours collaborating on this project, through weekends, evenings, and the wee small hours of the morning. Richard, you are world class. You have been a true teammate, and your professionalism, talent, and personality are simply one of a kind. It brings me joy to now call you a dear friend.